DALE AR

On Wings of Luck

From Outlaw Biker to Airline Pilot and Beyond Book 3

Copyright © 2025 by Dale Arenson Publishing LLC

All rights reserved.

No part of this publication can be reproduced, stored in, or introduced into a retrieval system, or transmitted in any form or by any means without prior written permission of the author or publisher.

ISBN-13: 979-8-9876398-2-5 Paperback

ISBN-13: 979-8-9876398-3-2 Hardcover

"Pilots are drawn to flying
because it's a perfect combination of science,
romance and adventure."

~ **Charles Lindbergh**

Contents

Introduction 1

Prologue **The Cabin** 3

Chapter 1 **Fire in the Sky!** 11

Chapter 2 **The Schoolhouse** 23

Chapter 3 **The Pressure Cooker** 35

Chapter 4 **Welcome to LaGuardia** 45

Chapter 5 **I Don't Want to Be Here** 53

Chapter 6 **California Dreaming** 61

Chapter 7 **The MD-80** 73

Chapter 8 **A Killer Reveals Itself** 85

Chapter 9 **Aviation Safety** 97

Chapter 10 **Living on the Line** 113

Chapter 11 **Can't We All Just Get Along?** 125

Chapter 12 **International Again** 139

Chapter 13 **The 767** 155

Chapter 14 **Captain** 179

Chapter 15 **Not Everything Goes as Planned** 189

Chapter 16 **I Have What...?** 199

Chapter 17 **The 737** 209

Chapter 18 **The Fun Never Ends** 221

Chapter 19 **The Triple Seven** 235

Chapter 20 **To Fly or Not to Fly** 247

Chapter 21 **How Not to Be** 255

Chapter 22 **Everything Changes** 265

Epilogue 271

Acknowledgments 281

About the Author 283

By the Same Author 285

Aviation Glossary 289

Introduction

At the end of my last book, *The Lucky One*, I had just been laid off from my job as a Learjet captain at Devarian Airways. They had heard I was interviewing with American Airlines, and since they were downsizing, that must have been a good enough excuse.

All the airlines were hiring, but with my past as an outlaw biker, I didn't dare to hope I had a chance with one of the major airlines. After a safari in Africa, the call of adventure was strong. I considered trying to find a job there as a bush pilot. It could be risky, as if I had not already had enough of that. The more I thought about it, the dangers on the ground from wild animals or political unrest, was probably not as big a hazard as working for an operator trying to save money on maintenance.

Then there was Australia, they didn't just let anyone in, you had to have a way to make a living, which I did. There were vast expanses of the Outback, pilots should be needed, and I was sure all the women looked like Nicole Kidman. Certainly, they would let me in, and I could find a job there.

I had now been a commercial pilot for five years and was willing to go wherever the jobs were. There had been that offer of running drugs from south of the border with unimaginable amounts of money to be made. It was very tempting, but the downsides were even more unimaginable. I never did call that number with the Miami area code. I still remember my late father's words: Keep your hands clean. I knew he meant it both literally and figuratively.

Prologue
The Cabin

The Cabin in the Woods

He stood in front of an old log cabin in the middle of a clearing in the woods without a clue as to how he got there. Looking up through the trees, the sky was cloudy, like it was going to rain, but there was a strange ray of sunlight illuminating the cabin like a light on a stage. Smoke curled out of the stone chimney. The moss on the roof and on one side of the trees told him one direction should be south, but right then, he really didn't care.

The cabin must have been at least a hundred years old. The smell of pine trees was pleasant, along with a whiff of wood smoke, and a gentle breeze ruffled his hair. He was neither hot nor cold. He took a deep breath and thought, "This isn't so bad."

Knowing he was expected, he climbed the short flight of stairs to the creaky porch and turned the brass knob on the old wooden door.

The inside was warm from the fireplace. On one side of the room, the only furniture was a large wooden desk behind which sat an old man with long white hair and a matching long beard, wearing white robes.

"Ah, right on time, come in," said the old man with a friendly smile.

"Why am I here?"

"Oh, didn't they tell you? You're dead."

"Yeah, yeah, I figured that out at the other place. But there it was all white and foggy. What am I doing here in the woods, in this cabin?"

"Well, this is my office, and I get to have it anyway I want; don't you like it?"

"Yeah, sure it's great, I guess, so why am I here?"

"So impatient… you have all the time in the world now, you know."

"Right… and who are you? Are you God?"

He laughed. "No, but I used to be an airline pilot."

"Isn't this heaven? I was expecting some pearly gates or something."

The old man scoffed, "Heaven? No, sorry, at least not yet. You're going to have to earn it if you want to go there."

"Earn it? What, I can't just be let in?"

"After the life you've lived? Did you really think it was going to be that easy?"

"Well, I was hoping… I wasn't that bad, was I?"

"If you'd been that bad, you wouldn't have gotten this far."

"Okay, so what do I have to do?"

"Why… you have to earn your wings of course. You have to be a full-fledged angel to get past here; we don't just let anyone in, you know."

"And how do I do that?"

"You have to look after someone on earth and keep him out of trouble and danger… Keep him alive."

"I have to keep someone else safe? Why didn't I have someone doing that for me?"

His bushy eyebrows curled downward, and the friendly smile left his face. "You did! It did little good, though."

"Oh… Well… So, at least I'm not in that other place."

"Not yet," he said matter-of-factly.

"Okay… So, do I have to watch over some little kid or something?"

"If it were only that easy. We picked you specially for this assignment because you were such a problem for us."

"I was?"

"You know you were!" There was that frown again.

Even though the room was not hot, he felt like he was starting to sweat. The crackling flames from the fireplace sounded louder than before.

"Okay, well, I'm here now, just tell me what I gotta do? Who's my assignment?"

"It's not an easy one. Like you, he has been quite a problem. Two of his apprentice angels have already quit; that's why we chose you."

"A problem… what is he, a serial killer or something?"

"Of course not; that would be easy—a one-way elevator ride down. No, he's a lot like you were. Motorcycles, guns, airplanes, we've had a hell… I mean a hard time keeping him alive."

"That doesn't sound so bad, but why is he special? Why go to this effort?"

"That's not my department, but let's just say someone upstairs has plans for him."

"And I didn't qualify for that?"

"Uhhh… No!"

Shaking his head, the prospective angel asked, "So, what happens if I fail?"

"Don't."

"But… if it doesn't work out… you wouldn't send me down there, would you?"

"No, worse, we'll send you back to be reborn."

Big sigh… "Alright, so, what's this idiot's name?"

"Dale Arenson."

Two years later

Showing up at the cabin in the woods, the apprentice angel knocked on the old wooden door. The familiar voice inside said, "Come in."

Stepping once again into the warm atmosphere of the cabin, the old man said, "Ah, you again."

Feeling strangely at home this time, he said, "Yes, sir, me again, hey is this place real? Or just an illusion?"

"It's as real as you want it to be. What can I do for you?"

"Oh man! This guy you've got me watching over, I just don't know… I think I've been with him long enough; I can see why the other guys quit. I don't think I'm up to the job."

"What's the problem this time? I told you he was a risk taker. All you have to do is keep him alive. That can't be so hard… is it?"

"You have no idea! You can't believe the chances he takes. Trusting his life to rattly little airplanes, flying around in the dark, and on fires in the mountains, he's making me crazy!"

"You want off the assignment?"

"Yeah, but… well, no, I mean, what would happen if I got another job instead?"

"I can't make any guarantees; that decision is above my pay grade."

"You get paid? Really?"

"No, it's a kind of joke around here."

"Oh… So, what would happen? Can't I just guard some little girl who just stays home all the time?"

"You think angels only earn their wings the easy way?"

"Well, I was hoping…"

"You're not up to the job then?"

"I didn't say that. I'm trying really hard, but there's this constant fear of failure."

"His?"

"No, mine. He keeps doing the most outlandish things. Bellying in airplanes and almost running into others, or running out of gas, or jumping out of helicopters, I'm not sure I can keep him safe."

"You've succeeded so far."

"Yeah, but my nerves are a frazzle. I didn't even know angels had nerves."

"Apprentice angels," the boss corrected him.

Taking a deep breath, he looked at the floor and sighed, "I was just hoping for another assignment."

"I'm afraid that's not possible."

"Okay then… I have an idea."

"You? You've had an idea?"

"Don't sound so surprised, Boss. Hey, what do I call you, anyway?"

"Sir will do."

"Okay, uh, Sir, can't we get him into a job that's not so dangerous?"

"That's up to him to take his life where he wants to go. It's called freedom. Freedom to succeed, freedom to fail. Our job is only to try to protect him along the way."

"But we can nudge him, right? Push him in the right direction? Open a few doors?"

"You haven't revealed yourself to him, have you? It is very much against the rules, you know. You could be fired immediately and sent back… or worse."

"No, no, of course not… well, there was one time when he may have heard me scream… but he didn't see me. I tried to make him think he was the one who screamed."

"Did he buy it?"

"I don't think so. He's not the screaming type."

"So, if we could, like you say, nudge him in another safer direction, what do you have in mind? Accountant? Teacher?"

"No, I don't think this guy would ever go for that. Just risking his life driving to work will never be good enough."

"What then do you think he would go for?"

"I was thinking… maybe airline pilot. You said you used to be a pilot. They have to keep people safe, so they stay safe, right? A win-win all around."

Stroking his white beard as he stared at the crackling fireplace, the old man said, "Ah, something near and dear to my own heart. It would be a safer job because he couldn't be racing around the sky like a cowboy. But we can't just put him there. He has to have the knowledge and be able to pass all the tests. We can't do that for him."

"So, you'll approve it?"

Turning his gaze back to the AA (apprentice angel), his brow furrowed, and his eyes narrowed.

"That's not up to me either. Are you thinking of this for him? Or just to make your life easier?"

"You call this life? I thought it was death."

"Don't go all semantic on me. You know what I mean."

"No… well, yes! But it would make it better for both of us, can't you see what I mean?"

"He'll never make it. He didn't do well in school."

Taken aback, the apprentice angel said, "You don't have faith in him? I thought that was what we were here for."

"We're here to watch over them, not live their lives for them. Besides, I don't know him. I've only watched occasional updates, mostly the stupid mistakes and miraculous survivals. Like those shorts on YouTube, they can be quite entertaining, you know."

"Tell me something I don't know…"

"You're the one who has spent the most time with him. The other two quit too soon. What's your opinion?"

"I think he can do it. It's hard to keep him focused, but as long as he stays out of jail, I think if we can point him in the right direction and maybe clear a few obstacles, he can do it."

Drumming his large fingers on the wooden desk, the old man pondered as he stared at the fire again.

Finally, he spoke, "Okay, we'll steer him to the airlines and see if that makes both of your 'lives' easier."

"I thought you said you had to run it up the chain of command?"

"I just did."

"Oh… well, okay, thank you."

"You're dismissed."

Chapter 1
Fire in the Sky!

"Do not fear failure but rather fear not trying."
-Roy T. Bennett

Boeing 727

The dark cockpit lit up with a bright red light with the word "FIRE" emblazoned on it, accompanied by a loud bell ringing. Immediately the Captain called out, "Engine fire checklist!"

The three of us bolted upright. My flight engineer seat, just behind the two pilots, was still facing forward. Having just taken off from Dallas-Fort Worth airport in our Boeing 727, we were already in the clouds at only five hundred feet in the air. We were in 'instrument conditions,' unable to see outside, flying only by the flight instruments and radio navigation.

The first officer yelled over the din of the bell, "Check essential power!"

The big airliner yawed back and forth as Ron fought to keep control of it. The asymmetric thrust of the remaining engines tried to roll the airplane onto its back.

Captain Ron shoved hard on the left rudder and started cranking in rudder trim to keep the airplane straight. Seeing the number three fire handle blazing, I reached to my panel and twisted the essential power knob and checked the load meter before announcing,

"Essential power on Gen one."

Ron said, "I've got the airplane and the radios, Bob, you and Dale run the checklist, and silence that damn bell."

My heart was in my throat as I grabbed the plastic-covered emergency checklist card from its slot, loudly announcing, "Engine fire, severe damage checklist." Without waiting for a response, I started reading the items on the list.

The bell clanged on as I yelled, "Essential power selector."

Bob, the First Officer, replied, "Generator One!"

Trying to focus and control my breathing, I responded with, "Generators one and two online."

I called out, "Number three thrust lever, close!"

Bob put his hand on the engine number three thrust lever and said, "Engine number three, verified?"

Ron replied, "Verified."

Yelling over the alarm bell, I called, "Number three verified."

Bob snapped the thrust lever to idle.

I called, "Number three fuel lever, cutoff."

Bob held the number three start lever and called out, "Number three start lever, verified?"

Ron called, "Verified!"

I said, "Number three verified," as he pulled it to the off position.

Ron said, "Silence that bell, would ya?"

Bob finally hit the button on the glare shield. Without the bell, I didn't have to yell quite so loud, but the red light was still shining brightly.

I said, "Engine number three fire handle pull!"

Bob pulled the fire handle back as far as it would go.

Ron said, "Dammit, Bob! You need to verify that before pulling it."

Bob said, "Sorry, Boss, I'm just anxious to get that fire out."

Still reading the checklist, I called, "Engine number three bottle discharge switch, push."

With his finger over the fire suppression discharge button, Bob said, "Ready, Boss?"

Ron said, "Hit it."

Bob pushed the button to shoot the fire suppression squib into the engine to try to put the fire out, but the light remained on. I punched the button to start the timer on my clock and said, "Bottle discharge light on."

The tower said, "American one-twenty-three, maintain five thousand and contact departure."

Ron grabbed the hand microphone and said, "Negative tower, American one-twenty-three, declaring an emergency. We have an engine fire, request immediate return to DFW."

Over the radio I heard, "Roger American one, two, three, climb and maintain three thousand and turn left to two seven zero, report fuel and souls on board. Do you want the emergency equipment?"

I heard Ron tell him yes, then he read off the numbers the tower had requested.

Turning us to the west started the rectangular pattern to take us back to land on runway 36L, the one we had just taken off from.

I tried not to think about the one hundred and eighteen passengers in the back, along with the three flight attendants, and braced myself as the captain rolled the Boeing 727 hard left. I vaguely heard him calling the flight attendants and telling them we were returning to DFW, and to prepare for an emergency landing.

Glancing at the clock, I told Bob, "That's thirty seconds, the firelight is not out, we need to fire the other bottle."

Bob agreed, flipping the bottle transfer toggle switch to the right. He hit the discharge button again to shoot our final squib of Halon fire suppressant into the burning engine. The firelight remained lit. I reset my clock for another thirty seconds.

I yelled through the confusion, "Captain, we're too heavy to land, do you want me to start dumping fuel?"

Ron said, "Not until that damn fire is out… we don't want to turn into a Roman candle!"

My mouth was as dry as British humor, and I wished for a drink of water, but there was no time, and we had none in the cockpit. I tried to focus on the checklist.

I hated this; I am a pilot! I'd been flying Learjets for two years before this job, and many pilot jobs before that. I should be up front flying this airplane or at least in the copilot's seat.

Here we are in an emergency situation, and I am sitting back at a panel, flipping switches and reading a checklist. It was not where I wanted to be.

I loosened my tie and unbuttoned my collar while trying to push those thoughts out of my mind and tried to focus on the job at hand. To keep the pilots informed and to get it on the cockpit voice recorder, I loudly read off the items pertaining to my FE panel as they were completed, "Galley switch, off, cargo heat outflow switch closed, number three pack switch off, number three generator field tripped, number three engine bleed closed."

I glanced nervously at the gauges on my panel to check the fuel balance just as Bob announced, "Fire light is out!"

Captain Ron looked back at me and said, "Dump fuel!"

I hesitantly said, "Don't we need to let Air Traffic Control know?"

Ron looked at Bob and said, "Tell ATC we're dumping fuel," then back to me, "Start dumping NOW!"

"Yes, sir, standby. How much do you want to go down to?"

Ron said, "To the standpipes, hurry it up, we'll be turning a base leg soon."

"Yes, sir!" I rotated my seat ninety degrees right to face the engineer's panel. Reaching to the rear bulkhead, I flipped open the small door that contained those taboo switches, the ones that poured your gas overboard. There is an old saying, 'The only time you can have too much fuel on an airplane is when you're on fire!'

I thought, *Well... here we are.*

Then I remembered the special 'Fuel Dump' checklist and madly turned the pages of the quick reference handbook until I found it.

I heard the tower say, "American one-twenty-three, turn left to one-eight-zero." I was running out of time.

Gently banking the airplane, the captain said, "Dale, I need the One Engine Inoperative Landing Checklist."

"Standby." Then I announced, "Fuel dump checklist."

Sweat seemed to burst out of my armpits as if it were from a spray can. Why the hell couldn't I just do things without reading them out loud from the checklist?

"Main tank number two boost pump switches all on!"

"Main tanks number one and three boost pump switches both on!"

"Cross-feed selector number two open, number one and three closed."

I struggled to breathe and pronounce my words clearly because my mouth was so dry.

I flipped switches and opened valves as quickly as I read the checklist.

"Fuel dump switches all open!"

"Fuel dump nozzle valve switches—open!"

"Fuel quantity—monitor!"

The tower said, "American one-twenty-three, turn left zero-niner-zero."

The captain rolled the wings level on the base leg just as I reached for the One Engine Inoperative Checklist. Bob called out, "Engine number two is winding down!"

We were now flying on just one engine. Ron said, "Shit! Secure that engine and get me the 'Two engine inoperative landing checklist,' we're about to turn final!"

The airplane slewed in the air again as Ron fought to control it. We were still in the clouds, and his only references were the flight instruments in front of him. He shoved in more left rudder and dialed more rudder trim, while adding power on the number one engine.

Once again, I wondered what I had gotten myself into and if we were going to make it out of this. Pushing those thoughts from my mind, I vaguely heard the tower tell us that the emergency equipment, the firetrucks, and ambulances, were ready and waiting for us.

As I grabbed the engine failure checklist, Bob, without waiting for me to read the items, said, "Engine number two thrust lever, verified?"

Ron said, "Verified."

I said, "Verified."

He smoothly pulled the thrust lever to idle and immediately put his hand on the fuel lever, calling, "Engine number two fuel lever."

At the same time, Ron and I called out, "Verified."

Bob switched it to the off position while Ron said, "Dale, I need that landing checklist, now!"

The tower said, "American one-two-three, turn left zero-three-zero, intercept the localizer for runway 36 Left and maintain two thousand, three hundred feet, cleared for the ILS."

Ron read it back.

In a gentle left bank, the captain rolled the airplane onto final approach, expertly intercepting the localizer beam, and increased the power on the number one engine to level off at twenty-three hundred. It was the only thing that kept us flying now. As we slowed, he called, "Flaps one."

The flap handle clicked into position, and Bob replied, "Flaps one."

I thought, *This might be a bit easier if it weren't at night.*

Fumbling through the laminated cards, I found the right checklist and quickly began reading, "Two engine inoperative landing checklist. Plan to use flaps five, V-Ref plus thirty knots. Intercept the glide slope…"

Ron impatiently snapped, "I know all that; get me a reference speed for flaps five, plus thirty at this weight."

Quickly doing the math, a combination of our empty weight, passengers, and cargo, plus the fuel I expected we would have, I came up with a number and both pilots set the bugs on their airspeed indicators.

Bob called out, "Glide slope is alive."

Ron said, "Intercepting the glide slope, give me flaps two. Dale, how's that landing checklist coming? Bob, what's the weather?"

Bob said, "Still two hundred overcast and a mile."

Panting and sweating, I tried to find my place and start reading again as fast as I could, "Pressurization set, cooling doors open. Seatbelt switch on?"

Ron replied, "On."

"Anti-ice?"

Bob called, "Off."

"Landing lights?"

Bob reached up and threw the switches on the overhead panel forward and called, "On."

"Altimeters?"

Both pilots said, "Set and crosschecked."

"Flight instruments and radios?"

Same response.

"Flap inhibit switch?"

Bob reached up and hit it, saying, "Inhibited."

At that time, a blue light started to flash on the instrument panel in front of the pilots.

Bob called, "Outer marker." I rotated my seat to face forward for the landing.

Ron said into the radio, "DFW tower, American one-twenty-three, emergency aircraft, outer marker inbound for three-six left."

The tower replied, "Cleared to land 36L American, emergency equipment standing by."

To the radio, Ron said, "Cleared to land three-six left." Then to Bob, "Gimme flaps five, gear down." Even though we were still descending, he added even more power to the number one engine to compensate for the additional drag.

As Bob complied, Ron called the flight attendants on the PA, saying, "Flight attendants, prepare for emergency landing."

I tried to finish my checklist.

"Ignition switches?"

Bob replied, "Continuous."

"Speedbrake lever?"

"Armed, green light."

"Gear?"

Both pilots said, "Down, three green," and checking the lights on the front panel, I repeated it too.

"Anti-skid?"

"Armed."

"Flaps?"

Putting his hand on the flap lever, then pointing to the gauge, Bob said, "Five, five, green light."

Once again, he glanced up to check that the inhibit switch was in its proper place.

I heard the tower say, "American 123, cleared to land."

I called out, "Hydraulic pressures and quantities checked."

As I looked to the right at my panel, checking both the hydraulic and fuel systems, I was horrified to see that we were still dumping fuel and that the imbalance was nearly out of limits.

I glanced forward to see that Ron was adjusting the aileron trim, automatically compensating for it.

Right then, Bob called, "Decision height."

At the same time, we descended below the weather, and the runway was right in front of us.

Ron calmly said, "Runway in sight, we're landing!" He had done a great job of flying a crippled airplane perfectly down the ILS.

I rotated my seat back to the right and saw the fuel dump was still in progress. Almost in a panic, I slapped down the gang bar to shut off all the switches at once and closed the crossfeed valves, instantly ending the fuel loss.

Flipping the last switches on American's proprietary mechanical checklist, I rotated my seat forward and said, "Gear's down, three green, rudder trim to zero—landing checklist complete."

The automated voice of the radio altimeter called, "Fifty, forty, thirty, twenty, ten."

Ron rolled the rest of the rudder trim to zero with his right hand, compensating manually with the rudders, then he reached up and eased the one remaining throttle to idle while raising the nose of the aircraft into a flare.

Because of the low flap setting, the nose came up higher than normal, but we were greeted with only a slight bump as the main wheels chirped onto the pavement. A perfect landing.

The speed brake lever slid back as he deployed the number one thrust reverser and applied the brakes. Bob said, "Nice job, Boss!"

I let out a big breath, realizing I had probably been holding it for a while.

As Ron slowed the airplane in the middle of the runway to little more than walking speed, he said, "Thanks, after landing checklist, please."

Suddenly, our whole world changed. Like stepping through a time warp portal or walking out of a dark movie theater into bright sunlight. The action movie was over.

The motion and the noise of the cockpit froze, and the runway outside the windshield disappeared. It became opaque, and all the lights in the cockpit came on. It was like daylight and very disorienting.

A disembodied, omnipotent voice that sounded like God said, "Not bad, you guys!" I thought I heard angels singing…"

The simulator slowly sank down on its hydraulic shocks, settling with a clunk as the check airman, who sounded just like the DFW Tower controller, got out of his seat and stood behind mine.

Putting his hand on my shoulder, he said, "Dale, it's a good thing you caught that fuel dump and turned it off before landing. That would've been a bust, you'd have failed. And you got lucky on the fuel imbalance; another five-hundred pounds and it would have been out of limits."

The two pilots were now sitting sideways in their seats to look back at the check airman and take their medicine.

"Bob, remember to always verify shutting down engine controls with the other crew members. We've had actual situations on the line where a good engine got shut down because someone was in a hurry. You don't want that to happen to the only good one you have left."

Bob looked at the floor and nodded.

"Ron, great job flying the airplane. Try to keep your crew more in line on the checklists, like that second engine shutdown."

"Yeah, I know, but we were a little rushed."

"You can always ask for delay vectors, you know. The fire was out. Hurry, but don't hurry too much. Your flight engineer is busy, so make sure he has enough time. And good job keeping the flight attendants informed. Did you call the company to let them know what was going on?"

Sitting sideways in his seat to look back at the check airman, Ron looked drained. I could see sweat stains under his armpits, like mine. He said, "No, I didn't have time. I was about to when that second engine quit."

The check airman said, "Try to make time; they need to know, and they're here to help, and a PA to the passengers would have been nice. Also, try to stay more aware of your fuel dumping situation."

Ron just let out a breath and shook his head.

Then back to me he said, "And you need to go faster on those checklists. You got the before landing finished before touching down, but just barely."

Go faster, I thought. I was going as fast as I could. *I'm not sure I'm cut out for this job…*

I just said, "Thanks, I'll work on it."

We breathed a sigh of relief when he said, "Okay, you all passed the checkride. Go back to the hotel and have yourself some beers."

A crew training in a Boeing 727 simulator

Chapter 2
The Schoolhouse

"Realize that you are greater than you've ever considered yourself to be."
-Norman Vincent Peale

American Airlines Flight Academy

Five months earlier, the third letter from American Airlines finally came in the mail. My heart was in my throat as I slowly slit the top of the envelope with a letter opener, taking my time, afraid of what it might say. To my utter shock, it offered for me to come to work, with a class date of December 23rd, 1986.

I couldn't believe it; I had convinced myself it would never happen. And it wouldn't have if not for the dare from my friend Jim Finley. Just over eight years since my first lesson and after so many close calls, here I was still alive and heading to the major leagues.

It was September, and I was still flying the hot rod Learjet as captain for Devarian Airways, also known as Bancjet because of the checks we predominantly carried. I loved the job, zooming all over the country, mostly at night with no passengers, no flight attendants, just cargo that didn't complain much. The pay could have been better, but I didn't care. It was a long way from my biker past and the construction jobs and further than I ever expected to get in aviation.

It was impossible to keep my mouth shut and not tell the news to other pilots I flew with. I told them the good news while asking them to keep it quiet.

But it did get back to the company.

On October 1st, after landing at Burbank in the morning, finishing a three-day trip, I was told to check with the flight office before I left. The new chief pilot named Brian said,

"You're being laid off as of now."

Just like that, after two years I was out the door.

He called it *downsizing*. I called it firing.

I wasn't exactly surprised. I had just turned down the offer to get type rated in the Falcon 10s and 20s, plus there were about 20 guys that had been hired after me since I'd been there. Obviously, seniority meant very little. Devarian had already given us a pay freeze, then a pay cut on top of that. They had been losing contracts to other lower bidders. Times were tough.

I had almost three months before my class date, so I tried to find another job with jet companies like Clay Lacy in Van Nuys or other jet charter outfits. They were impressed with my qualifications and experience, but they would then ask me to sign a paper swearing I had no commitment to any other companies on penalty of perjury. I couldn't, so no one would touch me.

Between Imperial Airlines and Devarian, I hadn't had a vacation in four years, so I just applied for unemployment and enjoyed the time off. The pay wasn't that much lower than I'd been making.

Later I learned I could have petitioned the training department for an earlier class date. Not only would I have been bringing in a bigger paycheck, but I would have gained at least two hundred valuable seniority numbers. But no one told me since I wasn't part of a clique of other airline pilots.

About a year after I left, I heard Devarian closed its doors for good. I got out just in time. In fact, all four of the flying companies I had previously worked for went out of business after I left. I claim no responsibility whatsoever.

Earlier that year I heard on the news that a guy named Barry Seal had been murdered.

He was a pilot running drugs and guns and got mixed up with the CIA, DEA and Carlos Escobar and the Colombian drug cartels. I thought of my meeting with Mac and what that could have led to. I secretly patted myself on the back that I had never called that number on the card. Could that have been me?

The Big Time

At the tail end of the year, I showed up early on the morning of my class date two days before Christmas. I walked around the big, high-ceilinged entryway of the Hallowed Flight Academy in awe. Or at least, that's how it seemed to me.

I'd been there before, just walking through, going to interviews, simulator checks, and flight physicals. But now I 'worked' here. I was there to start training, the pinnacle of my flying career. I was hired. But not really. I was soon to find out you had to pass training to be hired, and there were more hurdles to come. Initially, it would take six weeks, IF you didn't screw up and get sent home.

When were you really hired for good? In a year, and in that time, there were more pitfalls and traps than in an Indiana Jones movie.

In the big lobby of the flight academy, there were lines of pictures on the marble walls of some of the well-known pilots who had worked for the carrier in the pioneer days. One was Charles Lindbergh, another was Ernest K. Gann, who later became a famous writer. I couldn't believe I was in their company.

Once again, the doubts came creeping back as I wondered if I belonged there. I insisted to myself that I was qualified with an ATP, three type ratings and almost five thousand hours, mostly in jets and turboprops. I knew I could fly, but I was about to get subjected to seemingly everything but being a pilot. I swore to myself that I could do it. I had to.

I was dressed casually, as instructed — in slacks — and, not as instructed, a longsleeved shirt, since I was afraid someone would see my club tattoo and start asking questions.

Directed to a room, I found eleven other new hires like me and was told to take a seat by one of the four instructors. After being photographed, we were given our ID cards and told to wear them at all times. Next, we were sent to a room to be measured us for uniforms, then issued a ton of manuals and paperwork. Everywhere you looked, there were pilots walking around with big black bags. They called them 'Kit Bags' and we were told we would need one and could buy them at a kiosk near the cafeteria, which we did on the first break. I had to wonder if the name came from the old song, "Pack up your troubles in your old kit bag..." Fully loaded with paper, they weighed twenty-five to thirty pounds and went everywhere with us. This was before the advent of wheels on luggage. Carrying a kit bag in one hand and overnight luggage in the other gave pilots a peculiar walk that made them identifiable even when not in uniform. We built up great shoulder muscles.

All new hire classes consisted of six pilots. They paired us in twos as training partners and living partners and said we would share a room at the hotel. It would be the only time in our careers when we would have to do that. Once out of school and on the line, we would always have a private room. The union was to thank for that! Many years ago, pilots on layovers had to share rooms, sometimes with a whole crew of navigators and flight engineers.

My roommate and training partner was Mike Philpot from Kansas City. An easygoing guy with a Midwest drawl. Like me, he had all civilian flight experience.

Bo Marciniw was American born and of Ukrainian descent. He spoke the language fluently. I was impressed, since I was still working on English. He was paired with the youngest in the class, Ned Quarterman, a cocky kid from Chicago. He was funny and smart, and I liked him right away.

Russell Dennis, the guy with two first names, was the oldest of our group and had the highest flight time since he had flown C-130 cargo planes in the Air Force. He was the only military pilot in our class and seemed a little different, but we accepted him anyway, military or not. Russ was teamed up with Greg from South Florida. They were a real odd couple. Greg was a laid-back guy, a little too laid back. He had been flying seaplanes and copilot on Convair 440s mostly to the Caribbean Islands, mostly in VFR conditions.

With three type ratings and five thousand hours, I had the second highest flight time and, along with Mike, who had some time in Lears, was the only other one who had flown jets. With no college degree, that may have been the only reason they gave me a chance. I'd read somewhere that back then ninety-six percent of airline pilots had at least four years of college.

I don't know how my classmates felt, but to me it was like winning the lottery. Looking back over the short five years from my first flying job as an instructor, it seemed a world away. Ten years prior to that, I was a new member of the Hangmen outlaw motorcycle club. At nineteen, just surviving that life seemed unlikely. More like a universe away.

I'd felt lucky to have each job I got flying airplanes. And now, here I was at the pinnacle of commercial aviation, a place I never expected to reach. Euphoria might be a proper depiction of my feelings, often feeling like I was living in a dream. But that was tempered by the realization that I could get canned at any minute if I didn't make the grade, or if they found out about my past. There was little time to marvel at my situation with everything that was being thrown at us.

After our day of indoctrination, the first hurdle would be the Boeing 727 ground school as a flight engineer. They told us up front that compared to other training programs at the Flight Academy, this one was the worst; like boot camp. It was a high-pressure environment with so much information thrown at us that a common phrase for it was, "Like trying to drink from a fire hose."

You were expected to learn everything there was to know about the 727, sometimes to a ridiculous degree. There were several different sub-models, and you had to know the differences too. The oral exam was in four weeks, and if you didn't pass, it was over for you.

Our team of two older ground school instructors were Don Reynolds and Lee Sheldon. Ned called Lee 'The Hammer' since he was exact and demanding. An excellent teacher. Don was too, but more laid back. They had been teaching the 727 to students for decades. It was their job to get us through the first phase of our training.

Every morning there was a prearranged schedule that we printed from a computer, the first ones I had ever delt with. The printout told us where to be and when. Part of our days consisted of classroom sessions with the instructors and others with inanimate mockups of the flight engineer panel. There were periods of self-learning with early (1986) interactive computer screens that taught systems and quizzed you on your knowledge.

Then there was the dark, cold PLATO Room (an acronym for Programmed Logic for Automatic Teaching Operations), where you individually watched slide shows while listening to a tutorial through a headset from a guy named Jock. He had a pleasant voice. We were sure it was specially designed to put us to sleep. Being nearly impossible to stay awake, we were convinced it was really a test to see if we could fly all-nighters.

A PLATO terminal in a museum

Sometimes at the 'Schoolhouse,' as we called it, we would see working pilots in their uniforms, there for recurrent training. They seemed happy and confident. We were envious that they had passed all of this and were now on the line, actually flying the airplanes that we were studying so hard to learn. They were who we wanted to be, the goal of our future self.

Our world revolved around the Boeing 727. It lived in our heads. Even when we weren't in class, it was all we talked about. At lunch or riding in the van to and from the hotel. While sitting around together studying late into the night. We never watched television and had no idea what was going on in the outside world. The hotel had a bar, but we didn't go there. We were sure there would be spies who would inform the company if we were slacking off, drinking a beer. We wouldn't take any chances of losing our jobs.

One day, walking into the flight academy, I ran into an old friend from Imperial Airlines. I said, "Hi Andre, what are you up to?"

He said, "I'm outta here. I'm quitting this place."

Stunned that anyone would give up this job, I asked, "Why would you do that?" "I've been offered a job with Northwest. They don't have a B-scale, so this place can go to hell."

"You can't be serious."

"Yup, hey I've gotta go catch my van to the airport. I'll see you around, good luck."

I watched him trot off to the waiting vans, then turned back to head to my class, shaking my head. I felt this was the only chance I would ever get.

Being gone over the holidays resulted in a lot of money spent on long-distance calls to home on the pay phone in the hotel's lobby. Sometimes there was a waiting line. I'd always come prepared with a pocket full of quarters. Finally, I got a prepaid phone card. There was also snail mail for letters and cards, but before the dreaded 727 oral exam we didn't take time to write.

Our primary source of food was the cafeteria at the flight academy, where we paid for our meals. Several times a day it was packed with pilots, flight attendants, classroom teachers and simulator instructors, ebbing and rising like a tide. After hours, dinner was usually what we called the B-scale buffet. The Holiday Inn was nice enough to provide a free-food happy hour every evening—tacos, spaghetti, hot dogs or hamburgers. It was a lifesaver since most of us had little money because there was a two-month delay before our first paycheck. Another option was the Jack in the Box across the busy four-lane road from the hotel. Crossing that was definitely the most dangerous part of the job.

Class 86-158
Front row: Greg, Ned, and instructor Don Reynolds
Standing: The author, Bo, Russ, and Mike
Rear: Instructor Lee Sheldon

There was a meeting room at the Holiday Inn where the six of us and other classes could study together. It was wintertime in Texas, and sitting outside was not pleasant. One evening, the Allied Pilots Union decided to hold a meeting there. Contract negotiations were going on and, as usual, they were contentious.

The union bosses wanted the new hires to get a taste of union politics, but all we cared about was passing the next test. We had gotten the word to be there; it sounded like an order. Bo, Mike, Ned and I seated ourselves at the back of the room, wanting to be as inconspicuous as possible. To our dismay, the union president and his entourage strode straight to the back of the room and called the meeting to order. Everybody had to turn their chairs around, and suddenly we were right in the front row. He was big, loud and profane, the other union thugs, eh, I mean bosses with him spread out on either side. They acted and talked more like Teamsters than airline pilots.

At the end of his lecture a new hire in the back of the room asked, "We can't join the union for another year; we just want to get through training. If line pilots go on strike, are we expected to strike?"

The union boss angrily glared at him and his high-volume answer was full of profanity: "IF WE GO ON F***ING STRIKE, YOU'RE F***ING EXPECTED TO f***ING STRIKE TOO."

Our ears were pinned back like a dog in a wind tunnel. Bo and I were wiping his saliva off our faces as we looked at each other thinking, "Yeah, right… we really want to follow this guy."

Later Mike said, "I wonder what would happen to anyone who crossed the picket line?"

Ned said, "They'd probably get run over by a Mercedes-Benz."

It was pounded into us from the start that the only thing that mattered was passing the oral exam. A two-hour grilling where you had to answer questions from a check airman on any aspect of the 727 that he wanted to ask. No multiple-choice written test.

If you did badly and the check airman felt you didn't understand a system, he would start probing further. Looking for your weak spots, he would find out what you knew and what you didn't know. And you were expected to know everything.

After four weeks, we had to take the test whether we felt ready or not. Five of the six of us passed, but poor Greg had been a weak link from the start. It seemed his favorite phrase in class was high-pitched: "I don't understand."

One evening before the test, we were studying the anti-ice and de-ice systems on the 727 when the topic of Air Florida Flight 90 came up. It was a 737 that crashed into the Potomac River in Washington, DC in 1982, four years earlier. 70 of the 74 people aboard were killed. The cause of the crash was that the anti-ice system had not been turned on by the pilots before taking off during a snowstorm.

Greg blurted, "Oh, hey, I knew that guy!"

Ned asked, "What guy?"

"The captain on that flight. We used to drop LSD together."

Mike and I looked at each other in disbelief, not so much that he had taken LSD, but that he would admit it in this environment.

After the oral exam, he was sent home, and we never saw or heard from him again. He'd been snatched out of our world; it felt like he had died. To me, failing this class, this job, would have felt like dying. We were not surprised when he didn't make it. But then, like life, there were no guarantees for the rest of us either.

Still, the five of us passed, and it was like a huge weight had been lifted from our shoulders. Our instructors, Don and Lee, took us out for dinner and beer at the famous Texas honky-tonk Billy Bob's in Fort Worth. It was like a 12-hour leave from prison. For the moment, the pressure was off. These were the first drinks we'd had in over a month. Life was good!

Don gave us the keys to his car to get back to the hotel when we were ready, while Lee gave him a ride home. He made me the designated driver. Damn! Now I could have only four beers instead of six. After all, it was Texas beer.

He said, "Just park it in the employee lot near the simulator building when you come in in the morning." We behaved ourselves though, still thinking we were being watched, and it might be a trap. The next morning, driving to the flight academy in a car instead of the usual van service made us feel a little special.

That didn't last very long. Next, we were thrown to the lions—I mean the simulator instructors, and the simulator was the lion's den. Remember this was always a high-pressure environment.

In a 727 cockpit mockup with Ned and Bo

Chapter 3
The Pressure Cooker

"Try and fail, but don't fail to try."

-John Quincey Adams

They are the original virtual reality. Even the old 707 simulators were amazingly realistic, and that has only gotten better. Sims are the biggest, most expensive video games.

You can completely forget that you've never left the ground, and the sweat is real.

You are not in danger of getting hurt or killed; worse yet, you are at risk of getting fired. Even for working pilots, you get a check ride every nine months or anytime you are transitioning to a new aircraft. If you do badly, the FAA gets involved. Screw up again, and they can pull your pilot's license.

The training consisted of operating the systems and learning to read checklists in an emergency, where the checklists are and how to find them quickly. You had to know immediately where every switch, valve and gauge was and how to operate them and what the operating parameters and limitations were on any system. In the simulator, it was always one emergency after another, a pressure cooker; you had to shower every night and do laundry every two days.

The scenario with the engine fire in Chapter 1 was the culmination of the last month and a half of training. The checkride! Simulator training and checkrides can be so rigorous that pilots who have been in real emergencies have said, "It was a no-brainer. Having already done it in the simulator, it felt like I had been there before."

As opposed to the tedium of classroom learning, I always thought that simulator training was fun, despite the stress you were actually getting to do something. But the flight engineer simulator was anything but that. You weren't flying, or pretending to. You were running emergencies, flipping switches and turning knobs and reading checklists.

My new instructor's name was Joe, and he was a short old man who smoked a pipe and always smelled of it. I have fond memories of my first instructor, George Jones, with his easy demeanor and his fragrant pipe aroma, but this guy quashed that. Joe seemed like he was never satisfied, and his attempts at friendliness seemed more sarcastic than anything.

I was coupled with a pair of pilots up front, nice guys who were volunteers to drive the simulator around and practice emergencies. It was a good experience for them while I was supposed to be learning. It seemed things were happening so fast. Problems would arise that I had to identify and find the right checklist and read through the procedure to rectify it. You had to know each system by heart to operate it properly. Then it was off to the next emergency.

The main systems included electrical—both AC and DC—powered by engine-driven generators, the APU, ground power, and onboard batteries. Fuel was supplied from three tanks and distributed to three engines via a crossfeed system that allows any tank to feed any engine; familiarity with the fuel dump procedure is also essential. The hydraulic system consisted of three independent systems, and it's important to know which aircraft components are powered by each. Environmental control systems managed pressurization and cabin temperature. Fire suppression systems covered both the engines and the APU.

Engine instrumentation included gauges for oil quantity, pressure, and temperature.

Joe would poke me in the back with his pipe and tell me, "Hurry up, you're not going fast enough, you're too slow, get with the program."

It would be nice to go at tour own pace to learn, then the speed comes later. But Joe wanted the speed up front. It was a pressure cooker.

I don't think I ever disliked someone so much, but then there are a lot of big egos and dislikable personalities in the aviation business. I was on that narrow edge of wanting to succeed at this job, and wanting to walk away, at least from being a flight engineer.

Simulator sessions at the panel were nightmares; hurry, hurry, hurry!!! Struggling to find the right checklists while the pilots waited patiently or sometimes impatiently. Go fast enough to keep Joe happy and not miss anything. Screw it up and do it all over again under that glaring, judgmental eye.

I looked forward to the check-ride so this would be over with, and I would be done at the schoolhouse. I yearned for the days of relative freedom, flying the Learjet back and forth across the country. I didn't care if it was at night; I'd been a captain, in charge of my aircraft without some self-important bozo poking me in the back telling me to go faster.

All the doubts came flooding back. I'd been worried about my past and arrest record catching up with me. I knew I could fly, but was I really cut out for this job? Working for a big airline? What would I do if I didn't make it here? This was the best job I'd ever had or ever may have. I had to be successful.

Finally, the big day of the checkride arrived. I'd read the checklists and emergency procedures over and over and studied with my friends in my class.

The checkride was a blur as one emergency popped up after another. The pilots up front were more experienced, but they were still patient as they sometimes had to wait for me.

I read the checklists and configured my panel as fast as I could and still felt like I was behind.

When it was all over, my shirt had sweat stains. I was glad it was over. The check airman waited until the pilots climbed out of their seats and left, then he said, "I'm sorry, but you failed."

I was stunned! How could this happen? I'd tried so hard! I just stared at him with my mouth open.

He said, "You're going too fast. You need to slow down, relax."

My mouth was dry, and it seemed like my ears were ringing as I still couldn't find the words to say anything. My big chance and I'd blown it!

To ease the silence, he tried to lift my spirits.

"Don't worry about it. You'll get a couple more day's training to tune up, then try it again. I'm sure you'll do fine next time," he said.

I said, "Next time?"

He said, "Sure, you'll get a couple of hours of refresher rides, then try it again. I'm sure you'll do fine."

So, I wasn't done yet. It felt like someone had just thrown me a life preserver, and I wasn't going to drown… yet. I thanked him and walked out.

In the huge building, carrying my kit bag down the long catwalk next to all the simulators, I saw Joe ahead of me leaning on the railing with his pipe, smiling. Or was it a smirk?

"How did it go?" he said.

Barely able to control myself, I just said, "I busted."

Letting a little scoff, he said, "I told you, you were going too slow."

I stared daggers at his eyes and said, "He said I was going too fast."

There was that little laugh again as he shook his head and looked away.

It was a good thing the check airman told me I had another chance. If I didn't think that, I probably would have beaten him within an inch of his life. But that would have been the surest way to fail. They would give me one more chance; if I failed that, I'd be done for good. Without saying another word, I walked away.

When I got back to the Holiday Inn, the other guys were in the study room. I was surprised to find that Russell, the former Air Force guy, had failed as well. They told me not to worry about it.

Mike and Bo said they got by, but it wasn't easy. Ned aced it so nicely; they offered him a job as a flight engineer check airman. He nonchalantly brushed it off, saying, "Nah, I just want to get on the line and fly."

The other guys went home for a 48, Russ and I stayed and continued studying. I went to the person in charge of training schedules and asked him not to put me with Joe again, and they granted it. We were squeezed in for a couple of late-night training sessions, then they gave us another check ride. I tried to relax and go at an even pace. It felt strangely easy.

When it was over and the check airman congratulated me, I thought, *Is that all there is to it?*

Russ passed as well. It was an enormous weight off our shoulders. I couldn't help but wonder if they made the check ride a little easier than normal, maybe they took pity on us since we had come this far.

The next day at the Flight Academy, a bunch of people were clustered around a bulletin board, looking at the base assignments for new pilots. We were no longer students; we were American Airlines pilots. Well… Okay, we were flight engineers.

Finding our class number 86-158, and our names, all five of us had been assigned to LGA—the LaGuardia base in New York. They always needed pilots because nobody wanted to be based there unless they already lived in the city. I immediately put in for a transfer to Los Angeles, and the other four guys requested Chicago. But we knew it could be months at least before those requests were granted.

Graduating from Phase One

The real thing

Next was a trip to the airport, where you got to see a real 727 up close. We were shown how to do an exterior 'walk-around' inspection. Until then, it existed only on paper, cockpit mockups and simulators. It was thrilling to see a real Boeing 727 in the flesh, or I mean aluminum.

You were again tested on your knowledge of everything inside and outside the airplane as a check airman randomly asked us questions. Everything was a test, and you still could fail and be sent home at any time, although it was getting a little more relaxed.

We didn't have our wings yet. It was a bit embarrassing to be wearing the uniform without wings on our chests. Kind of like an apprentice angel, I suppose, with no wings yet to show your status.

The next day we showed up in operations at the Dallas-Fort Worth airport in uniform for an IOE, or Initial Operating Experience. The IOE was like a check ride, but without all the emergencies. You were on a real airplane with a real crew and real passengers in the back on a regularly scheduled trip with a flight engineer check airman looking over your shoulder.

His job was not only to evaluate your performance and knowledge of aircraft systems, but also to teach you all aspects of line flying that weren't covered in the schoolhouse.

Mine was three days and twelve legs, jetting around the eastern United States from Jacksonville to Detroit to Chicago and it seemed everywhere in between.

It was late February 1987, and the winter weather was awful. It seemed we did instrument approaches on every landing. The pilots were working pretty hard, and I was totally lost the whole time, sitting back at my panel with no charts to keep track of our position. Everywhere we went, there was always snow or rain, depending on how far north or south. Most walk-arounds happened in pouring rain or ankle-deep slushy snow on the ramp. It helped that we had been issued uniform raincoats, but my shoes never dried out for the whole three days.

The captain and first officer were great guys, and I was totally impressed with their skill at flying the 727. They never used the autopilot except during cruise. They were the best pilots in the business. I, however, was not having fun. My flight engineer check airman named Mike didn't seem to like me. He was not friendly and seemed to be scolding rather than teaching me what I needed to know about flying the line. It seemed he felt it was his job to make my life miserable.

Flight engineer panel of a Boeing 727

Sometimes poking me in the back if I wasn't doing something fast enough to please him. I wondered if he had learned this from Joe. Giving him a beatdown right there in the cockpit was tempting—but out of the question. There would be witnesses.

It felt like I was back in the simulator again, but at least there were no emergencies to deal with. If there were, I would have been fully prepared from all the training. The workload on the engineers' panel and pre-flights for four legs a day, one after the other, was not my cup of tea. I thought the airplane was cool but wanted to be up front flying it. I thought back to the more relaxed flying coast to coast in the Lear.

There was a saying in the airlines on three-man crews; "The copilot has the best job. The captain has all the responsibility, and the flight engineer does all the work. All the copilot has to do is fly every other leg and flirt with the flight attendants." I was dying to move up to the right seat.

One funny thing happened on my IOE, at one airport on a quick turnaround I was outside on the ramp, after my interior preflight, with my AA issued uniform raincoat buttoned and pulled tight around my neck against the cold wind and my black dress shoes wet from walking in slush. I'd just finished my walk-around and was about to climb the stairs to the jet bridge when it started pulling away from the jet.

I ran up the steps, struggled with my key, then burst through the door and told the agent, "I'm supposed to be on that airplane."

She looked at me as if I came from Mars.

Having looked inside the cockpit and seeing three pilots, she assumed they were good to go and closed the door.

She apologized and brought the jet bridge back and opened the door. As I walked into the cockpit, the two pilots were amused and chuckled about it. Mike just frowned and said, "What took you so long?"

I survived the IOE, but even more importantly, so did Mike.

American Airlines jets at LaGuardia with the old 'Ice Cream Cone' tower

Chapter 4
Welcome to LaGuardia

"This isn't a fairy tale, it's New York City."
–Alex Flinn

It seemed magical sitting inside the huge cockpit of the DC-10. I was in the jump seat just behind the captain. The big window to my left stretched from below my seat to just above the top of my head, and felt like a sliding glass door. In the dim light and all the dials and switches on all the many panels made it look like the inside of a spaceship as we rocketed toward planet New York.

It was my first time in a '10.' There were five of us, along with several hundred passengers and ten flight attendants in the back. The flight crew consisted of two pilots up front and the flight engineer at his panel. I envied him; it was a more modern airplane than the older 727 I'd just qualified on. The other two of us were commuting pilots in the jump seats. The engineer had commented on how easy his job was.

In the Learjet while at Devarian, I had flown into Newark and Teterboro right across the river many times, but this felt different. We would be landing at La Guardia. I didn't think a DC-10 would fit onto those small runways. As we descended toward the megalopolis of Manhattan, the lights of the city at night were overwhelming. It was quite a sight, like a terrestrial galaxy in its own right. We were low, about twenty-five hundred feet. You could see the Empire State Building in midtown, and as the Twin Towers went by, it seemed you could touch them. As we passed over the city, you could see down into the long corridors of streets lit mostly by the headlights of cars.

I marveled at the crew and their nonchalance as they handled that big bird easily and confidently. They were not as impressed as I was with the view, having seen it many times before.

It was the middle of winter, cold and crisp, and the air seemed to sparkle. I commented, "There has to be at least a million lights."

The copilot dryly observed, "Well keep this in mind: for every light you can see, there is at least one toilet."

The other guys laughed. Talk about spoiling an image! The city below just went from a sparkling planet in space to nothing more than a dirty town full of sewage.

I had hopped a ride to my new crew base, LGA for La Guardia. It was supposed to be my new home indefinitely, until I could transfer out, preferably to the west coast.

Once on the ground, I was on my own. I'd have to find a place to stay, as cheaply as possible. Again, I wished I were back in my Learjet, living at home in sunny Southern California.

The King's Inn

My blue company-issued uniform raincoat was buttoned under my chin with a scarf wrapped around my neck and my hands shoved deep into the pockets against the zero-degree temperatures. White clouds from my breath trailed behind me as I walked. I wished I had a hat.

The winter had swooped down from the north with a vengeance. The whole city seemed frozen. The only hat I had was my uniform cap, but I wasn't going to wear that in public unless I was at work.

My toes were numb in my running shoes as I stepped over patches of ice on the dark sidewalk, making my way up 87th Street coming back from the diner on Astoria Blvd, back to the King's Inn Hotel.

It was February 1987, and the crime rate was high. People had told me not to go out alone, especially at night.

I didn't have much choice. There was no restaurant at the King's Inn, and I couldn't afford a cab. So, I took the walk twice a day while I otherwise had nothing to do except wait in my room for a call to fly a trip somewhere, hopefully somewhere warm. I was on reserve, having to be available to fill in for sick calls or for whatever reason there might need me.

There were a bunch of new pilots on reserve, like me.

The first block of the half-mile walk from the hotel was an industrial district, deserted at night and very dark. On the second there were long, strange-looking buildings. On both sides of the street, they took up the entire block. Individual apartments or maybe condos, I suppose, but you could have walked the whole block on the roof without having to jump once.

On this block there were streetlights, and some of them were even working; that was a plus. There was a bluish glow in most of the windows from televisions. No one else was out.

The cars parked at the curb were not new. A working-class neighborhood in the city of Queens. I walked as fast as the slippery traction on the sidewalk would allow.

As I stomped along, my head was on a swivel, scanning for threats. I wondered once again if I really wanted this job. I thought I had, and it seemed like I'd made the 'big time,' and I had worked very hard to leap all the hurdles they had thrown at me. But just a few months ago I was a captain on a Learjet. Making more money and living at home in Southern California.

Now, I was at the very bottom of the totem pole, working as a flight engineer, which I didn't like, and having to pay for a hotel room in a city I could do without. I was seriously wondering if I'd made the right decision. A few years prior while at Imperial Airlines, flying out of Los Angeles, I had met flight engineers who were retiring, never having upgraded to copilot, let alone captain. They had been hired as pilots, but upward movement had been so slow, they never got to fly the airplane. It was probably just as well since after nineteen years, as one of them related, they'd probably forgotten how to fly, anyway. Deregulation of the airlines was supposed to change that, and all of us newly hired pilots were counting on it.

At the end of my frozen hike, I was grateful for the warmth of the lobby of the King's Inn. It was empty, and the clerk did not look up from his desk behind the bulletproof glass.

After bounding up the stairs two at a time to the second floor, I walked into my room and heard the already familiar sound of a headboard rhythmically hitting the paper-thin wall and the sounds of people going at it. The hotel had an hourly rate.

I hung up my coat, and rather than turning on any of the five local channels on the television — here was no cable, I flopped onto the bed, picked up a book and put in my company-issued earplugs.

The King's Inn was practically across the street from the famous LaGuardia Airport. You couldn't walk to it because of the Grand Central Parkway, but the hotel had a shuttle, so fortunately there was no need for a cab.

I was starting my first month at my new crew base, 'on the line' as a real American Airlines pilot. The next morning, I would report for duty.

The iconic American Airlines hangars, built in the 1930s

At 7:00 AM, I found myself in the iconic old antique hangar at the chief pilot's office, standing in a line with my four remaining buddies from our training class. Seeing them again made me feel not quite so alone in the city. Plus, there were six more from the class immediately senior to us.

We were given our seniority numbers, which would rule our lives for the rest of our careers. I think mine was 6,250 or so. It would change almost every month, as any pilot ahead of you retired, got fired or died. Sometimes new hires quit when another airline without the two-tiered B-Scale. You were now in a long line that figuratively shuffled forward over the years, dictating which seat in which airplane you could fly, or in what base. More on that later.

The people who upgraded to captain were not necessarily the best pilots. It was just that their number came up. And that day at La Guardia, we were at the very end of that line.

In my previous job, I had been making twenty-five thousand dollars a year. First-year pay at American was only eighteen thousand dollars a year, fifteen hundred a month before taxes, of course. As a probationary pilot, you could not yet be a union member, meaning you had no union protection if you got into trouble. The company could fire you at any time for the slightest mistake.

Eleven of us stood proudly in our new uniforms with our hats on. One other person in the room, a secretary, sat at a desk in a corner of the old office pounding away on a typewriter as Captain Ross Saddlemire, one of the two Chief Pilots of the New York base welcomed us and went down the line pinning on our wings, then shaking our hands with congratulations. It was a great feeling. We had graduated; we finally had our wings.

He explained; "Being based here in New York, you'll be on reserve and will be expected to cover all three of the airports of this base. Here at LaGuardia, Kennedy and Newark, and be available in no more than an hour's notice."

Ned asked, "How are we supposed to do that? We don't have cars here."

"That's your problem. There is plenty of public transportation here; the whole city is built on it. There's the subway, buses, and cabs. You'll learn how to use it. Just be where you're supposed to be when you're supposed to be there. You don't want to get fired for being late."

It wasn't that far to any of the other airports, but we were to find out that in New York City traffic, depending on where you were living, it could easily take an hour to get to the other two airports.

We just said, "Yes, sir!"

Then he said, "Oh, by the way, I need two volunteers for DC-10 International Flight Engineer." Looking at the two most junior guys, Bo and Ned, he said, "You two are it."

They both groaned as a small dark cloud came over the exhilaration of getting their wings. They wanted to get on the line and go to work, not go back to school for another month and learn about a new airplane. In unison they asked, "Do we have to?"

The Chief shrugged, "I just need two warm bodies. I don't care who it is."

I raised my hand and said, "I'll take it."

Art, a guy from the other class said, "Put me down for that too."

The Chief said to both of us, "It's yours. But you're still based here till the end of the month. The class won't start until mid-March."

Bo and Ned were relieved that they didn't have to go back to school. I felt just the opposite. I didn't like the 727 FE panel, and I didn't want to rent a place to live in New York, in the winter, and be available at three different airports, hopping around the East Coast, doing five to six legs a day in a lot of bad weather.

While I stayed at the King's Inn, Bo, Ned and Mike found a crash-pad in Brooklyn with other pilots and flight attendants. With limited bedrooms, it often involved sleeping on a couch or the floor. Everyone wanted to work as much as possible so they could eat for free on the airplanes and sleep in proper beds at layover hotels.

Sometimes when we had days off together, we would venture into the city. I was sort of the designated tour guide since I had been there many times, having spent entire weekends at the condo in Englewood, New Jersey, when I was with Devarian. We had the Lincoln Bobcat crew car at our disposal to explore, but we had learned the subway as well.

Bo and I in the New York subway. I wasn't really thinking of mugging him. Ned took the picture.

Chapter 5
I Don't Want to Be Here

"If I can make it there, I'll make it anywhere."
-Frank Sinatra

I used to say that New York was like a zoo; a very interesting place to visit, but you don't want to live there. I couldn't wait to transfer to California so I could live at home. Los Angeles was not a 727 base, but they had DC-10s. I hoped that by the time my training was up, my transfer would come through. Having just jump-seated in the cockpit, I knew how automated it was compared to the 727, which at that time was twenty-three years old. It seemed a lot back then because of the older technology.

The DC-10 was only seven years newer but was more modern. Technology was taking off; computers were suddenly being used in everything. Even the cars were talking, "Please fasten your seatbelt. Your door is ajar." People hated it.

Because of the computerization, the big wide body was a piece of cake to fly, but it did have a rather bad reputation because of several high-profile fatal crashes. At least the school was said to be easier than the Boeing boot camp.

I was happy to have this opportunity so quickly, but first I had to endure a month in New York in the dead of winter. That whole month, I only flew one trip in my current position as a 727 flight engineer. We called it a Buddy Ride. It was a three-day trip with an experienced flight engineer. My guy was named Andy. He was a good guy and not a check airman. For a change, I wasn't being tested.

On one of those days, according to my logbook, we flew six legs, seven hours and thirty-nine minutes, and my notes say, "Rain, snow, ice, wind-shear and minimums," meaning nasty weather, risky winds and the clouds were as low as they could be while we were still able to land. In other words, it was lousy flying and hard work, especially for the pilots up front.

The flight engineer on your Enhancement Flight was just supposed to show you the ropes and help to get you indoctrinated to day-to-day operations and Andy did a good job of that. He had me operate the panel on some of the legs and with no emergencies it was easy. I helped with the preflights and walkarounds and finally got to be part of the crew, not under the gun.

During a layover, sitting in the lounge of a hotel in Fort Wayne there was a conversation among the pilots about having a beer on layovers. The

FAA requires eight hours 'bottle to throttle.' For example, if you fly at 6:00 AM, you can't drink past 10:00 PM the previous night. But American had its own stricter rules of twelve hours. Most pilots thought it was crap and would abide by the more lenient FAA regs. But we didn't work for the FAA.

There was concern about getting turned in by flight attendants on your crew if you were seen breaking the company rules. Apparently, that had happened. But it was common to ignore the company's more stringent mandate. Being on probation I observed the twelve hours. Not long after, the union got American to observe the eight-hour limitation. This was long before random drug and alcohol testing as they do now. In 2019 United Airlines instituted a twelve-hour rule for its pilots after a crew got caught showing up for work over the legal limit.

That three-day buddy ride with its multiple legs and bad weather reinforced my feelings once again that I did not want to do that job, on that airplane, out of that base. I couldn't wait to get to the DC-10. I anticipated that I would be flying to Hawaii, the only international destination out of LAX at that time. Of course it is not another country, but being 'overwater,' that's how they designated it.

The gentleman's airplane

After surviving a month at the King's Inn, which is still there, I went back to training at the Flight Academy. Now instead of paying for a hotel room in freezing New York, I had a company provided room a lot further south at the Flagship. Owned by American Airlines, left over from the days when the company invested in hotels to house passengers and crew members. It turned out to be a losing proposition and the Flagship was probably the only one left. The pilots that stayed there called it the Black-Flag, after the bug spray.

When I showed up back at the schoolhouse, Art Arceneaux, the other guy in New York who volunteered was there as my training partner. He was from New Orleans, or as he pronounced it, Nawlins, Loosiana. He had a million jokes about the fictional Cajuns Thibodeaux and Boudreaux, pronounced Tibido and Boodro. Though he spoke normally most of the time, he could do the Cajun accent perfectly. He was hilarious and a joy to train and hang out with.

Throughout an airline career, some of the most memorable people are the ones you do a month of training with, because you spend so much time together. But that can work both ways, it can be good or bad. In my memory, most of mine were good.

I never minded training on a new airplane, new information, new procedures, a new world to learn. After doing so badly as a kid in school, and my turbulent past, I was surprised to find myself so eager to learn. It turned out all I needed was to be interested. Maybe I wasn't so dumb after all.

It was the last airplane designed with a flight engineer. The first thing they told us was, "The DC-10 is a gentleman's airplane, and this is a gentleman's school."

It felt like it too. Compared to the 727 it was more modern and highly automated. A much easier job for a flight engineer. There was even an auto-land system, it could land itself on autopilot, but for now that was for the pilots up front.

All airplane transition schools consisted of a month. Two weeks of ground school and two weeks in the simulator, usually five days on and two days off where you could fly home, for free of course. Like working at a restaurant where you get to eat free.

During the two weeks of ground school, remembering the stress of the 727 orals, Art and I studied our butts off and made sure we were ready for the dreaded oral exam.

The pressurization system especially, so easy to screw up on the older 727's was a piece of cake. It seemed it all was.

In the evenings instead of having out noses in the books, we spent our evenings in the hotel bar drinking beer with me listening to Art's Cajun jokes. Laughing so hard at times my sides hurt.

Instead of being individually under a microscope, Art and I were told we would take the test together. We wondered; Is this some kind of trap?

Sitting side by side in the small room behind a table, the walls were covered with pictures of the cockpit. The flight engineer panel, the pilot's flight instruments and the overhead panels. Everything we had been learning for the last two weeks. The check airman came into the little room, looked at his watch and said, "I've got a golf game starting in half an hour, do you guys have any questions?"

In unison we said, "No."

"Okay, you passed. Congratulations gentlemen."

With that he walked out. Art and I stared at each other in disbelief.

Finally, he said in his funny fake Cajun accent, "Well I'll be danged Thibodeaux, I guess this rally is a gentle man's *aeroplane.*"

Engineer's panel of Aircraft #AA135 (DC-10), featuring the proprietary mechanical checklist on the left. Photo courtesy of Airliners.net.

After another forty-eight, meaning a two-day R&R, instead of coming back to the Flight Academy at DFW, we were told to catch a flight to Miami.

American had just purchased some assets, like routes, from Pan American Airways, a long-time competitor. They were downsizing before finally shutting down flight operations altogether. The only thing left is the Pan Am Flight School, possibly in the same building where we trained. In one of them, there were several DC-10 simulators. Located on NW 36th St on the north side of Miami International Airport, it is the last vestige of the company. I am sure the DC-10 sims are long gone.

It was still wintertime, 1987. Our buddies from our new hire classes were still in New York, freezing their butts off, paying to live in crash pads and flying the old Boeing 727, hoping to be assigned trips to fly so they could eat for free on the airplanes while laying over in nice, paid-for hotel rooms. Meanwhile, Art and I were catching rays by the pool at our resort hotel in Miami Beach, studying our aircraft manuals part of the day, then spending several hours each day in the Pan Am simulators, with a pair of pilots up front, training as well. It's a big cockpit, which was a good thing because six of us were crammed in there: Art and I, the two pilots, the FE instructor, and the pilot instructor. In the evening, it was off to a bar for dinner and drinks.

Life can be tough, but somebody's gotta do it.

Paul Stephens, an old friend of mine from Alaska, is one of those 'positive thinking' entrepreneurs who helped me to change my life. He now lived in Orlando, and among other things, was a diving instructor. He came down and taught us to scuba dive in the hotel swimming pool. Then on a day off we went to the Florida Keys and drove out in his inflatable boat.

Diving into the clear waters of the Keys, we explored a new world with all kinds of fish, like barracudas and moray eels. We caught lobsters to cook for dinner. It was a great day and a world away from the cold northeast. This airline life was starting to look pretty good. If only we'd had email or texting back then, I could have sent selfies of sitting around a swimming pool or scuba diving to the guys in New York.

The check ride in the simulator was as easy as the ground school oral, and by the time the training was over, my transfer request to Los Angeles had been approved. Finally, I was going home!

Chapter 6
California Dreaming

"Not all those who wander are lost."
-J.R.R. Tolkien

The big DC-10.

Although I had been assigned International DC-10 Flight Engineer, LAX had no openings for international, so they put me on domestic operations. Which means within the United States but included Canada and Mexico, while 'International' to Hawaii was the same country. It was backwards, but that's how they operated it. Go figure. I wouldn't be flying to Hawaii yet.

After months of training, then sitting reserve in New York, and more training, by May 1987 I was finally on the line as a domestic DC-10 flight engineer. It was great. The winter weather was gone, and the job felt easy. The pilots up front were laid back and relaxed and always seemed to want to go out on layovers and have a good time. The flight attendants were friendly, and the food was good. I even had a table to set my tray on.

Best of all, I was based in Los Angeles and living at home. I didn't even mind the two-hour drive to the airport, if you're lucky. But it could easily turn into three or four hours if you weren't. If you found you were going to be late because of an accident or who knows what, the LA freeways didn't need a reason.

You had to get off and find a phone booth to alert crew scheduling, sometimes in a not so nice part of town. There seemed to be a lot of those. I hated getting off the freeway to find a phone. It made you even later. Years later, that problem was solved with the invention of cell phones, but back then it was a struggle.

You had to leave enough time after arriving at the employee parking lot for the bus ride to the terminal and operations. It was better to arrive two hours early than even five minutes late.

Frequently we flew non-stop to Boston, Miami or New York. Sometimes on the JFK run, we used the call sign American 'One' going west bound. It actually originated in London, flying to Kennedy, then LAX, then on to Honolulu. American 'Two' went east, Honolulu—LAX—JFK—London. Once again, it made me feel like I'd hit the big time.

Pilots are often treated to sights that earthbound people never get to see; even passengers with their little windows rarely are treated to spectacular sunrises and sunsets seen from high above. Moonless starlit nights with a bright Milky Way, looking edge-on into the galaxy from seven miles above our planet. Thunderstorms take on a different perspective when seen from the air. It can be right outside the window, just for us, it seems. Those are some of the special times of being a pilot.

From a distance we can marvel at the beauty and the power of an enormous thunderstorm, sometimes a whole line of them, flashing bolts of electricity sometimes nonstop. During the day, there are impossibly white clouds above, while being dark and threatening below. But at night, they can be black and invisible, lurking in the darkness until it lights up, making their presence known. Like a snake ready to strike if you get too close, the flash, like a rattle, serves as a warning, "Stay away." They can surprise you if you are not watching the radar. A close bolt of lightning can light up the cockpit like an arch welder. All we could do was shut our eyes to the brightness, trying to preserve what little night vision we had left, but there is frequently no time. That's usually when the 'thunderstorm lights' are turned on, making the cockpit almost as bright as the flashes outside.

The storms seem safe at a distance but have been known to throw hail out the top, traveling as far as thirty miles from a cell, hitting airplanes like white machine-gun bullets in clear air.

For the people below, they can be devastating. Spawning deadly lightning, heavy rain and tornadoes. Storms can attack, every bit like monsters, spreading death and destruction in their path without a care of whom they hurt.

Then there are the quiet, peaceful and rare moments. Like seeing the northern lights, or Aurora Borealis. Depending on your latitude and the time of year, it can be a fantastic display of mysterious nature, just doing what it does. All we can do is watch in awe. Sometimes seemingly right outside the window as if you could touch it, shimmering and changing colors. It is beautiful and completely benign.

Seeing them on the ground in Alaska years earlier, I was always amazed there would be so much motion and color but not sounds. There should be music, a symphony perhaps. Or drum rolls and cymbals crashing. It was like going to a concert and somebody pulled the plug on the speakers.

Saint Elmo's Fire can be spooky, like mini-lightning bolts dancing around your windshield. It's a static discharge caused by ionized air molecules, creating an eerie luminous plasma glow. Occurring in moist, electrically charged air, like near a thunderstorm, it doesn't happen very often, but it is memorable when it does.

Sometimes, these incredible images happen on the ground as well. One morning after an all-nighter, having landed at JFK, or Kennedy Airport, formerly known as Idyllwild. I got to my hotel room at the Hilton on the north side of the airport. Closing the door and putting my bags down, I walked to the window and threw open the drapes.

It was like the curtain rising on a stage to reveal an unforgettable sight. Almost right in front of me, it seemed, was an Air France Concorde. The supersonic airliner was in a hard right bank; after doing the Canarsie VOR approach, it was in the turn to line up on runway 13 Left. Even through the glass and the insulated hotel room, I could hear the roar of the massive engines.

The whole picture appeared at once: the long, narrow fuselage, tiny windows, swept wings, drooping nose, and long landing gear, with a beautiful blue and gold sunrise in the background. It was an incredible moment that almost took my breath away. It would have made a fantastic photograph if I'd had a camera handy. But it went by so fast I wouldn't have had time to get the picture. All I could do was stare in awe as he swept past, rolled level and descended toward the runway.

Whether we were flying Transcons, or hopping in and out of hubs like DFW, or ORD (Chicago), and smaller locations like Houston, Detroit or Toronto, I always enjoyed the flying because I was going into many different airports and cities from what I'd done on the Learjet.

By August, my transfer to international had come through. Now instead of going to the east coast and our big hubs, I was off to Hawaii.

Going International

Honolulu

Wearing my nylon shorts, a sweaty T-shirt, and running shoes, I panted as I sailed down the sidewalk to the tune of *Eye of the Tiger* by Survivor. Maybe it was the endorphins. I was in the paradise of Ala Moana Park, surrounded by tall palms, majestic banyan trees, and wide green lawns. Just across the busy boulevard stood the hotel and shopping mall that shared its name.

It was August, and the weather was warm and humid. I could see Diamond Head in the distance beyond Waikiki, looking like a postcard. Fat doves pecked at the grass or sat in the trees as seagulls whirled noisily above, and waves crashed on the beach. I couldn't hear any of it under the headphones of my Sony Walkman cassette player. It was just another perfect sixteen-hour layover in Honolulu and a world away from the northeast in the wintertime. Maybe being a flight engineer wasn't so bad after all.

Most flights arrived during the day, and when it was clear, which seemed most of the time, the view of the deep blue ocean and the emerald-green islands was breathtaking. Even though you were busy, you could glance out the cockpit windows and hurriedly take it in.

It looked just as good on the ground. The beach was a short walk from the hotel, and often you would get a view of the ocean from your room with that salt air breeze if you opened the sliding glass door. But you were subjected to almost constant car alarms going off in the nearby mall parking lot. On the back side, it was quieter, and you could see the luscious green mountains behind the city.

To eat or go shopping, the Ala Moana mall had just about everything. At McDonald's, they sold Spam and eggs with rice for breakfast, a World War Two leftover, perhaps. Having grown up on Spam, I thought that was cool. It was often on the menu at restaurants too. Japanese food, which I love, was also popular. You couldn't swing your surfboard without hitting a sushi restaurant.

It was usually a quick five-hour flight, and you were done for the day. But sometimes, after arriving in Honolulu and unloading most of the passengers, we would fly a turnaround to Maui and back—about twenty minutes each way. Three legs and landings instead of one. Still better than domestic flying. A lot of pilots and flight attendants thought it was the best job in the company. I had never been to Hawaii before, and I loved it. The tropical atmosphere, palm trees and ocean breeze reminded me of when I was a kid in South Florida.

When it was time to head home, during the exterior walk around, I was always in awe while looking up at that enormous airplane. I think you could have put a whole Learjet inside one engine. And it was always warm and pleasant.

Aluminum Overcast: Kicking the Tires on a DC-10

It often felt surreal, especially while on the ramp at Maui or Honolulu. Visions of Ernest K. Gann's *The High and the Mighty* came to mind.

Sometimes on the flights back, often at night, sitting in a dark cockpit, when it was quiet, I would think of that movie and the similarities. Here I was, flying an airliner from Honolulu to the west coast. They were flying to San Francisco, not LA, but I also thought of how different it was. They were in a DC-4 with four radial engines with propellers at eight or nine thousand feet, doing one-hundred-seventy miles per hour. Here I was on a big threeengine jet at thirty-seven thousand feet, streaking along at almost six hundred miles per hour, spending only five hours in the air compared to eleven back then. Things had changed a lot in just thirty years.

Prominent in Gann's story is the dramatic sounding 'point of no return.' It was my job to figure where that was for each flight based on the winds, aircraft weight, fuel use and a dozen other factors, including the phase of the moon and whether or not it was an election year. However, by then we called it ETP for Equal Time Point. It's the point where, if something goes wrong before it, you return to your departure airport; if it happens after, you continue straight ahead.

Today, the ETP is listed on your flight plan, figured out by computer. Flying to and from Hawaii, there is only one. With other destinations, you might have three or more. The west coast to Hawaii is the longest overwater route in the world, with no alternate landing spots in case of an emergency.

Earnest Gann was a great writer, and many of his books were made into movies, the dream of every writer. So here I was, living the dream of working for an airline, although not actually flying yet. I could not even have imagined it when I was living the life of a biker. At the end of one trip as we were saying goodbye before leaving the flight deck, the captain named Hank, who was a real good guy, turned to me and said, "Don't lose your good attitude."

I was taken aback; I didn't know I had one. I was just happy to be there, but I appreciated him taking notice, and I always tried to remember those words. Especially because a short time later he retired and a month after that, while helping a friend repair his roof, he fell off and was killed. To survive a lifetime in aviation, and then when he was finally going to relax and enjoy retired life, he was gone. It seemed so sad. Fate Is the Hunter, as Ernie Gann would say.

All new hires were pilots, our uniforms sported three strips, even if we were working as flight engineers. There were some old flight engineers who were not pilots, they wore two stripes, so we called them Two Stripers. Not having to retire at sixty like pilots, they could work forever. Some of them were seventy-five years old and had been flying for at least fifty years. Starting out as Air Force mechanics, then going to flight engineers, then retiring and going with the airlines. Many were collecting social security, plus an Air Force pension along with their AA paycheck. It was said they were making more money than captains on the 10.

They were incredibly knowledgeable about the aircraft systems and could seemingly do the job in their sleep, since I heard from other pilots, they did that a lot.

A suspenseful cockpit scene from the classic aviation movie, *The High and the Mighty*

Surviving Probation

Back on the ground in LA, there was still that whole six-month 'board' thing waiting for me. As a new hire, they monitored you and had captains fill out evaluation reports to make sure you were up to speed. Sometimes riding with you on the line watching you work, and in interviews in the flight office. Six months after your hire date, you were called on the carpet before the local chief pilot, and he would grill you on aircraft systems, procedures and company or FAA regulations. If he felt you were inadequate in any way, he could fire you on the spot. Remember, you had no union protection.

`The chief pilot at LAX was a hard-nosed, old-school guy named Ralph Sirek. A former Air Force fighter pilot who had flown F-105's over North Vietnam, he was the kind of guy I had read books about. He had no tolerance for anyone he felt was a slacker. Supposedly, twenty new hires had been fired in the last few years, and nineteen of them had been at Los Angeles, mostly at their six-month or eleven-month board hearings. One, it was said, because his hair was too long, although I suspect it was more than that. Hair can be a statement, or an attitude.

I knew pilots who lived in Southern California who refused to bid into LAX until they were off probation, specifically because of Captain Sirek. I flew with him once on a trip to Honolulu. He was a no-nonsense guy, not friendly, all business, but he wasn't the terror I had been told to expect.

When it came to upgrading, the conventional wisdom was to stay at the engineer's panel and keep your head down until you were off probation. Then, if seniority allowed, you could move to the right seat.

I never listened to conventional wisdom. Although I enjoyed the DC-10 and flying to Honolulu, I still had that burning desire to fly, so I bid for MD-80 copilot as soon as I could, in LAX of course. In December 1987, it came through and I was sent back to school for the third time in a year.

I picked the 80 because it was the only airplane American flew out of Ontario, which was closest to my home, only an hour and without the awful Los Angeles freeway traffic.

After another month of training, two weeks in ground school and two weeks in the simulator, by late January I was back on the line in the right seat of the DC-9. But before I even got on the line, I was called in for my last board. Unlike being a flight engineer, I felt confident answering questions about being a pilot.

Captain Sirek didn't fly the MD-80, so he didn't ask system questions; he focused on approach charts and FAA regulations. With only a little bit of sweaty palms, I passed the eleven-month board. Now I would fly trips as a copilot out of Ontario, California. I was a pilot again, not a flight engineer. I could even hold regular schedules and not have to be on reserve. I had made another hurdle, and being off probation, got a big pay raise. From eighteen thousand a year to about forty-five thousand. Life was good!

Having joined the Allied Pilots Association, I could now be part of its credit union, so I thought it was time to buy my first ever new car. When the lady in the office asked what equipment and seat I was in, she entered it into the computer and told me I could borrow up to seventy thousand dollars. Wow! No wonder some pilots were driving Corvettes!

I bought a Honda Civic.

MD-80 cockpit

Chapter 7
The MD-80

"Treasure this day and treasure yourself, neither will ever happen again."

-Ray Bradbury

I was finally back at the controls, a window seat, not a flight engineer panel. Looking back, I think the 727 is a great airplane, but I wanted to 'fly' it, not just flip switches.

The check airman on my IOE was a cool guy named Dick Gilliam. He had me fly all seven legs of the three-day trip. It included a diversion to Baltimore because of bad weather while trying to get into Philadelphia. When we finished back at Ontario, as a joke he signed off my little pocket logbook with "Okay for solo, S-80 only."

The MD-80, meaning McDonnell Douglas DC-9-80, was also called the Dash 80 or, as American liked to call it, the Super 80—and sometimes the Mad Dog. In the 1980s, it was the darling of the airlines. It had almost the same seating capacity as the 727-200 but was powered by two more powerful Pratt & Whitney JT8D engines that produced nearly as much power as the three engines on the 727. It used significantly less fuel and, when introduced in 1980, became the most fuel-efficient airliner in the skies.

Modern and highly automated like the DC-10, the MD-80 was not necessarily easier to fly. It could autoland and had a rather complicated flight guidance panel, plus autothrottles. Some pilots, like the 727 guys, were apprehensive about flying it. The old 72 was just easier and straightforward, and they were used to it. But I embraced it, seeing that as the future. I worked to learn as much as possible about the various flight management systems. I didn't avoid it as some of the older pilots did, but I certainly didn't blame them; it was hard to trust those newfangled things called computers.

It was more fuel efficient and, like the 727, featured a rear air stair plus a retractable stair at the front entry door. It could operate without a jet bridge or pulling up ground-based stairs at smaller airports. Those rear stairs always reminded me of the boarding ramp on the Millenium Falcon in Star Wars.

As part of the B-Scale agreement with the union, AA management promised to buy hundreds of them, creating rapid upward movement of pilots that had been stuck in the copilot or flight engineer's seats for years.

American started operating the Mad Dog in 1983. It was the workhorse of the fleet, which by 2003, with just over 100 planes from Trans World Airlines, had grown to 362, making the AA MD-80 fleet alone larger than some major airlines.

In the mid to late 80s, the movement up the seniority list was so rapid, there were flight engineers who had not flown an airplane in many years, suddenly upgraded to first officer, then after a few months, they were in the left seat as a captain in the 80 which was the junior equipment at the time. Sometimes it was rather apparent. Even as a junior copilot, it was obvious that I had more stick time in recent years than some captains I flew with. But that was rare; most of the guys I was paired up with were excellent pilots. And most were good guys too, but there are always exceptions. Who you're working with can make or break a three-day trip, or a whole month. For me, flying the airplane was easy. The hardest part was getting along with the more unusual personalities. As an ex-biker, kicking their ass was simply not an option. Using tolerance and patience became a valuable exercise in controlling my redheaded temper.

I was happy in my current position, flying big jets all over the country and off probation. I could relax and focus on the job. All that apprehension and worry about whether I could do the job was mostly behind me. Now, I just needed not to screw up and tried not to think about all the ways you could still lose your job.

In training, one of the things we learned immediately is the difference between procedures and techniques. A procedure is how you must do something; a technique is how you may do something. It can be annoying when a pilot you are working with replaces the former with the latter. As a copilot, it was your job to learn the procedures and fly the airplane the way the company expected you to.

As an FO, being 'creative' was not allowed. Making up your own techniques, thinking you knew more than the people who designed how the airplane should be flown, was stupid. If you did, it was the captain's job to correct you and demand that you do it the right way. If you still didn't, and word got back to the chief pilot, you could get fired. And you should.

However, when you sometimes fly with a captain who would make up their own techniques instead of using proper procedures, it is not the first officer's job to tell the captain how to fly. I know. When you question them, they don't like it. Their egos are already out of control in thinking they have a better way. But unless they are doing something completely unsafe, the FO will usually put up with it and look the other way.

Accidents have happened where the captain is doing something wrong, and if there is no evidence on the cockpit voice recorder that the copilot said anything, they can be found equally at fault for letting it happen.

I flew with captains who could be very annoying with their techniques, but usually not dangerous. They are supposed to provide a good example to the copilot, not show them how creative they can be. Everyone is a teacher. Not only how to be, but how not to be. All of life is like that.

There was one who would always go below the glide slope on short final, and I would always call it out loudly to put it on the cockpit voice recorder.

He said, "Oh, you have to go below the glide slope to get this thing stopped."

I said, "No, you don't!" He kept doing it despite my protests, so I put in a request not to fly with him.

Rather than going to the company, there was an office within the union called Professional Standards where you could report bad pilots. But when you did, and told them their name, the answer was always, "Oh yeah, we know all about him."

Then the obvious question was So, why haven't you done anything about it? It could be frustrating; the union would frequently protect bad pilots.

In my opinion, one of the perks of flying for an airline was crew meals. Some people will laugh at this, since 'airline food' has gotten to be a joke, but none of the outfits I had worked for previously offered food for pilots. We got the same meals as first-class passengers. Head and shoulders above what they used to serve in coach. On the wide bodies, I thought it was especially good. Okay, maybe because I had grown up poor, and thought Spaghetti O's, especially with meatballs, was a big deal. My perspective may have been a little skewed.

When I left home at fifteen on my first motorcycle, I often lived on fast food or canned goods, so I wasn't picky. During a training session at the flight academy, we stayed at a hotel in Arlington, Texas, right next to a Waffle House. I'd never seen one before, so I gave it a try. Walking in the door, I was greeted by a waitress and the smell of waffles, bacon and maple syrup. I liked it right away. They had, and still have, an excellent grilled chicken sandwich, and back then their micro-thin steak and eggs was only about four dollars.

I went there a lot, partly because it was such a short walk. One day on the van riding into the flight academy, I overheard another pilot talking about it.

He said to the guy next to him, "Have you been to the Waffle House?"

His buddy replied, "No, I'd never go in a place like that."

"Good, don't! That's the worst greasy spoon I've ever seen. All you smell when you walk in the door is grease."

I thought to myself, are we talking about the same place? But then I like McDonald's too, and I've heard people say that was the worst place ever.

I flew with some pilots who would simply never eat crew meals, no matter how good I thought they were. Whether they just didn't like them, or maybe they believed the rumors of flight attendants spitting in their food, I didn't ask.

The Mad Dog—McDonell Douglas MD-80

Instead of driving two hours to Los Angeles, if you're lucky, Ontario was only an hour from where I lived. There were none of the congested LA freeways. Many of the schedules I got were three days on, four days off, with four trips per month.

Unlike on international flights, the flight attendants on the S-80 were newer, younger, friendlier, and more motivated—a whole new environment. Unlike the Honolulu flights, which were the easiest job in the airline, and the best layover, those trips went to the most senior crews, except for, as I had experienced, new flight engineers.

Many of the FAs on the 80 were new hires, happy to be there and full of enthusiasm. Sometimes they even went out with us for dinner and drinks. One captain I flew with was named Vic. He was a great guy, but even though he was a former Air Force fighter pilot, he couldn't ever seem to land the airplane very well. For one entire month we had a cute little Japanese-American number one flight attendant named Nori, and she would tease him unmercifully about his awful landings. He was such an easygoing guy he just smiled and took it. Maybe he was used to it.

After the problems with the DC-10 hydraulics, and newer airplanes that were 'fly by wire,' the Super 80 seemed safer with its control cables to servo tabs and anti-servo tabs. The flight controls were not hydraulically boosted or electrically controlled. The 727 and 737s have hydraulically boosted controls, and they still have a manual reversion as a backup, which is hard to use, but better than nothing. Even though it handled like a truck, the MD-80 felt more honest and dependable. As the years went by, flight crews either hated the MD-80, or they loved it.

The cockpit was quieter than the 727, which was designed in the 1950s, partly because the engines were so far back and a newer model of the same JT-8's on the 727. It was more comfortable for the lucky people sitting in first class. However, if you were a passenger or flight attendant sitting in the very back between those two big motors, it was a loud, constant pulsating growl that never stopped until you got to the gate.

I'd heard some pilots say it was hard to land, but I never experienced that. I've probably made some of my best landings ever in that airplane. Even though it had a Performance Management System or PMS, you still had to figure your descents and fix crossing altitudes by doing the math in your head.

The 727 was probably the last 'pilots' airplane before automation took over certain tasks. American retired the 727 in 2002 after flying it for thirty-eight years. Then the MD-80 was an old airplane, having been with the company for nineteen years.

There are several computerized safety measures that have improved safety immeasurably, Traffic Collision Alert System, or TCAS, and Enhanced Ground Proximity Warning System, or E-GPWS to name a couple.

Computers on airplanes have made flying them easier and safer than ever. But it has also made pilots more complacent. It's human nature that when someone or something is going to do a job for you, you can relax. For pilots, that can be a problem. If someone or something suddenly decides not to do that job for you because you are out of practice, will you remember how to do it? At a moment's notice? Or a split second?

It's called automation dependency, and it was even a problem almost forty years ago.

I can assume it has only gotten worse. When I was first flying the MD-80, it was a basic VOR-only airplane with basic round flight instruments, which were no different from anything else I'd flown, like Lears and Falcons at Devarian, or even Cessnas. That was the standard in the aviation industry at that time. Unlike the 727, the '80' had autothrottles and could land by itself. The autoland feature was designed, and even required, to be used when landing in foggy conditions where the pilots can't see to do it manually. We would practice it in the simulator regularly because if it didn't work right, you had to be ready to take over. Once again, you faced the pressure of split-second decisions. Even though you had to know how to do it, it was rare to perform that maneuver under real conditions.

In 1981, Boeing launched the 767, one of the first airliners equipped with cathode ray tube (CRT) displays. CRTs or small display screens with flight instruments and moving maps, giving you a tremendous advance in situational awareness as to your location; where you are and where you are going. That technology quickly spread to other airplanes, eventually making its way to the MD-80. It never got the laser ring gyro navigation of the 767, but later GPS, or Global Positioning Satellites, came along and simplified things even more. It's the same as what we use in our cars nowadays.

Even though automation dependency has become a problem, the most dangerous year to fly was 1972 when, according to Wikipedia, 2,373 people died worldwide in seventy-four crashes.

Automation was originally limited to an autopilot that kept the airplane at the selected altitude and heading. World War Two bombers like the B-17 and B-24 and the civilian DC4/military C-54 were so equipped. They were very basic but reduced fatigue from the monotony of hand flying for hours at a time. The early jets like the Boeing 707 and 727 weren't much different. Pilots hand-flew the aircraft to altitude, engaged the autopilot for cruise, then disengaged it for descent and landing.

As a copilot on the MD-80, it was not unusual to fly with a captain that had come from the 727. He would say in the initial briefing that he didn't use the automation. At first, I was annoyed, thinking that he just didn't understand it well enough, which may have been true in some cases. So, they flew as if they were still on the 727—no autothrottles, no autopilot, no flight guidance system. When reaching cruise altitude, they would turn on the autopilot and autothrottles for cruise flight, and when starting the descent, they would shut off the automation and fly it all the way to landing. Despite my bias toward embracing automation, their flying skills genuinely impressed me; they were usually smoother and more precise than if the autopilot had been on. At that time, the 727 guys and girls were the best 'stick and rudder' pilots in the business.

Though my attitude was to learn the automation and procedures as thoroughly as possible, because of my admiration for these true pilots, I tried to make it a point to hand fly most of at least one leg on a three-day trip to keep in practice.

On the other side of that coin, there were the guys who had been flight engineers for many years when the upward movement started. When they moved to the right seat, it was often on a highly automated aircraft like the DC-10 or 767 and possibly flying international trips like to Hawaii, not multiple hops per day like most domestic flying. They may have spent only six months there before upgrading to captain on the MD-80. There were times it was obvious they had not flown much in a long time. Things were moving so fast, it wasn't unusual to fly a new airplane with a new captain.

***

In 1987, Continental 1713 was a DC-9 taking off out of Denver Stapleton on a snowy November afternoon. The captain had been with Continental for nineteen years, but had upgraded three weeks prior and had only 166 hours in the DC-9.

The first officer was newly hired, with 3,000 hours of total flight time, but no prior jet experience. He had left another flying job where he had had problems with passing check rides, but Continental was not told that when he was hired. He had 36 hours in the DC-9 and had not flown at all in the last twenty-four days.

A lot of mistakes were made by both pilots, but the captain is ultimately responsible. The copilot over rotated and stalled the airplane on takeoff. They crashed back onto the runway, killing twenty-eight of the eighty-eight people onboard, including the pilots. After that, the FAA put out new regulations about pairing low-time pilots together.

***

In the last days of December 1991, the Dana Viking, a Scandinavian Airlines MD-80, lined up on the runway at Stockholm, Sweden.

After takeoff, both engines began experiencing compressor stalls and surges. The captain properly reduced power while struggling to control the aircraft, but the autothrottle system reversed his decision and increased to full power. As a result, the engines started to disintegrate and catch fire.

Spewing pieces of turbine blades and other engine parts across miles of snow-covered forest, the plane was losing airspeed and descending. The captain did an incredible job keeping the aircraft in the air until there was no other option. Spotting a clearing in the forest, he managed to belly-land the big jet, which slid along the rough terrain, the long fuselage breaking into three pieces. Incredibly, everyone survived.

Jet engines are very reliable; losing one is unusual enough, but losing both at the same time was unheard of. What could have caused this catastrophe?

The aircraft had come in from Zurich the night before and sat outside with 5,600 pounds of cold-soaked fuel in the wings. During the night there was rain and light snow, making it necessary to deice the airplane before takeoff. They did that twice to make sure, and they got most of it, but when inspecting the wing, the deice Forman did not notice the clear ice hiding in plain sight at the wing root, where the cold-soaked fuel had been coldest.

Clear ice is invisible. Even if he had looked straight at it, he might not have seen it.

Ice on the wings has been a problem in aviation since the first pterodactyl tried to take off in a snowstorm.

When the airplane lifts off, the wings flex when the weight transfers from the wheels to the wings. When that happened, the ice layer broke and left the wing. If the engines are under the wing like most jets, nothing happens. On earlier versions of the DC-9 that was not a problem, but the MD-80 was so long that now, in the nose up attitude on takeoff and the engines being further back, they were in the perfect location to ingest that ice.

Many MD-80s had taken off in clear, blue-sky conditions, only to have their engines ingest ice, resulting in damage. It happened on an AA flight out of Ontario with a captain named Tony Moore. A really good captain and a nice guy who I'd flown with. Taking off westbound from runway 26R, both engines immediately started surging and losing power. With the airspeed dropping, Tony was afraid to try to turn the airplane to make a pattern back to the runway, instead of allowing the autothrottles to go to full power and destroying the engines, he disconnected them, pulled the power back, declared an emergency and drove on straight ahead toward LAX. That's probably what I might have done, but the FAA disagreed, they thought he should have landed at the nearest suitable airport, which was Ontario. But they made it, and it was one more lesson about ice on the wings.

But why were they getting ice ingestion into the engines in clear air conditions?

It turned out that the MD-80 would 'make its own ice.' With 'cold soaked' fuel in the wings, it would literally pull moisture out of the air to form clear ice on top of the inside section of the wing. The area right in front of the engines. Not good!

It became a requirement for whoever was doing the walk-around, usually the FO, to climb up on the wing, via specially made ladders provided by the ground crews, to check for the presence of ice. Just looking at it was not enough; you had to run your foot across the surface of the inner portion of the wing to make sure it was free of ice.

Eventually, they came up with a heated 'blanket' in that location on the wing that would melt any ice if the OAT (outside air temperature) was below a certain level. The problem went away. They did not yet have those heaters while I was an FO.

Chapter 8
A Killer Reveals Itself

> *"Whatever you want to do, do it now.
> There are only so many tomorrows."*
> -Michael Landon

About to face death, the pilots peered into the murky conditions after dropping below the cumulus clouds. They could see ahead, but not well. The heavy rain on the windshield made it difficult. They were alert and tense, knowing this would be a risky approach. Highly competent, they were one of the most experienced crews on the new Lockheed L-1011.

The first officer said, "Lightning coming out of that one."

They had forty-seven seconds left to live.

***

First you hear the rain, light at first, then crackling loud like popcorn, pounding on the outside of the cockpit, then it gets dark, even in the daytime, then you hear the thunder and sometimes see the bright flashes. Suddenly the airspeed increases, so you pull back the throttles as you enter the deadly trap being set by the killer drawing you in.

You're on final approach, perfectly aligned with the ILS glideslope, almost safely on the ground, but the trap is about to be sprung. The killer has you in its sights.

***

On August 2, 1985, a large, three-engine widebody Lockheed L-1011 operated by Delta Airlines was cruising in the clear blue sky. The towering white clouds all around them looked both beautiful and ominous. Threading their way through the white columns was one thing; having to descend into them was quite another.

The current destination was Dallas-Ft. Worth airport and on the ground, it was one of those typical summer days, hot and humid with occasional rain and thunderstorms.

The crew was watching the onboard weather radar while dodging cells, the air traffic controller gave them a heading in the descent straight toward a bad place.

The captain said, "I'd rather not fly through that; I'd rather go around it."

The controller said, "I've had about sixty aircraft go through there and had a good ride, no problem."

"I can see a cell now on a heading of two-four-zero," the captain replied.

"Okay, Delta one-ninety-one, you're cleared to deviate right and intercept the Blue Ridge zero-one-zero radial inbound."

They descended from the bright blue sky and white clouds into a dark grey world, with rain beating on the windshield and turbulence. Ted, the captain, and Rudy, the copilot, were two of Delta's most experienced pilots. On this leg, Rudy was flying the airplane as a mysterious, deadly force was taking shape in their path.

It was almost six in the evening, and despite the cloudy weather, the temperature on the ground was one-hundred-one degrees Fahrenheit and sticky. Typical Texas in the summer.

Lockheed L-1011 Tristar

The radios crackled with the announcement, "Attention all aircraft, there is a little rain shower just north of the airport..." Then the captain switched the radio frequency.

What he didn't hear was, "... There's a little bitty thunderstorm sitting right on the final." But that little thunderstorm was building rapidly.

With superior radar, the weatherman in approach control would have noticed the growing storm and could have warned pilots, but at the time it got to a dangerous level, he was in the cafeteria on a meal break.

Delta 191 checked in with the tower and was told, "Wind 090 at 5 gusting 15."

Sounds easy enough…

As the big plane got kicked around in turbulence, one of the passengers was worried.

He tightened his seat belt, saying it was so quiet in the cabin you could hear a pin drop.

Others were concerned too.

Now on final approach, while Ted was watching his radar scope, they dropped out of the cloud layer and Rudy said, "Lightning coming out of that one."

"Where?"

"Right ahead of us."

The monster was waiting for them.

The Learjet ahead reported a smooth ride, but he later told investigators, "It was the heaviest rain I've ever seen before or since. We used the whole runway and turned off at the end." The trap was set, and Delta was walking right into it.

Using 13,400 feet of runway for a Learjet is unprecedented, but he did not tell the tower to warn other aircraft.

As Flight 191 entered the microburst, the airspeed increased. They'd been instructed to maintain 150 knots to stay behind the Lear. Ted said, "Watch your speed." Rudy pulled the throttles back.

The rain grew louder, and the cockpit darkened as they hit the leading edge of the microburst. The airplane began to shake, and the airspeed increased further. Rudy pulled back the throttles again to maintain the assigned approach speed. Turbulence shook the airplane up and down, side to side. Suddenly the airspeed fluctuated wildly, then dropped to almost stall speed.

Ted yelled, "Push it up! Push it way up!"—meaning the throttles, the engine power. After four tours in Vietnam, Nick, the flight engineer, was no stranger to stress. Feeling frustrated, he echoed, "Way up!"

The airplane seemed to recover, the airspeed increased, and everything was looking good.

They were already too low when the bottom fell out again and the vertical speed went to over two thousand feet per minute down at four hundred feet above the ground. A severe right crosswind hit and pushed them left as the plane rolled hard right. Rudy fought to recover.

On the cockpit voice recorder, the captain yelled, "Hang on to the son of a bitch!"

"You're going to lose it all of a sudden."

"There it is…"

Ted yelled, "TOGA!" Meaning hit the 'Takeoff/Go Around' button, which gives you full power. But it was too late; those were the last words on the cockpit voice recorder.

They impacted the ground just short of Highway 114 and plowed across that road through evening rush hour traffic rolling on the landing gear. Amazingly killing only one person in his car, William Mabry, who had just left work and was on his way home.

Continuing past the road, the plane lifted off again and flew for a second, but then it settled onto the rough ground. The ride was now like a very rough off-roading experience or, as another passenger described it, like driving on flat tires. Now on airport property, they plowed across the open ground beyond Highway 114. They might have made it, but having been pushed to the left by that nasty right crosswind, they were now in line with two giant water tanks.

The landing gear collapsed, and they had no way to steer, now sliding on the belly of the aircraft.

At approximately 150 miles per hour, they impacted one of the water tanks. The plane broke into many pieces and burst into flames. The rear part of the fuselage holding the last ten rows broke off and spun backward across the field. 138 people died, including Ted, Rudy, Nick the flight engineer, seven flight attendants, and William Mabry, who was in his car. Three flight attendants survived. Of the 152 passengers, 128 lost their lives; the rest miraculously survived. Don Estridge, the IBM executive, and his wife were among those who did not survive.

In 1975, an Eastern Airlines Boeing 727 crashed while attempting to land at John F. Kennedy Airport in New York. The cause at the time was a mystery.

In 1982, another Boeing 727—Pan Am Flight 759—crashed on takeoff in New Orleans. They weren't the first, and they wouldn't be the last. The National Transportation Safety Board, which investigates all aviation accidents, didn't know why it happened and labeled it an "Act of God."

At first, the NTSB thought it might be lightning having hit the airplanes. But the advanced Flight Data Recorder on the L-1011 revealed detailed data on exactly what the storm was doing every second, and with this information, they were able to expose the killer.

A microburst is very localized and resembles a waterfall of water and wind. If you try to fly through it, first you get a headwind, then a downdraft, then a tailwind, plus the turbulence. It's all bad! And it's a trap you may not escape from; you need to run from it.

Avoidance is the only way to fight it.

After Delta 191, the FAA hurried to install Terminal Doppler Weather Radar systems at large airports. DFW was one of the first.

Since 1964, investigations have found microbursts to be responsible for 26 airline accidents costing over 500 lives.

With special new detection equipment on a modified 737 in 1991, the FAA went hunting for microbursts. With dozens of technicians onboard, they risked their lives as they flew into dangerous microbursts to get the data required to prevent these accidents in the future. After testing several different systems, they found the forward-looking Doppler radar was the only one that could reliably detect a microburst ahead.

Today, forward-looking Doppler radar is standard equipment on airliners around the world. In the early 90s, I was introduced to the new warning system during recurrent training sessions. With advanced detection equipment and pilot training, microburst accidents have become a thing of the past.

This quote appears at the end of the Mayday: Air Disaster episode on Delta Airlines Flight 191, titled 47 Seconds Until the Catastrophe: "Captain Connors and First Officer Price lost their fight against the microburst, but their struggle exposed and disarmed an invisible killer."

***

Virtual Reality

An American Airlines simulator in 'flight'

Even though it was hard work, for the most part I enjoyed simulator training, but not the microburst scenarios. It was scary, loud, rough and unpleasant. Even though you know you're not going to die, the sweat was all too real. Over the rattling, shaking and the simulated noise of rain or hail, the pilot not flying had to loudly call out the flight instruments, airspeed, altitude and vertical speed indicator to the pilot flying who was trying desperately to hang onto what seemed more like a bucking bronco than an airplane, fighting to keep it right side up.

We would always be in the clouds; the pilot didn't have time to look at anything but the attitude indicator. Of course, in real life, you might be in clear conditions and look out the window, but that was never the case in the simulator. You trained for the worst-case scenario, which meant you were almost always in the clouds at night.

The thought of going through this in the real world was almost enough to make you walk away and pursue your fortune in stamp collecting.

Simulator flight training is the original virtual reality. Even the crude early Link trainers were very effective at teaching instrument flying to pilot trainees in World War Two.

However, modern trainers were so realistic that, years later, when I saw the 'Holodeck' on Star Trek, I thought, *That's the future extension of flight simulators.* Thanks to the lessons learned from Delta 191, we were taught about the dangers of wind shear and microbursts, how to avoid them, and how to respond if we were caught in the trap.

Back on the Line

The final leg of the day, it was dark when the flight attendant burst through the cockpit door in a jovial mood, we were on our way to Buffalo, New York, she asked excitedly, "Are you having wings and beer tonight?"

The captain said, "Sure."

I said, "Wings? What's that? I've never been to Buffalo before."

She said, "You've never had Buffalo wings? No Kidding? You're in for a treat, you've gotta join us for wings."

I asked, "Sounds good!"

"Everyone goes for wings in Buffalo."

I looked at the captain, he nodded enthusiastically and smiled.

"Okay, I'll be there."

We stayed at the Williamsville Inn and they, probably like every other bar and restaurant in Buffalo, claimed they had invented the wings. It was very old with dark wood paneling on the walls, but neat and comfortable. The rooms felt like they were in the basement, a window in the upper part of the wall was at ground level. They had a cozy dim bar and restaurant where we had dinner sometimes, and it was always Buffalo Wings and beer. In the early 90's, the televisions in the rooms had three channels, all of them local, and two of them Canadian. If you practiced, you could understand them.

They signed off at ten O'clock at night. But the hotel had a 'crew room' and it had a new channel called CNN. Something called cable, and they did live news from all over the world. Right then it was the Gulf War in 1990.

The airline crews started congregating there rather than the bar. The waitresses would come and take our orders. If it wasn't Wings and Beer, the rest of the rest of the room looked at you like you didn't belong there. A plant. A spy perhaps. Not just us at AA, other companies as well.

How did you want your wings mild, medium or hot? I always chose hot. One night there was a Delta crew sharing the room with us, flight attendants and all. We put our orders in and watched the war on live TV. The Delta crew had a first officer that appeared to be Asian, they can be as bad as Mexicans when it comes to hot food. He ordered his wings 'Volcano' hot.

The waitress's eyes widened, she was dubious, "Are you Sure?"

He said, "Yes, the hotter the better."

We chuckled and shook our heads in disbelief, now we had to stick around to see what would happen next in the small room with the old console TV. When his order showed up we watched with great interest.

The bombs on television were going off with regularity, sometimes dropping with extreme precision through windows or down chimneys. We were all amazed, but not as much as watching the Delta FO eat his wings.

The cold beer didn't seem to be cooling things off much as his glasses started to fog from the heat. Or maybe it was from the sweat on his face.

We laughed so hard; it was better entertainment than the live war on television. He was a good sport and laughed with us as he sipped beer to try to cool off while sweat poured down his face and soaked his shirt. He said the wings were hotter than he expected, but he continued to eat, and we continued to be impressed.

To our amazement, he finished the whole plate, a dozen wings as hot as they could make them.

Buffalo Wings

The Wings from Hell

I figured I could take on any hot wing out there, until one night during a layover in Stamford, Connecticut. I stopped at a packed bar. It was a weekend. I ordered a beer and a dozen wings.

The bartender asked, "How do you like 'em?"

I said, "Hot."

He said, "Are you sure? Hot is hot!"

I confidently said, "The hotter the better."

Hesitantly, he said, "Okay."

This is the East Coast, I thought. *How hot could it possibly be? I'm from the West Coast.*

When the wings arrived, I tore into the first two like nothing. When I picked up the third, my mouth was going into thermal runaway like a battery on a Learjet or a Tesla. A whole beer could not cool my mouth, my lips, my tongue. So, I hoarsely ordered another beer.

The bartender brought it with a sympathetic smile. The fire still wouldn't go out. I nervously looked at the fourth wing, holding it until my fingers started to burn. My mouth was crying, 'No mas, no mas!'

I could feel the inferno descending into my stomach and suddenly worried if I'd drunk enough beer to drown it. Then I wondered if I would be fit to fly tomorrow.

Is this legal? What would the health department think? What would the fire department think?

I tried to eat another wing, alternating bites with huge gulps of beer. After the fourth wing was gone, I realized I was too. It was no use. Hoping flames would not shoot out of my mouth, I ordered another beer to look like I was still enjoying my meal, although I think my watering eyes gave the game away.

After the third beer, the fire was almost under control, so when the bartender wasn't looking, I left the money for the bill and tip and slinked away in defeat, leaving the other eight wings smoldering in the basket. I think if the lights had gone out, they would have glowed. I didn't even care if they burned a hole through the bar and possibly caught the whole place on fire.

I don't know how they got them so hot; soaked them in plutonium, perhaps.

For a moment, on my way out, it occurred to me that I could make extra money by lighting people's cigarettes with my breath. But I just wanted to get out of there.

Chapter 9
Aviation Safety

"Flying is learning how to throw yourself at the ground and miss."
-Douglas Adams

Airliners crashes are getting to be a thing of the past, at least in the United States and Western countries, meaning Europe, the UK, Scandinavia, Canada and Australia. But it wasn't always that way.

Okay now, all of you airline pilots out there, don't make me a liar.

There are many developments besides the forward-looking Doppler radar that are making commercial aviation safer. Autoland is one of them. All modern jetliners have the ability to land themselves on autopilot, track the centerline and brake to a stop in the middle of the runway. It is in fact required during very low RVR, or runway visual ranges (fog). It would be too dangerous to allow the pilots to do it.

It sounds easy to let the airplane land itself, but it's not. It is very tense and necessary to practice often in the simulator, where something always goes wrong. We do it often. You don't just sit back and relax and let the airplane take care of itself. The procedure must be monitored very closely to ensure everything is working correctly. If anything in the automated system gets out of limits, the crew is required to take over and go around. It demands split-second decisions close to the ground.

There are different levels of requirements for various visibility limits. I will put the descriptions of categories and requirements in the pilot glossary at the end of the book.

On some planes, they now have an emergency Autoland, to be used by a flight attendant or passenger in case the crew is incapacitated. Kind of the United 93 situation, or the movie Airplane. Perhaps one day an A.I.-controlled airplane will argue with us like HAL 9000 in 2001: A Space Odyssey, but we're not there yet... Or are we?

Imagine you're a passenger, looking out the window at thick fog as the airplane comes in to land. You can't see a thing, and then suddenly you're on the ground, almost before the runway lights even appear. In that moment, the pilots probably weren't flying the airplane; the computers were.

One thing we practice constantly on any multiengine airplane is the specter of losing an engine, which is most dangerous on takeoff, but still tricky at other times.

On takeoff, if an engine quits before V-1, takeoff decision speed, you have to have enough runway left to stop. If it happens faster than

V-1, you must take it in the air. With one engine at full power and the other one suddenly going to idle, the asymmetric thrust will roll the airplane over on its back and fly into the ground, ruining your whole day. There have been many accidents that have happened this way, hence the simulator practice.

Still, when we talk about "losing" an engine, we generally mean that it quit or stopped running. There is a story about a pilot who wrote in the logbook that they had lost the number two engine. A wiseass mechanic wrote they had found it under the left wing.

In 1990, a Northwest Boeing 727 was flying from Miami to Minneapolis when the number three engine, the one on the right side of the tail, wound down, so they followed the checklist and secured the engine. With two engines still running, they diverted to Tampa and landed. Walking out of the airplane to inspect the engine, they were amazed to find it gone!

The next question was, where did it land?

Just the year before, in 1989, a Piedmont 737 lost an engine after takeoff. And in 1987, a US Airways 737 experienced the same issue. Both planes landed safely, and the problem was traced to faulty, worn-out engine mounts.

In 1985, an American Airlines 727 was flying from Dallas–Fort Worth to San Diego. The three-engine jet arrived with only two of them still on the airplane. Fortunately, the escapee was found in a remote area of desert near Deming, New Mexico.

In 1974, a National Airlines 727 almost dropped an engine on Sierra Blanca, Texas. It seemed to be an issue with Boeings for a while, or poor maintenance practices. But the engines don't hold up the airplane; the wings do.

All of these flights landed without incident, and nobody was hurt, even by falling engines, which weigh about three thousand pounds.

And then there was American Airlines Flight 191 at Chicago...

***

Mid-air collisions have been around ever since man invented aviation. If there is more than one plane in the air, someone will find a way to hit it. Like most pilots, I'd had my share of close calls.

As airplanes filled the skies, mid-airs became all too common, especially around airports. An Aero Mexico DC-9 collided with a four-seat Piper over Cerritos, California, in 1986. In 1978, a PSA 727 hit a Cessna over San Diego. Unfortunately, this was nothing new. A United DC-7 and a TWA Constellation ran into each other over the Grand Canyon in 1956 and again, the same two carriers, a United DC-8 four-engine jet and another TWA Constellation collided over New York in 1960. No one survives mid-airs of airlines.

These accidents finally led to the development of TCAS, the Traffic Collision Avoidance System. There hadn't been another major mid-air collision in the United States since its development, until recently.

I was flying for American when it came onboard, and I can testify to its effectiveness as it has given advanced warning of possible collisions many times in the crowded skies all over the world.

But even TCAS would not help if pilots didn't follow instructions. If two planes are on a collision course, one TCAS will issue a verbal command, 'Climb, climb now,' while the opposite one will command, 'Descend, descend now.' They are called Resolution Advisories.

There used to be a dark joke that if a pilot screws up, the pilot gets killed. If an air traffic controller screws up, the pilot gets killed.

The air traffic controller never gets killed. But not always.

In July 2002, on a dark night over Europe, a DHL 757 carrying cargo was flying north from Bahrain to Brussels. Meanwhile, a Russian Tupolev 154 was on its way from Moscow to Barcelona, almost full, mostly with school kids. They were on a holiday as a reward for doing so well in their studies; they were the brightest kids in their school.

Both aircraft entered the airspace of an overworked controller at 36,000 feet. Each was equipped with TCAS, which worked as designed, issuing the warning: "Traffic, traffic."

DHL's TCAS instructed its pilots to descend, and they began doing so. The Russian plane's TCAS told them to climb.

At the last moment, the controller noticed the conflict. Trying to help, he told the Russian plane to descend. There were five pilots in the cockpit. After a couple of seconds of confusion, the Russian captain followed the controller's instructions to descend.

The airplanes exploded on impact. Torn apart, they rained debris and bodies over onehundred-seventy square miles of the German and Swiss border. Everyone on board both airplanes was killed. For a week, recovery teams were finding the bodies of children in gardens, wheat fields, cornfields, and forests.

It has been surmised that Russian pilots are more prone to follow orders from the ground, which is probably why they ignored the TCAS instructions.

Over ten years prior, at the flight academy, I had been trained on TCAS when it was first installed. We were told, if not ordered, to trust and obey the TCAS no matter what. If the Russians had done that, the accident would not have happened.

But the story doesn't end there. Eighteen months later, a Russian architect, who had lost his entire family in the crash, his wife, son and daughter, showed up at the home of the air traffic controller who was on duty that night—the guy who told the Russian airplane to descend.

Hysterically confronting him over the accident, he then pulled out a knife and stabbed the controller to death. The killer was put into a mental institution.

It turned out our dark joke was wrong. Sometimes air traffic controllers do die when they make a mistake.

It has been thirty-nine years since the last airliner had a mid-air collision in America. Tragically, it happened again on January 29, 2025, when a regional jet operating as a feeder for American Airlines collided at low altitude over Washington, D.C., with a U.S. Army Black Hawk helicopter. It shouldn't have happened, but many safeguards were overlooked, and mistakes were made. As usual, no one survived.

American Airlines Flight 965, flying from Miami to Colombia, was partly responsible for the development of the Enhanced Ground Proximity Warning System, or E-GPWS. It allows pilots to see terrain depicted on their navigation screens. The NTSB calls it CTIF for Controlled Flight into Terrain. Flying a perfectly good airplane into the ground or into a mountain used to happen all too often. In the 70s and 80s, it was the leading cause of airline accidents. Now it is mostly a thing of the past because of the computerized terrain database.

The worst airline accident in history was in 1977 at Tenerife in the Canary Islands when two fully loaded 747's, one was Pan Am and the other a Royal Dutch KLM. The KLM was taking off and hit the Pan Am jet on the runway in the fog. It was the fault of the KLM captain. Ground control radar would have prevented it. It was available at most airports even then but was not installed at that airport.

***

As a pilot, it might sound like you could relax and enjoy the job, but the truth is, in the airline industry, you can never relax. Your job is never guaranteed. There are flight physicals, once a year for copilots, twice a year for captains. No medical license, no job.

On recurrent training, there are check rides that you have to pass, plus surprise line checks by either company check airmen or an FAA inspector. It's like having a cop in the back seat while driving your car. At any of these times, there are pop-up questions about aircraft systems, FAA regulations or company rules. If you can't answer them, they dig deeper to see what else you don't know.

There are random drug and alcohol tests done when you finish a trip, so you better be clean. If you don't pass, you will be not only fired but prosecuted. These are mandated by Congress. Most of us think they should be subjected to the same rules.

For captains over forty years old, an EKG is required every year. If you don't pass it, you lose your medical certificate. An EKG does not tell the doctor if you will have a heart attack, only if you have had an issue, like a mild one you didn't know about.

If you screw up and damage an airplane — like clip a wing or make a hard landing — you will almost certainly be fired. Call in sick too often or show up late too many times and you'll be gone.

Today, if you tell the wrong joke to the wrong person and they get offended, you're outta there.

There are probably a hundred ways to lose your job. The stress of the job is not just flying the airplanes; it is in part walking the straight and narrow path, trying to do everything right, all the time. Of course, that was never my style, so I had to work at it. The discipline was good for me.

Simulator training was fun. Check rides, on the other hand, were work. The sim instructors could make anything happen. Engine failures, hydraulic or electrical failures are all routine. When I was hired, they would give you multiple emergencies to deal with at the same time. At some point, you would get overwhelmed. Later, the union stopped that. They could make part of a wing fall off, or the landing gear may not come down. The more you train for it in the simulator, the easier it is to handle it if it happens in real life.

Security

As pilots and flight attendants, we were trusted and allowed to bypass security when we came to the airport. Everyone understood we were there for the safety of the passengers and the airplane. That all changed on December 7th, 1987.

At PSA, Pacific Southwest Airlines, a ticket agent named David had been fired for fraud and theft, but he still had his employee I.D. card. It turned out he already had a lengthy criminal record before transferring from Buffalo, N.Y., to Los Angeles. He had hidden that from the company. His boss, who fired him, lived in San Francisco and commuted to LAX to work. The agent planned to get back at his boss.

David brought a gun to the airport, bypassed security and boarded Flight 1771. At their cruise altitude of twenty-two thousand feet, he killed his boss, then, pushing his way into the cockpit, he shot the number one flight attendant before shooting the two pilots. The BAC-146, a very safe four-engine airplane, went into a nosedive on that cloudless day in December. It and everyone onboard were obliterated. Forty-three people, all but one innocent, died from this useless act of domestic terrorism. The government called it workplace violence. I suppose that is true, since there were no political aspirations involved.

Either way, it was just plain old murder.

I was flying out of L.A. at the time. News crews filmed us at security. The next day, the footage on television showed how airline crew members were allowed to bypass security, as if we were the problem. TV anchors said the problem was that flight crews were not going through security.

The next day, I watched the news reports with amazement as the media implicated flight crews as a security threat. The killer had been a corrupt ticket agent with a criminal record who was to blame, not a crew member. He had been in charge of the ticket counter and passenger safety, not the airplane. He was a criminal who had been caught. He didn't care about anyone's safety.

Yes, I had a criminal record, but I had worked hard to make the transition to trusted crew member, and I was proud of that status. I had come full circle to a place I never thought I'd be. I was entrusted with the safety of the passengers and multi-million-dollar airplanes.

Like all flight crew, I took it to heart.

Shortly after PSA 1771, the FAA mandated that all pilots and flight attendants go through security and be searched along with the passengers. All of us were pretty unhappy about it. Pilots don't need a weapon to crash an airplane. My new position as an airline pilot was not to be trusted anymore.

But for now, I was happy to be off probation and flying as copilot in a big jet, based an hour from my home. Maybe I did want this job after all. The trips I flew spanned the entire country and into Canada. Laying over in almost every city with an airport big enough for the MD-80. I still spent a lot of time in the big cities, from Los Angeles to Boston, Miami to Seattle and everywhere in between.

Most captains were good, and some were an absolute pleasure to fly with. Working with them didn't seem like a job; at times I was amazed I got paid for it. Some were good enough pilots, but had no personality. Like a human autopilot. I had already been a commercial pilot for a whole six years, and felt some of them were questionable, lousy at flying and landings and poor at decision making.

While flying with one of the better captains, we were talking about the well-known problem captains. I asked, "How do these guys get by?"

The answer was, "The union protects them, and will get their job back if they get fired… as long as they don't kill someone."

As mentioned, some did not have much recent flying time since the upward movement started. Still others were perfect pilots whom I wished I could work with all the time.

One of the things that made me a good pilot was starting out in tail-draggers. I wasn't afraid to push hard on the rudder pedals when necessary, unlike some military pilots who were used to flying jets with yaw dampers that handled it for them, at least to a degree. Those early designs were meant for the Dutch roll, but some pilots got used to flying with their feet on the floor and not using the rudder. Rather than put in a lot of rudder and cross-control the airplane on crosswind landing, they would land in a crab, into the wind.

In some fighter jets, pilots had been taught that way, crabbed into the wind. Or navy pilots on aircraft carriers, who always landed into the wind. It was hard on the landing gear and tires. With the center of gravity ahead of the point of friction, which is the main wheels, it'll straighten out. But fighters are short and relatively light. On a longer, heavier airliner, the airplane would still straighten itself out, but it was a rough ride, often resulting in snide comments from the passengers and even sometimes the flight attendants.

If you did that in a taildragger, you would ground loop and crash. In an airliner, landing in too much of a crab could collapse a landing gear. Someone is going to notice that.

Any airport can have vicious crosswinds at times. Ontario, California, is one. During certain times of the year, the Santa Ana winds would come howling out of the north, sweeping down the San Gabriel Mountains and right across Ontario's east-west runways. In this case, we are landing east, and the wind is from the north—a left crosswind.

It's turbulent on the final approach, and you're working pretty hard at it. First, you're crabbing into the wind, flying partly sideways to line up with the runway. At the last minute, just above the ground, you shove in a lot of right rudder away from the wind. If the crosswind is really strong, you might use all of it. The airplane will want to roll to the right, off the centerline. At the same time, you crank in a lot of opposite aileron into the wind, sometimes all of it. Whatever it takes to level the wings. Touching down on the upwind landing gear is also a good technique. The possibility of dragging an engine was not a problem, just a wingtip.

Landing to the east on runway 8R, with my right leg straight out and the control yoke full left. I held the column back almost into my chest. Pulling the nose up while easing the throttles to idle. Cross-controlling the airplane is hard; you have to muscle it around, especially the manually operated controls on the MD-80. At times, I've had full deflection of both rudder and ailerons in opposite directions, all while battling turbulence. The Super 80 responded perfectly, and I would usually get a pretty good touchdown. Cross-controlling like that is nothing but a sideslip into the relative wind. The '80s were good at it.

Air California 737-100, sometime in the 1960s

It can be a problem when two pilots in the same cockpit have been trained to fly the airplane by different companies. There are different procedures, different techniques and different attitudes.

In 1978, before deregulation started, there were ten major airlines and about forty regional or local airlines. When the Civil Aeronautics Board or CAB stopped governmental control over the airlines, it turned into a free-for-all. Like fish in a tank, the big airlines started growing and eating the smaller ones.

Sometimes American just bought the routes, like Eastern's Caribbean and South American routes and Pan Am's in the Pacific. But AA also had a habit of buying whole companies. They would then get rid of the airplanes and the routes and keep the employees, merging them into the workforce.

In 1987, when I transferred to the MD-80, American Airlines bought AirCal, formerly Air California Airlines. I was a bit biased about it because it negatively affected my world in a couple of ways. Rather than tacking the new pilots onto the bottom of our seniority list, they were fully merged into it. Which is probably a standard practice, but it pushed me down approximately 250 numbers.

American was an international flag carrier. AirCal was a small regional airline like Southwest Airlines, only smaller. First it was only in California, but after deregulation, it expanded operations to the West Coast as far north as Anchorage and as far east as Chicago.

The pilots who came onto our seniority list ahead of me, delaying my upgrade to captain for years. What was worse, many of the AirCal captains started bidding onto the MD80; they mostly lived in Southern California. They came into the LAX, Ontario and Orange County bases. I ended up flying with most of them. They could be great guys and excellent pilots, but not all.

I was surprised to hear many of them complaining about being bought. They hated American. In my mind, they had just won the lottery. Instead of only flying narrow bodies around the West Coast, they could (and did) fly wide-body jets worldwide for a lot more money.

I think there was a lot of "big fish in a small pond" syndrome. Now they were a small fish in a very big pond, and some didn't like it.

There was also another matter of 'standard procedures' that some of them didn't like. When a company teaches you how to fly their airplane, they want it done a certain way, for safety and efficiency, so everyone knows what to expect. Not all, but a few AirCal pilots were disdainful of AA's standard procedures, thinking they knew how to fly an airplane better.

On rare occasions, they could go to the company and prove that their way was better, and the company might adopt a new procedure. I've seen that happen. But in too many cases, it is laziness or just arrogance. As a copilot, if you question them, their defense is to get very angry.

Wanting to be the best pilot I could be, I embraced standard procedures for several reasons.

First, to pass checkrides and IOEs.

Second, so the captains I flew with would see I'd been paying attention in school and was up to speed—no surprises.

Third, to stay out of trouble by doing things the company's way. They can't fault you if you're following their instructions.

Unfortunately, some AirCal captains didn't see it that way. They weren't new-hires.

They'd been doing things in the cockpit their way for years and didn't like having to change. Sometimes it was just being sloppy. I flew with one captain who completely disregarded our standardized procedures. It was so frustrating I questioned him about it.

He responded, "I don't need this f**kin company to tell me how to fly my f**kin airplane!"

I said, "It's not your airplane. It's the company's airplane, and they are paying you a lot of money to fly it."

For a time, American kept the short north-south routes along the West Coast. We flew them for years in MD-80s even after they got rid of the old 737s. I was always grateful to go eastbound when I could. In addition to the short hops, they were often one-day trips, starting and ending in Ontario. Instead of laying over in a hotel room, I had to drive home at night and be there the next morning to do it all over again. It felt like I was back at the commuter airline, Imperial.

Eventually, they phased out even the old AirCal routes along with the airplanes, and the only thing left for all the money they spent was the employees. It wouldn't be the last time.

To be fair, some AirCal pilots were great guys and good pilots. One in particular was more by-the-book than most AA guys. You can never cover everyone with one blanket. I flew with some great captains and excellent influences, as a pilot and as a person. There were too many to mention, but one comes to mind. His name was Read Mecleary, he was True Blue, in other words hired by American, not brought in from another airline.

We got along great; I flew the whole month of September 1991 with him. We talked about all kinds of topics and had a lot in common. He said he had been a Navy pilot, (Naval Aviator), and I wished I had asked him more about it.

A year later, it was election season. Ross Perot was running for president and his choice for vice president was James Stockdale who had been a POW in North Vietnam. One evening a show came on the television introducing Stockdale to the American public. He had been awarded the Medal of Honor for his courage and fortitude while being held as prisoner. As I watched, as fellow POW came on to talk about his friend James Stockdale. It was Read Mecleary!

I was shocked. I had flown a whole month with the guy and he never mentioned having been a POW in North Vietnam. What a humble man. I was embarrassed that I had not asked more questions about his military service. But for his part, perhaps he was happy not to talk about it.

One thing that really annoyed me about flying narrowbody domestic routes was changing airplanes. It seemed to be AA's version of musical chairs. Every time you flew into a hub, you would switch equipment. You might fly four legs a day and operate four different airplanes. Each time having to vacate your gear out of one airplane. You had to hurry through a large terminal like DFW or Chicago, get to another gate, and if your airplane has arrived yet, start all over again. Do another cockpit preflight, another walk-around, adjust the seats, test the oxygen mask. If you weren't already running late, it could very well make you late.

Sometimes for the whole day.

For example, after flying into DFW from LAX, the paperwork might say that your airplane is scheduled to do a turn to Palm Beach and back. Yet you change to another one that is going to Miami and back. "What's the difference?" we would ask. The company told us it was maintenance requirements that dictated where the airplane went. So why couldn't we go with that airplane instead of this one? We never got a logical answer.

The union complained to the company about it, but nothing ever changes. Maybe it's better by now.

Hubs are for the convenience and profitability of the airline, not for the convenience of the passengers. It's not very convenient for the pilots either. But I have to admit, there are no direct flights to London from Lubbock.

Chapter 10
Living on the Line

"Once you have tasted flight, you will forever walk the earth with your eyes turned skyward."

-Leonardo Da Vinci

Mount Washington, the highest point in New Hampshire, has a weather reporting station. While there is no airport, it has some of the worst weather you will find in the country. High winds, freezing temperatures and blowing snow and clouds with sometimes zero visibility. My favorite prank was pulling up the Mt. Washington weather, changing the identifier to our destination, then hitting Print Screen to show it to the captain and watching his face as he read it.

One thing I liked was the long layovers. Frequently thirty hours or more, in places like New York or Detroit. For example, you might fly in Friday evening, stay all day Saturday, and then leave Sunday morning. You could bring your spouse and have a whole day to yourselves.

In order to avoid the hub and spoke system and five legs a day AirCal routes for a month, I bid a line out of Los Angeles that did all-nighters to Dulles, just outside Washington, DC. Not because I liked flying all night, but the layovers were thirty-nine hours long. Enough time to rent a car and tour the Gettysburg Battlefield or hop on the Metro and see the monuments and other sights in downtown DC, which we did on different trips. It was like a mini vacation, except that you're getting paid.

On one long LaGuardia layover, I brought my wife and, after a nice dinner in Times Square, we saw the play Phantom of the Opera. I had never been to an opera before. Earlier that day after what seemed like miles of walking, we were crossing through Central Park. It was a beautiful warm day, and the sun was shining through the watery sky. The concrete cliffs of the buildings surrounded the green oasis of the park. We were taking a break in the shade of a huge oak tree when, out of the corner of our eyes, we caught sight of a squirrel bounding our way through the overgrown grass. He stopped about five feet away and stood up on his hind legs, looking at us. Not wanting to scare him, we held very still. Slowly turning our heads to look at him, we finally realized it wasn't a squirrel; it was a large New York rat.

Surprised, we both burst out laughing, which made him turn around and scamper back the way he had come. Perhaps people sometimes fed them, and he was looking for a handout.

Still, we felt lucky he didn't pull a knife and demand money.

Central Park, New York

Another favorite layover was in downtown Detroit at the 'City Within a City,' the Westin Hotel, now known as the GM Renaissance Center Hotel in the huge GM building right next to the Detroit River. Not that Detroit was a great place to visit. In the 80s, crime was high there too.

But the hotel had a huge mall with five levels of shopping, restaurants and even movie theaters at the bottom. You could spend a long layover, especially during a cold winter, and never leave the hotel. If you did want to go out, there was the free people mover, or automated, elevated monorail. The station was right outside the hotel. You could go to restaurants like in Greektown and never have to walk on the streets.

I don't think Detroit was as bad as Hollywood portrayed it in the movies, like Robocop or The Crow, but then I didn't feel daring enough to venture into the city at night to find out. Besides, I had a job to show up for.

Detroit's iconic GM Renaissance Center

If you wanted to walk city streets and feel safe, you could go to Canada. It was literally just out the window of the hotel. A stone's throw from the entrance was a tunnel under the river. You could buy a dollar ticket for a bus ride to Windsor, a journey of about three minutes. It was like going back to 1950s America and seemed more like a small town than a big city. It is the only place in the country where you can go south from the United States to get to Canada. Today, there is a bridge across the Detroit River.

Except for bidding trips out of LAX, usually driving one hour to Ontario once a week was a piece of cake, especially when I thought about all the people in the Orange County and Los Angeles basin sitting in traffic on freeways twice every day. I felt for them, but I was determined not to do that. If I weren't flying, I think I would have hired onto a tramp steamer, or maybe as a ranch hand in Montana.

In my experience, the MD-80 performed flawlessly. There were mechanical issues of course, but no emergencies, a tribute to the airplane's reliability and the company's maintenance crews. I liked flying the Mad Dog; it was straightforward and honest; it felt safe. But domestic routes were a lot of work. I was already getting spoiled. There had to be a better way.

Back to the 10

After four years on the DC-9-80, I was ready for a change. I'd never flown one kind of airplane that long. Hell, I'd never stayed in one place that long. Even my parents didn't when I was a kid.

Some pilots hate transcons, saying they're long and boring. They appealed to me, having done them on the Lear and as flight engineer on the 10. I felt it was easy and relaxing. One takeoff and one landing, then it's off to the hotel. Laying over in New York and Honolulu already seemed nostalgic instead of Little Rock or Pittsburgh. Plus, I couldn't help but admire those huge airplanes. After the pocket-sized Learjet, the DC-10 seemed enormous. It was the largest airplane in the AA fleet, other than the 747SP's which were already being phases out. When I saw the big tri-jet on the ramp, looking up at those little guys, way up there in the cockpit, I knew it would be my next airplane. Knowing their workload was easier, the pay was better and their layovers were nicer. Only this time, I would get to fly it!

My training as first officer on the DC-10 started in January 1992. I had been with the company for just over five years. The school was like the flight engineer course had been; it was still a gentleman's airplane. After two weeks of ground school on systems, which I had already learned, and two weeks flying the simulator, I was ready to go. Being a McDonaldDouglas product, much of the flight guidance system was similar to the MD-80, only older.

With most of the gauges, buttons, knobs and switches of the various systems being back at the FE panel, it was a lot cleaner up front. It was a heady experience for a high school dropout and ex-biker to be piloting a wide-body jet for the world's biggest airline. Once again, I couldn't help but feel lucky but kept that to myself. I tried to act as if I belonged there.

Unlike the '80 with its mostly manual controls and servo/anti-servo tabs, the 10s flight controls were hydraulically boosted. It also felt light and responsive, more like a Learjet than the huge airliner that it was. But there was no 'manual reversion' to operate the flight controls manually like the MD-80, 727 or 737, which was a comforting safety factor.

Today, the newer airplane's flight controls are electrically powered, which saves a lot of weight. If all electrical power is lost, the backup source is PMGs, or Permanent Magnet Generators on the engines. Even if the engines are not producing power, as long as they are spinning or windmilling, the PMGs can produce electricity solely designated for the flight controls.

One weakness of the DC-10 that came to light early on was the hydraulic flight controls. If hydraulic fluid were lost, you could find yourself up a very fast creek without a paddle. It was later fixed with the installation of check valves to prevent the loss of fluid, but only after hundreds of people had died. In the simulator, we were given the chance to try to land under the same conditions of having no flight controls. I crashed. Everyone crashed. No one was able to duplicate what those guys did that day. Fortunately, it was not a test we had to pass.

The flight training was easy, and the simulator was a piece of cake. Pretty soon I was off on an IOE. In the real airplane, while sitting on the ground, I was amazed at the view from what seemed like a second-story window. In the air, the controls were so light. After flying the heavier controls of the MD-80, I initially overcontrolled it. The check airman told me to rest my arms on my knees and fly with my fingers. It worked to smooth out my pilot-induced oscillations.

There was a saying that the copilot of the DC-10 had the easiest job in the industry. "The captain has all the responsibility, and the engineer does all the work. All you have to do is fly every other leg, eat your crew meals and flirt with the flight attendants." But flirting has never been my forte.

It was such a good job, there were two very senior AirCal captains who bid DC-10 international first officer and stayed there for the rest of their careers until they retired. They were numbers one and two on the FO seniority list and flew with some newer captains junior to them.

It's possible that I was able to hold the right seat on the Ten because many pilots didn't want to fly it because of its bad reputation. There had been a lot of accidents over the years. It got off to a bad start in the '70s with some design flaws that were quickly fixed. The accidents continued in the '80s, not all of which were the airplane's fault; many were pilot error. The American Airlines Flight 191 at Chicago was largely the fault of maintenance, not the plane or the pilots. But then again, there was that hydraulic design.

I was as comfortable flying the DC-10 as any airplane I have flown and trusted it, even on those iffy windy landing at night in Maui after a long day of work. It was responsive and did what you asked it to do. It was a big pussycat.

One of my favorite approaches was at Kennedy Airport in New York, the Canarsie VOR to 13 Left or Right. Landing frequently in the morning after an all-nighter, with the sun was coming up as we drove in over Jamaica Bay on a 041 heading. Dropping lower and lower over an industrial area until crossing the DMYHL fix, then descending again. You must see the runway or at least the lead-in lights if it's foggy. Finally, at about five hundred feet, you roll into a twenty-five to thirty-degree banked turn just inside the Aqueduct Racetrack to line up on either runway. You roll out of the bank and short final and your wheels touch down on the concrete. It's fun.

Again, there were no openings for international first officer yet, so initially I would still be domestic. That was okay with me; it meant transcons and laying over in some of my favorite cities like New York and Miami. Often at operations in Boston, the captain would show up with a box of fresh lobsters. He could afford it. If you weren't doing trans cons, it was usually only two legs a day and again, we would frequently swap airplanes in hubs. But remember, the flight engineer had to do the preflights and walk-arounds.

In addition to the three of us in the cockpit, instead of three flight attendants in the back, we had ten. When we went to the layover hotel, we didn't take a van; we had a bus.

In New York City, we stayed at the Milford Hotel, just off 42nd Street and near Times Square. We called it the Mildew. After a flight attendant was murdered in her room, the pilots and flight engineers started escorting groups of flight attendants to their rooms. She would prop her door open with her luggage and search the room while we waited in the hallway. In the case of the murder, the killer had hidden under the bed until she closed the door. They always checked under the bed.

New York City then was an interesting place. Walking out the front door on 7th Ave, you could be accosted by drug dealers offering you anything you want. Twenty feet away would be a NYPD cop just standing there. The first time it happened, I looked at the cop wondering if he saw what was going on, then I realized he was probably being paid to be there by the drug dealer.

After a short walk, turning the corner put you on 42nd Street. The namesake of the 1933 movie, it had a magic all its own. Or at least it used to. In the late '80s, it had more decay than magic. There were several movie theaters showing X-rated movies in between the seedy bars and peep shows and head shops selling drug paraphernalia. Crowding the sidewalk were drunks, druggies, pimps and more drug dealers. The few diners didn't look fit to eat in. Buying hot dogs from the ubiquitous street vendors was a lot safer. Finding a respectable diner seemed miles away, perhaps in Toledo.

Looking out the windows from the room, it was not unusual to see open curtains in other nearby buildings, sometimes with nude people walking or lying around their apartments or having sex. A local custom, perhaps?

From my days with Devarian, I knew the subway system very well; for a small price, you could easily get around town to visit Central Park, some of the museums on Park Avenue or Grand Central Station. Finding a restaurant in a nicer part of town was easy too. I always used to think of visiting New York as going to the zoo. It was an interesting place to visit, but you wouldn't want to live there. I enjoyed exploring the city. It was not unusual to see a celebrity, an actor or musician, walking down the street.

On one layover when my wife came along, we rented a car to see more of the town. That was a mistake. Driving in New York traffic was bad enough. There were a million yellow taxi cabs with dents all over, like they had a kamikaze attitude. And finding a place to park turned into a nightmare. What you did find was always expensive. There was no such thing as free parking. On a whim, we drove to the Bronx to see if it was really like they said. It was. It looked like a war zone. Rusted-out hulks of cars that had been there for months, possibly years. There were deserted buildings with broken windows and trash everywhere; the only thing missing were shell holes in the walls. We didn't stay long. I started trying to get layovers in Miami or Toronto, places where you didn't feel you needed a bulletproof vest.

It was always interesting. Sometimes you wondered why you were getting paid for this, flying big jets and having mini-vacations in cities all over the country. After all the hard work, long hours and low pay of previous jobs, it really made up for the hard work to get here.

I was enjoying the huge, roomy cockpit, the easier workload, the good food and the higher pay. Even domestic flying was good. I felt I had to pinch myself to make sure I was really here.

Like on the narrow bodies, we got first class meals. I don't know what they're like now, but back then I thought they were quite good. On the Ten, they were even better. Before takeoff, the number one flight attendant would take drink orders. At first I thought that was cool, just like when you're in first class. No Champaign though. After takeoff, the door would open and a metal tray, called an insert, would be slid across the floor into the cockpit with cans of the selected drinks, plastic cups and a bag of ice, then the door would slam. We were on our own; the flight attendants were done with the cockpit until the meals needed to be delivered. I found that many wide-body flight attendants did not like pilots. For a variety of reasons, some of them quite justified.

A typical meal comprised appetizers of caviar and lox with all the trimmings, followed by entrees usually including filet mignon cooked perfectly, baked salmon with an awesome sauce, or maybe a pasta dish—so we all ate something different. Dessert, if any was left, was an ice cream sundae complete with hot fudge or caramel, whipped cream, and nuts. The only thing missing was an after-dinner martini. It sure beat the sack lunch you might have remembered to bring for the Devarian all-nighters from Burbank to Teterboro. No wonder the older captains were called wide-body captains; they had rather wide bodies.

I had never had caviar and thought it was great. But we didn't always get the greatest service. After all, the passengers came first. On one transcon leg when the flight attendant brought up the crew meals, the captain asked, "No caviar today?"

She replied, "We're all out."

He said, "Okay."

After we ate, the flight engineer went back to the lav. When he returned, he said that as he passed the front galley, he saw the number one flight attendant eating caviar straight out of the jar with a spoon. The captain just laughed and shook his head.

I was surprised at how the company used the big widebody jet. In addition to transcons and international, they also had a lot of short hauls, like Chicago to Detroit, DallasFort Worth to Houston. Maybe they were short of the smaller airplanes for those routes, or wanted to lessen the frequency. It was okay with me; sometimes the shorter flights break up the monotony, but you get fewer chances at those good crew meals.

Chapter 11
Can't We All Just Get Along?

> *"Everything is dangerous, my dear fellow.*
> *If it wasn't so, life wouldn't be worth living."*
>
> -Oscar Wilde

Perched on the edge of my chair, I watched in stunned silence as all hell broke loose on ABC Channel 7's live news out of Los Angeles. It was April 29, 1992.

Four police officers had just been acquitted of the brutal beating of a black man after a police chase on the freeways of L.A. The four officers were white; the black man's name was Rodney King.

It wasn't dark yet, but fires were starting, and the looting had already begun. A mob at an intersection was attacking motorists. Several innocent truck drivers had just been dragged out of their cabs, robbed and beaten. One was hit in the head with a brick and another with a fire extinguisher. They nearly died.

I was on reserve as a DC-10 first officer based out of LAX; Los Angeles International Airport. I thought to myself, *I hope nobody calls in sick. I'd rather not have to drive there anytime soon.*

Just then, the phone rang. It was Crew Scheduling. "I have a trip for you leaving tomorrow at 1328, Los Angeles to Miami."

I had no option of declining, passing, or deferring. With a big sigh, I just said, "I'll be there."

When packing my usual bag for a trip, I added something extra. A Ruger single-action .44 Magnum. Not your ideal gun for self-defense, but it was the only handgun I owned at the time. This was California, a state that frowned upon citizens carrying guns.

As I watched the news, more businesses were set on fire. Police cars were being attacked, and instead of calling for backup, they did a one-eighty and got out of there. The LAPD abandoned the citizens of South-Central Los Angeles to the rioters.

The riots got bigger and more violent as the evening progressed. Police and firefighters were being shot at. Mayor Bradley established a 'dawn to dusk' curfew and called for a state of emergency. The violence spilled out of the south-central area as far north and west as Hollywood and Westlake, and as far south as Long Beach and San Pedro.

I thought, *Well, this is going to be fun.*

***

The next morning found me driving alone on an empty freeway while listening to non-stop news on the radio. There were reports of snipers shooting at cars from the overpasses, so I kept a sharp eye out. With no cops in sight, I saw no reason to obey the speed limit as I flew along westbound on the recently completed 105 freeway. I wanted to be as fast a moving target as possible, so I stayed in the center lane where I could swerve in either direction if necessary.

There were no traffic jams, and I found myself thinking, "Maybe there are some advantages to this rioting thing."

Passing the 710, I could see columns of smoke rising into the air on both sides of my route. Ground zero was Florence and Normandy, and I was well south of that, but surprised to see that much smoke. It was a strange sight, and it looked like all of Los Angeles was on fire. The feeling was surreal, like I was in a disaster movie. I kept glancing up, looking for airplanes on final to LAX, but there were none. No police helicopters either.

With the loaded .44 resting under my seat, I was of course breaking California law and taking a big risk of going to jail and ruining my flying career. But at that point in time, going to jail was the least of my worries. My first priority was staying alive, and although that ridiculously overpowered revolver would be little help in a confrontation with a mob, it provided at least a small amount of psychological comfort.

It was an eerie feeling.

Here I was, trying to turn my life around. I was walking the straight and narrow.

Unlike my old life, I was trying to be responsible but carrying a gun while heading into what seemed a war zone where, according to the radio, there were no police if you needed them. It was like the Wild West—you were on your own. I had no cell phone. Back then, you had to stop and find a phone booth. I secretly wished I had brought some motorcycle club brothers with me to have my back. Maybe I should've called them. They would have come with glee, ready to jump headlong into the fire. The hell with the reason. It would have been another adventure. But I never considered involving anyone else. I had to do this alone, and I had to get to work.

At that moment, it felt like me against South Central Los Angeles.

There was no one else on that six-lane super-slab. I had driven that road many times, even in the middle of the night, and had never been all alone on it. I couldn't help but think of the Arby's commercial, "Where is everybody?"

The 105 Freeway ran through the middle of South Central. No wonder there was nobody else on this road. I really wished I'd gone out of my way to take the 405 instead.

The news said the cops had all pulled back to guard their headquarters, the Parker Center in downtown Los Angeles, so I was pushing my little Honda Civic to the limit, doing over one hundred miles an hour. I didn't even know it would go this fast. I was constantly changing lanes and didn't even have to use my turn signals, scanning rooftops and overpasses looking for the snipers that had been reported on the radio.

I spent about twenty minutes with my heart in my throat. Then after getting to the airport employee parking lot, I puffed up my chest and said to myself, "That was nothing!"

Arriving in operations and meeting Captain Neil Fitzmorris and flight engineer Jack Anderson, we each shared our stories of the fun ride to the airport. I mentioned having brought a gun, and they said they had too. Hearing the conversation, another pilot in the operations room said, "Didn't you know, it's riot season?"

I said, "What do you mean?"

He said, "Yeah, you know, California is a four-season state. Fire season, flood season, earthquake season and riot season."

He laughed, but no one else did.

We read reports that rioters had been shooting at police helicopters and airplanes landing at LAX. The airliners had to fly right over the area where all the turmoil was. They were low and slow at that point and made an easy target. The airspace east of the airport was shut down. The FAA was only allowing flights to take off to the west, over the ocean, and land to the east, also over the water, so as not to fly over the city.

Airplanes need to take off and land into the wind as much as possible, especially jets. The prevailing winds at LAX are out of the west about 98 percent of the time. So normally you are taking off west and landing west. Departing Los Angeles would be no problem today.

The DC-10, despite having had some issues early on, was a great airplane to fly. Relatively modern with three huge engines, when on the ground, you felt like you were looking out the window of a four-story building.

It didn't take long to board the passengers onto our airplane; it was almost empty. Apparently, most decided not to try to come to the airport that day. After my tense drive, I sympathized with them.

We took off as Flight 1440, a non-stop to Miami. Pulling into position at the end of Runway 25 Right, we noticed half a dozen police cars on the other side of the fence, guarding Aviation Boulevard for the departing airplanes like us. Climbing out over the ocean, we started a slow turn back to the east. It was one of those clear blue sky, Southern California days, and we could clearly see the air over the city was filled with black and grey smoke. Flames could be seen on the ground in many places. It looked apocalyptic, and it was hard to believe this was happening.

Shaking his head as he looked out his big left-side window, Neil said, "This should all be over by the time we get back tomorrow."

Jack said, "I hope so. I don't want to have to drive through that again."

Four hours and fifty-one minutes later, we touched down at Miami International Airport. After unloading our small number of passengers, we rounded up our ten flight attendants and boarded the bus for the layover hotel, a Holiday Inn, right on the beach. It was just a short stroll down the boardwalk to the famous Fontainebleau, where we would go for dinner.

With the flight crew and some of the flight attendants, it seemed a world away as we sat at a table near the swimming pool. The palm trees swayed in the warm evening breeze as we ate and drank mojitos. I always enjoyed laying over in Miami.

After dinner, we moved out to the open porch bar with the ocean breeze rustling the palm trees overhead and ordered more drinks. They had a television, and it was tuned to CNN, the first cable news channel. We watched the unrest continue. It appeared the situation was getting worse. City hall and the police headquarters, Parker Center, were surrounded, and the rioters were trying to set it on fire. The violence had spread to the San Fernando Valley. It felt strange to sit in a nice hotel and watch the chaos and mayhem going on at our home base.

***

The next day was May 1st. Just after noon found us pilots again sitting in the cockpit at the gate at Miami International. With the flight attendants and passengers onboard, the plane was nearly full, and we were all set to go. Jack had completed his preflight and walkaround, and I had finished adjusting my seat. We monitored the company frequency, waiting to be given the green light.

Coming from the operations office, Neil walked in the open cockpit door and said, "The ground-stop to LAX is still in effect. The airspace to the east is still shut down, and the winds from the west are thirteen to fifteen knots, we can't land with more than ten. They're waiting either for the winds to change or for the chaos to settle down so they can open up the east side. With any luck, maybe they'll let us go."

We sat in the cockpit at the gate and waited. Hour after hour went by. Unlike the nonstop coverage from CNN, we got sporadic reports from the company. It didn't sound good.

Instead of dying down, the violence was increasing.

I suggested flying the plane and passengers to Ontario and bussing everybody to Los Angeles. The company said no.

At the gate in Miami

Jack was particularly nervous. He said, "I really want to get going. I live in the Valley, and my wife is home alone. Last night she said she could smell smoke and hear gunshots."

"She should get out of there," I said.

"I already told her to go to her parent's house in Ventura; she's on her way there now."

Neil said, "Good move. Nobody knows how far this will spread or how long it will last. I live down in Laguna, but I'm eager to get home too; my wife is scared."

The cockpit door was open so passengers could come up and ask questions or show their kids the cockpit. Our number one flight attendant walked in and said, "Captain, the passengers are getting antsy. Can you give them another update on when we can expect to get going?"

Nodding, Neil picked up the big telephone-shaped handset from the back of the center console, pressed the push-to-talk button and started another PA to the folks in back.

At about four o'clock and after several more announcements, the company decided to cancel the flight. Amid groans and complaints, the passengers were deplaned and were on their own for the night. The airline doesn't put them up if the delay or cancellation is beyond its control. All of us crew members were sent back to the paradise of the hotel for more mojitos and dinner. Don't you hate it when that happens?

Of course, we watched more CNN. Open gun battles in broad daylight were being televised, mostly between Korean business owners who stood their ground and defended their stores. The death toll rose with every report.

As we watched, Rodney King made a public appearance. Dressed in a suit and tie, he looked a little bewildered due to all the violence happening in his name. He spoke briefly, pleading, "Can't we all just get along?"

Rodney King
His book, The Riot Within is worth reading

I felt sorry for him; he was tall, soft-spoken and good-looking. He seemed like a nice guy. A private guy who had gotten himself into a public mess and now was trying to help make it all stop.

The second night showed no signs of slowing down. Mayor Bradley was calling in the National Guard, and President Bush declared the Insurrection Act in order to send in the Army and Marines.

Turning in, I slept fitfully, dreaming of chaos and Armageddon. Being trapped in a city in flames, trapped somewhere I didn't know. Trying to find my way to somewhere I still didn't know. Running from crowds, running from the flames.

I woke up to bright sunlight; a gecko was clinging to the window screen looking innocently at me. I could see a palm tree in the distance, and then a seagull flew by my window. I was saved after being lost in my dreams. The gecko didn't try to sell me insurance.

The three of us with our mob of ten flight attendants showed up at the airport ready to get to work, only to find our flight had been canceled. Now we were scheduled to deadhead as passengers back to LAX. Another crew would be our chauffeurs.

No problem! Sit back and relax, some of us in first class. Passengers paid thousands of dollars for this. Instead, we were getting paid. It was one of the major perks of the job. Even the flight attendants got to be waited on. It didn't happen very often, so we enjoyed it when it did. Read a book, eat a meal, maybe sleep—there were no in-flight movies then. Life was good. I never minded deadheading.

Arriving at LAX, the winds were light enough for us to land to the east, over the ocean. As we passed the city on the downwind leg, I looked out the window from my passenger seat. I could still see some thin columns of smoke. Nowhere near like it was three days before. It looked like it was over. On final approach, I gazed down at the surfers on the waves, seemingly without a care in the world, oblivious to the troubles just a few miles away.

***

It was one of those clear blue-sky California days as I pulled out of the employee parking lot on the west side of the airport. I decided not to take the 105 Freeway back. This time I would play it safe and instead go up Interstate 10 on the north side of ground zero to avoid most of the festivities.

Turning right from Aviation Boulevard onto Century Boulevard, I headed for the 405. After the underpass, I made a right 270-degree loop onto the long circular on-ramp to go northbound.

Traffic was still light as most people were wisely staying home and avoiding the area. As I merged onto the freeway, I was surprised to see a long line of big military trucks, the kind with the green canvas covers on the back—troop carriers. It was the Marines. They were lumbering along in the middle lane as I merged into the right lane.

Pacing along beside one of the trucks from my little Honda Civic, I craned my neck to look way up at the guy sitting in the right seat of the cab. He was African American and wearing full combat gear. He was staring down at me, and his face under his helmet appeared grim.

I wondered how he felt about being deployed to a war zone in his own country. It must have been a bizarre feeling, and I didn't envy him.

We stared awkwardly at each other for a couple of seconds. I could have just accelerated away, but instead I smiled and raised my hand in a wave. Breaking into a big grin, he raised his hand and vigorously waved back.

This encounter only lasted a couple of seconds, but it was a special moment I've always remembered. Though no words were spoken, it was a silent "Thank you for coming to the rescue of the city." His returning smile said, "You're welcome." At least, that's how I took it. I gave him a salute, and still with that big smile, he saluted back.

Marines from Camp Pendleton arrive in Los Angeles

Then I accelerated away, passing the long line of trucks, feeling content with the brief connection I had just made. The arrival of the Marines and soldiers gave me the sense that it was all over. The problem was fixed, and the riot had ended.

In just a few miles, I was turning eastbound on Interstate 10. Traffic was light for that time of day, but it seemed like the city was getting back to normal. There were no black smoke columns rising into the air here. Up ahead I could see the tall buildings of downtown L.A.

Minutes later, I saw an off-ramp sign that said Normandie Ave. I'd been hearing that name on the news for the last four days, and my curiosity got the best of me. I got the bright idea of pulling off the freeway and see how things looked. A little riot tourism, you might say. I thought, *It doesn't look that bad. There's no smoke, and besides, three branches of the military are here, right? After all, how many people get to drop in and see what everyone has been watching on the news all over the world?*

I hit my turn signal and swung onto the off-ramp. Driving down it, I immediately realized my mistake. The intersection at the bottom of the offramp was clogged with cars; the traffic light was not working; the electricity was out all over town. There were people walking all around, and I was the only pale face in sight.

My first instinct was to try to back up the offramp to get back on the freeway, but that option was crushed as a large truck came up behind me. I had nowhere to go but forward.

There were no police and no soldiers to be seen anywhere. I could feel my hands getting clammy on the steering wheel. My only salvation was straight ahead, on the other side of Normandie. Within rock-throwing distance was an on-ramp leading back to the 10 freeway, but getting to it was another matter, as the intersection was clogged with cars.

Shaking my head, I felt like a fool for getting myself into this pickle. To make matters worse, I was still in uniform—a white shirt, with a tie and epaulettes on my shoulders. Worrying perhaps I could be mistaken for a cop, I started pulling off the tie and epaulettes. I thought about the six-shot revolver under my seat, but quickly dismissed it, knowing it would do no good against a mob. It turned out this was not over. I found out later that the violence would go on for two more days. Sixty-four people would be killed and over two-thousandthree hundred would be injured.

There were and are a lot more good people in that city than bad, and those good people suffered terribly from that event. But during those six days, there certainly were a lot of bad people.

Fortunately, there was no angry mob here. I tried not to make eye contact with anyone but couldn't help it when I saw people staring at me. Probably wondering what this idiot white boy was doing here. I looked back and smiled; they didn't smile back. I turned up my air conditioning so they wouldn't see me sweating.

The traffic jam at the intersection was moving very slowly when it moved at all. It seemed to take an hour to get across it to the on-ramp, which at that moment looked like the stairway to heaven. I slowly nosed through the traffic jam. When someone would let me in, I would smile and wave a thank you. They did not respond; the mood of the drivers was sullen. I couldn't blame them. Their lives had been turned upside down, and these were probably just everyday folks, certainly not the ones causing all the death and destruction.

Eventually, I got through the tangle of cars and thankfully stomped on the gas to speed up that beautiful on-ramp. All the terrible images of what could have happened began to melt away like a bad dream. Then I thought about all the poor people who lived there. At least I could leave, but they had nowhere to escape to. It would take months, maybe years, before their lives would get back to normal. I felt very sad for them, and a little guilty that I could run away from Los Angeles, and they could not.

Once back on the freeway again, I realized my shirt was soaked with sweat despite the air conditioning. I felt very lucky and stupid at the same time, amazed at my carelessness. I thought I had dropped the old habit of getting into dangerous situations.

John Wayne said in *The Sands of Iwo Jima*, "Life's tough, but it's a lot tougher when you're stupid."

I said to myself, "I know what you mean, John."

Chapter 12
International Again

"Flying is hypnotic, and all pilots are willing victims to the spell."
–Ernest K. Gann

I flew domestic on the Ten for exactly a year. My last trip was a long layover in Toronto with nothing to do on the last day of the year, followed by a flight home on January 1, 1993. After that, I was back at the schoolhouse for international training. We learned how to read latitude and longitude coordinates for over-the-ocean navigation, perform fuel checks, complete position reports, and calculate ETPs—Equal Time Points—which I had originally learned as a flight engineer.

Pilots and flight attendants together were required to bring a swimsuit so we could jump in the big indoor pool and learn how to climb into a life raft and locate the emergency supplies. Practicing in a calm pool was a big difference from doing it in a dark, pitching ocean, but AA didn't have one of those available in Texas.

The pool and cabin mock-ups at the American Airlines Flight Academy

As mentioned earlier, at the time, the DC-10 out of Los Angeles was strictly flying to Hawaii, which was considered the longest overwater flight in the world. While Canada and Mexico are classified as domestic, Hawaii—despite being part of the United States—is not. Go figure. For a time, American operated LAX to London using DC-10-30s with longer range, but that route had been discontinued by the time I got there.

Back then, the MD-80 was just a VOR and NDB airplane. The Ten had the same old round gauges but more advanced navigation. We learned to use the different systems on the two models. The Dash 10 had the Omega system. It was ground-based and very old. At least it seemed that way. Designed in 1971 by the U.S. Navy for its ships, it consisted of eight transmitters around the globe. The receiver triangulated low-frequency radio waves to provide your approximate location and get you close enough to pick up a VOR station. Its accuracy was between one and two miles. More than enough to find Hawaii. The same system was on the Learjets I flew for Devarian.

The DC-10-30s were equipped with the more modern INS, or Inertial Navigation System. It was more precise, but I was surprised at how well the older system worked.

Today's satellite navigation is accurate to a few feet.

A few days later I was on my international IOE. I enjoyed plotting the Lat-Long fixes, thinking back to the old days when a navigator had to take fixes off of stars to confirm their position. It was a great feeling descending into the islands again, watching emerald-green Oahu getting better and better with the deep blue ocean all around. Only this time I had a window seat. The layovers at the Ala Moana Hotel now felt familiar, and I already knew the best places to eat. Each layover was like a mini-vacation. Most of the time, you would get a room with an ocean view and a salty breeze if you opened the sliding glass doors to the balcony.

Faced with the same noise of car alarms from the nearby mall parking lot, I started to opt for the backside of the hotel. It turned out that just across a narrow alley there was an apartment building with large floor-to-ceiling windows and sliding glass doors facing the hotel. I was surprised to learn from the other pilots that there were pretty women who liked to walk around their apartments quite free of any clothing and with the curtains open. It seemed they were strippers who worked at nearby nightclubs. Free advertising perhaps? I didn't mind since there was no cover charge.

My routine of running in the park next to the beach was back. Then, I went for breakfast at McDonald's to have Spam and eggs with rice. I wondered how I could continue to do this job and layover anywhere else.

On my third trip to the islands, my captain was none other than Ralph Sirik. The guy I had been so wary of as a new hire. But the trip was uneventful. I guess he figured if I had made it this far, I was okay. Or perhaps he flew this trip to make sure I knew what I was doing. Either way, we got along fine; he was actually a good guy. The chief pilots only flew Hawaii out of LAX, so it was good to get to know the bosses on a first-name basis, just in case. Most pilots avoided them like the plague.

My ideal schedule on the MD-80 out of Ontario had been three days on and four days off, one trip a week, four trips per month, eight hours total driving. On the Ten international, the trip schedules were written two days on and two days off. Seven trips per month. Since I lived a hundred miles away, it was a two-hour drive each way, fourteen hundred miles total to and from the airport. That meant at least twenty-eight hours spent in some of the worst traffic in the country. At times it felt like I was in my car more than I was on an airplane. So rather than bid a line, I was lucky enough to hold reserve. Filling in for sick calls or schedule interruptions, sometimes on a moment's notice, but usually it was for a trip the next day.

Sometimes I'd be off for a week or more at a time. My neighbors wondered if I even had a job. I used to jokingly complain to friends that after being off so long, I actually had to go to work and fly to Hawaii. I never got any sympathy.

There were three flights a day to the islands. Two were just one leg over, then straight to the hotel. But the last flight did three legs; after HNL, you would unload most of the passengers, then take off to Maui. That airport could be tricky, landing on a 7,000-foot runway in gusty winds, often in the dark. It was a challenge. But I never saw anyone screw it up and have to go around. Both legs were light on fuel and passengers, and if you were flying the more powerful Dash 30 version, it climbed like a rocket. It felt to me like a giant Learjet. We didn't get that high, flying past Molokai, looking down at the much more arid island on the way over, then it was back to Honolulu for the night. You didn't mind the extra legs because the short flights were fun.

One of the most popular shows of the 1980s was Magnum P.I. Filmed in and around Oahu, it offered viewers an escape to paradise from the everyday humdrum of life and work in the continental United States. It probably boosted tourism to the islands and ran for nine years. I thought it was great. When I had to go to work, I got to go there, to paradise!

Being on reserve left me plenty of time off for one of my hobbies, horses. When I was a kid, I'd always loved horses, but owning one was out of the question. As I got older, I never seemed to stay in one place very long, so for years it was too impractical. Finally, for the first time in my life, I had a steady job and income.

One day, I was riding my favorite big grey Quarter Horse gelding, Doc, in the San Jacinto Riverbed, several miles from my house. The soft sand was good for his feet and gave his muscles a good workout. When my pager went off, I knew it was American Crew Scheduling. They were the only ones with the number. I had to find a payphone right away.

I put Doc into an easy gallop, and we charged up the steep bank of the riverbed. Looking around, I found I was far from town, with the only civilization around being a trailer park. Thinking there must be a pay phone there, we took off on the dirt road beside the riverbed until we found an entrance to the community that had a golf course.

Enjoying some time off with Doc

We trotted around the mostly deserted streets looking for a payphone; thinking there must be a clubhouse around here somewhere.

An older woman was watering her flowers in front of a house with a golf cart in the driveway. I reined Doc to a stop. She looked at me as if I had just ridden out of a Clint Eastwood movie. I asked. "Is there a payphone around here? I need to call my company."

She said, "No need for that. You can use mine."

Thanking her, I swung down and tied Doc to her white picket fence, hoping desperately he would not spook and tear it apart.

Walking into her tidy mobile home, she pointed out the phone in the kitchen. I dialed the number of crew scheduling and was relieved when they said the trip was for the next day, so I didn't need to worry about dropping off my horse and rushing to the airport. The nice lady asked if everything was okay. I said, "Yeah, I just have to fly to Hawaii tomorrow."

She was not sympathetic.

Thanking her profusely, I walked back out to Doc and breathed another sigh of relief.

He was waiting patiently, and her fence was still in one piece. He was such a good horse.

I decided it was time I got a cell phone. After coming back from the trip, I went shopping. My first one was the Motorola 'Brick.' It was as big as a World War Two walkietalkie, and they charged ninety cents per minute. I was better off with the pager.

One particularly hot day while sitting in the air-conditioned cockpit at the gate, I watched the rampers working and sweating way down on the ground. I thought back to Alaska and doing construction work, long before I had learned to fly. In the house through the pine trees on the next lot lived my neighbor, who worked for Wien Air Alaska, the hometown airline. He was a baggage handler and mentioned they were hiring, so I got the phone number from him and gave them a call.

The lady answered, and I said, "I'd like to apply for a job as a baggage handler."

She said, "Do you have any experience?"

"As a baggage handler? No."

"I'm sorry, we can't use you."

I said, "I have a strong back, and I can read. What more is required?"

"I'm sorry, we only want people with experience."

I stared at the phone for a moment before I hung up. This was 1977, and I'm pretty sure there were no computers involved. I was confident I could do the job, but they wouldn't give me a chance. I tried not to feel rejected and unwanted. Because of my background, I wondered if I could ever improve my life.

Later, still trying to break out of construction, I answered an ad in the paper for cabin service cleaning the airplane cabins between flights and delivering meal carts. They said I was overqualified.

I didn't tell them I was a high school dropout with an arrest record and working as a carpenter and hanging sheetrock. Still not yet a pilot. I didn't feel overqualified.

Now sitting in the cockpit of a DC-10, looking down at the ground crews, I couldn't help but think that could be me. They wouldn't let me throw bags or clean the airplane, so I ended up flying them instead. Go figure.

Like all international flying, I spent many hours sitting in cruise flight with the autopilot on, crossing that vast ocean, trying not to think of all the things that might go wrong. Pilots learn to trust their airplanes, and we bring our passengers along as they trust us. But all the things that could go wrong never did. Despite its bad reputation, the DC-10 was extremely reliable, and, other than minor mechanical hiccups, it never gave us a problem. In April of '93 a Dallas-Ft. Worth crew coming from Honolulu crashed one of our DC-10s at DFW while landing in a rainstorm. The NTSB faulted the captain for mishandling the braking on the wet runway. They went off the side of the runway, and the airplane was damaged beyond repair, but no lives were lost. Like many DC-10 accidents, it was not the fault of the airplane.

One of the things we practiced in the simulator was emergency descents. If you lose pressurization at altitude, everyone can die without oxygen. We practiced putting on the masks and getting down to breathable air as quickly as possible. The emergency oxygen for the crew and passengers lasts only a short time.

In November 1993, the flight attendants went on strike, but the pilots' union did not join them. The company tried to operate a normal schedule using administrative flight attendants and a few picket line crossers. The unions call them scabs. It didn't work very well. Thousands of flights were either canceled or flown empty in order to move the airplanes where they were supposed to be. Passengers would call reservations to see if their flight was going, and the company would tell them yes, no problem. They would come to the airport only to find their flight canceled, or worse, get to a hub only to be stranded. It was a nightmare.

Like the passengers, we were told our flight to Honolulu was going fully loaded. At the last minute, the agent told us we had no passengers because we had no flight attendants, and we were to leave on schedule. So, we did.

Being so light, we climbed right to 42,000 feet and stayed there. The captain sent Bob, the flight engineer, back to the eerily empty cabin and down the narrow elevator to the downstairs galley, where the food was stored and cooked. He came back saying the airplane was fully catered. Bob figured out how to work the ovens and cooked us filet minions, I think we each ate two of them. Then there were the ice cream Sundaes. I never thought you could have too much; of course, I was wrong. It was a good thing we didn't eat like that all the time.

On a break from the cockpit, I took a tour of the huge cabin. With nobody there, it felt like a *Twilight Zone* episode. It was my leg to fly, and we had nobody in back to scare, so I had a bright idea. I said to the captain, "Hey Cliff, how about if we stay up here a while, then do a practice emergency descent?"

Cliff, who was a good guy, thought that might be fun. He said, "Sure, let me clear it with ATC."

Into the radio he said, "Honolulu approach, American thirty-one, we'd like to stay up here a bit longer and then do a practice emergency descent if you can clear the airspace below us."

To our surprise, the approach controller reacted as if this was an everyday request. He said, "Roger American thirty-one, I'll clear the airspace below you, just let me know when you want to start down."

Instead of figuring our normal three to one descent rate, three miles for every one thousand feet, we thought one to one should work. Doing the math, we counted down the minutes, then notified ATC we were ready.

He said, "American thirty-one descend and maintain one-zero thousand at your discretion."

Counting down for the descent, we started the practice emergency maneuver. With all systems working normally, we didn't have to put on our oxygen masks.

I pressed the button on the flight guidance panel for the autopilot to hold Mach .85, the maximum number for the speed brakes to be extended. Then smoothly pulled the throttles to idle. With the island of Oahu ahead and to our right, the nose dropped smoothly down toward the water as I extended the speed brakes to full up.

As we plummeted downward, I was glad there were no cylinder head temperatures to monitor and keep warm. Jet engines were so much easier.

The windscreen was filled with the blue Pacific as the airplane shuddered and rumbled in its controlled fall from altitude. The ships on the ocean slowly grew larger. The descent rate exceeded the 6,000-feet-per-minute limit on the vertical speed indicator. At the twenty-six thousand crossover mark, I punched the button on the flight guidance panel for IAS, or indicated airspeed at three hundred-twenty knots instead of Mach. I could have done three-fifty except for the speed brake limitation. Descending through twelve thousand, I stowed the speed brakes. The autopilot had already captured the altitude to level off at ten thousand feet. Dropping thirty-two thousand feet of altitude took about five minutes.

It worked out great. The other pilots thought it was interesting to get to do it for real and agreed that despite the extra crew meals, this was the highlight of the flight. Because of simulators, not many people get to fly a real airplane simulating an emergency situation.

After landing at Honolulu, a bus arrived at the bottom of the stairs leading to the jet bridge. Ten flight attendants sneaked on board so they wouldn't be seen in the terminal. Union members would take their pictures, and they'd be ostracized for the rest of their careers. I'm sure they were. Anyway, it's impossible to keep something like that secret. Their supervisor came to the cockpit, introduced herself, and said we didn't need to talk to the flight attendants or know who they were. It was all rather cloak and dagger. We then took a handful of passengers to Maui and returned almost empty. On arrival in Honolulu, the flight attendants disappeared onto the bus, never to be seen again.

The next day we flew an empty airplane back to the coast, once again fully catered.

One summer afternoon I arrived at the gate in Los Angeles to a hot airplane. Walking into the cockpit, instead of doing his job getting the airplane ready, the flight engineer was sitting on one of the jump seats reading a newspaper. I looked at him questioningly, and he pointed to the engineer's panel, where a red "Do Not Use" flag was on the switch for the auxiliary power unit, along with matching flags on the APU circuit breakers. With no external air hooked up, we needed the APU to provide air conditioning.

With a shrug, he said, "The mechanics are working on it."

The passengers were already boarding, and it was not pleasant in the cabin.

I climbed into the right seat and started getting the navigation radios set up, hoping they would be finished soon.

The captain arrived. He was a very senior guy and popular with the flight attendants. He had his usual bags of chips, dips and snacks he would pick up at Trader Vics on his way to work. Feeling how hot it was, he was immediately upset, not wanting his passengers to be uncomfortable. He also looked at the relaxed engineer, who again pointed out the "Do not use" flags.

"The hell with that," the captain said. He pulled the flags off of the APU switch and the circuit breakers, pushed them in and started the APU.

I said, "That's not a good idea, boss."

He said, "I don't care. I'm not going to have an airplane full of sweating passengers."

About thirty seconds later, the cockpit became a hornet's nest as it was filled with angry mechanics demanding at the top of their lungs to know who started the APU.

Captain Arrogant responded with equal anger, yelling back at the mechanics, "I did. This is my f**king airplane, and I'll start it if I want to."

The head mechanic yelled back as if the passengers weren't listening just outside the open cockpit door, "We were f**king working on it! Someone could have been hurt or killed, you idiot!"

The captain came out of his seat and went nose to nose with the mechanic. I thought there was going to be a fistfight right there. I wondered who would win. Suddenly the big DC-10 cockpit didn't seem so big.

The engineer looked like he was trying to make himself small. I glanced out the side window, wishing I weren't there, and wondered what the passengers must be thinking. I thought, *Should I step in? Or let him get his ass kicked?* I stayed out of it.

This went back and forth for a bit before the mechanic stormed out of the cockpit and off the airplane, vowing to take the issue to his boss. When they left, Captain Arrogant had a few choice words for them, as if they were the ones who were wrong. I was glad no mechanics got hurt; that was a very bad move.

I imagine the captain had to explain himself to the chief pilot. I expected to hear from the flight office about my side of the story but never heard another word about it.

I was on international reserve, and sometimes I got sent to other bases to cover trips. In May of 93 I was deadheaded to Dallas-Fort Worth and spent the night. The next morning, I met my crew. The captain was from LaGuardia and in his fifties. His first name was Rock, and he sounded like a mobster to me. Craig, the engineer, was a young guy based in DFW, and me from LAX. Both Rock and Craig were great guys, and we all got along fine. Our crew was thrown together, and this is where Americana training really worked. If everyone uses standard procedures, you could take crews from different bases and make everything work.

The trip started early out of DFW to Miami, then on to Santo Domingo, the main city of the Dominican Republic. It is on the eastern side of the island that is shares with Haiti.

Then we returned overnight to Miami.

Rock, the captain brought along his pretty daughter, Emily. At sixteen, she was a cross between a girl and a lady, charming, innocent and funny. She accompanied us on the whole three-day trip. On one leg, Rock let her sit up in the cockpit during cruise.

Getting into Miami in the early evening left us plenty of time to relax at the hotel, have dinner and drinks next to the beach with palm trees swaying in the breeze.

It was another long, lazy layover. Twenty-four hours later we flew one leg back to Santo Domingo, getting in just before seven. We loaded onto the bus with the cabin crew bound for the hotel. The flight attendants loved Emily and treated her like a communal daughter. The bus driver warned us not to leave the hotel, especially at night. He said in his broken English, "Eet ees not safe." We were okay at the resort hotel, or on the bus to and from the airport, but not anywhere else. His warnings were very solemn, so we took them to heart.

Long after the movie *Saturday Night Fever*, America had gotten over the whole disco scene, but not Latin America. They were still firmly in its throes and loving it. The DJ with a record player in the nightclub played nothing but. It was Bee Gees mania, complete with glitter balls spinning from the ceiling. It was a blast from the (recent) past. Moving to the patio, we enjoyed Mojitos, Daiquiris and Margaritas. The warm humidity and lush tropical environment of ferns, banana trees and bamboo blending with the colorful tiled walls and Spanish architecture made this place seem a world away. It was like a vacation.

The next morning we flew back to Miami, then back to DFW, and the trip was over except for my deadhead back to LA.

It was a fun trip. I was hooked on international flying.

In the Pacific, the routine for navigation was to bring a ready-made sheet of the half dozen oceanic tracks, then after takeoff ATC would assign you one and direct us to an entry point. We were to stay on the track and not change altitude unless given permission by AIRINC, which we called on HF radio. At certain points, we'd make position reports at fixes designated on the track. You did this by plotting the Lat/Long (latitude and longitude) coordinates on the Omega or INS readouts, then radioing them to AIRINC as a position report. They needed to compare closely to the numbers on the chart. It was the job of whoever was not flying the leg to make those plots and position reports.

One day I was flying with a captain who was known to be a problem. Many copilots had him on their 'do not pair with' list so they wouldn't have to work with him. Of course, someone called in sick, and I was assigned to the trip.

He did a few quirky things, but I didn't think much of it. Once over the Pacific on our way to Honolulu, I was flying that leg. When we hit the first fix, he made no move to plot our position, so I questioned whether he was going to do it.

He angrily grabbed the chart and said, "You want me to do the plot? Here, I'll do all of them for the whole trip." He proceeded to arbitrarily mark Xs at the required position reports for every point on the track for five hours in the future, then threw the clipboard onto the center pedestal.

I was shocked and stared at him for a moment. Amazed that he would blow it off like that. I took the chart and said, "I guess you won't mind if I do it then." I did the plots and position reports for the rest of the flight, which was probably what he wanted. When I got home from that trip, I added his name to my 'do not pair with' list, like most of the first officers on the base.

You could say it is axiomatic that the bigger the airplane, the bigger the ego. Most of the captains I flew with on the Pacific route were great guys, and I had a fun time. I've seen some very big egos on smaller airplanes too, and not just with captains but with copilots.

Maybe it's just a pilot thing.

Like on the transcons, the food was great. The flight attendants on the Pacific routes were very senior. It was the highest-paying FA position with the best layovers at the airline.

They did not wear standard uniforms but Mumu's, which to me looked more like bathrobes, and were strained at the seams. Most of them were grandmothers, and the common pastime on the bus going to the hotel was exchanging pictures of grandkids. Still, most of them were very nice, and I didn't think they deserved the secret nickname of 'Sea Dragons.'

By the time I got hired, passengers were no longer allowed to smoke on the airplanes, but the pilots still could. I'm sure the union pushed for that. In the early '80s, when I worked for Imperial Airlines, flying mostly out of LAX, we used to see United DC-10s. They were painted white with red and blue stripes down the middle of the fuselage. In front of the left wing was the cabin outflow valve, where all the pressurized air from the cabin is metered out during flight. There was a long brown streak on the left side of the airplane emanating from that outflow valve. It was tar and nicotine from cigarette smoke.

There was a funny story I heard about a captain on the 727 who was a chain smoker. He always had a cigarette going in the cockpit. So, the copilot and flight engineer would wear their oxygen masks and smoke goggles the whole flight. It was very uncomfortable, but they had microphones in the masks to communicate through the intercom. They were trying to make a point, but I think when they did that, the captain smoked even more.

Eventually, the company said that pilots could no longer smoke either. I think there were a few old captains who retired rather than quit.

In his great book *Fate Is the Hunter*, Ernest K Gann talked about not only the seniority system with its long slow line but also the pecking order of pilots. Even back then, the military pilots were at the top of the heap, with fighter pilots and test pilots being the owners of the biggest egos and holding the most respect. Then there were the cargo pilots and, lower than that on the totem pole, were the helicopter pilots, who I think have the hardest and most dangerous job. Like Gann, I was at the bottom of that totem pole, which is reserved for civilian pilots. "No formal training," as one military guy once said to me.

Believe it or not, there was a time when I thought I might have a shot at being an astronaut. I know that sounds crazy, but someone had written an article about the space shuttle in the early nineties. He said the shuttle would become so routine and there would be so many flights, NASA would not need highly trained astronauts to fly them; they would use commercial airline pilots.

Certainly, I would volunteer for that, and I started fantasizing about going into space.

Asking other pilots what they thought about it, most said, "I'd never do that. It's too risky." So, I thought if the senior guys didn't want to do it, I might have a chance.

I began to have visions of the Pan Am space plane in the movie *2001: A Space Odyssey* or flashing my Hangmen motorcycle club tattoo for a picture with the earth in the background.

It was fun to imagine, but of course it never happened. Still, it was exciting for a while to think I might have a shot.

I loved flying the Ten and laying over in Honolulu, but all good things must come to an end. In the early 90s, there were several factors that led to wanting to leave California. Too many to count, but some were, the traffic, the dirty air, the politics, the cost of living, housing and registering vehicles. And then there were the earthquakes. If nothing else, they were a good excuse. The main plan was to get out of California, where I had lived most of my life and thought I'd never leave.

Another reason was to be able to buy a place with some land to keep our horses, and the biggest one for me was to be able to upgrade to captain many years sooner than if I stayed in high seniority LAX.

One of the nice things about working for a major airline was the choices. Which airplane to fly and where to live. If you want to commute to work, you can live practically anywhere. I didn't want to commute, and I didn't want to live in the New York area, or Boston, or Charlott, or Chicago, or Miami, or Nashville, all hubs and crew bases. With horses, Texas seemed ideal. Flying over miles and miles of empty land, looking down, I thought it would be the perfect place to live and ride the open plains.

The DC-10 in DFW was very senior, and I would almost never be able to hold it, so the obvious thing to do was bid to the Boeing 767 as first officer. It was time to say goodbye to the Big Ten and Hawaii.

American Airlines was the launch customer for the DC-10 and continued to fly it for twenty-nine years before retiring it in 2000. To my knowledge, there are no passenger DC-10s left flying in the world today. Despite the B-52s and KC-135s being older, the U.S. Air Force has retired their KC-10s. The only DC-10s left flying are being used for aerial firefighting.

Chapter 13
The 767

"Change is inevitable, growth is optional."

-John C. Maxwell

The Boeing 767

I spent the month of June 1994 back in the schoolhouse learning about the Boeing 767. It would be domestic again, just in the States. There were four models: the -200, the -200ER for extended range, the -300, which was longer and heavier with bigger engines, and the 757. On a given day, you could be flying any of them.

It was very modern, and I was excited to be flying the newest airplane in the fleet. A double-aisle wide body, it was almost as big as a DC-10. It had two huge fuel-efficient engines and was simpler and easier to learn. Unlike the old round gauges for flight and engine instruments, the front panel had six big state-of-the art, cathode ray tubes or CRTs, computer screens. A primary flight display and navigation screen for each pilot, plus two screens for engine displays and other airplane systems. It was space-age stuff.

The ultra-modern Boeing 767 flight deck

Navigation was the new ring-laser gyros. The same system that they used on the space shuttle. They were far more accurate than what was on the Ten. The heart of the airplane was the flight management system, or FMS. It was brand new, so I focused on learning to use it.

At that time, it was the most advanced airliner in the world. It could fly itself and land itself, as long as you pushed the right buttons.

I was getting closer to the Star Wars universe than ever. Even so, GPS satellite navigation for civilian airplanes had not been invented yet.

A navigation page of an FMS

In 1989, American also bought 757s. The cockpit designs were so similar they were flown under the same type rating, so we trained on both. But they felt like completely different airplanes. The 767 was a widebody and felt like a big jet, more like the Ten, while the 757 flew like a sports car. It was a narrowbody with powerful Rolls-Royce engines. The first thing you noticed when you got on a real airplane was the way you stepped down into the cockpit. In the DC-10 you stepped up, and like the Ten, the nose wheel was well behind the cockpit, so the captain had to allow for that when taxiing.

Like a lot of pilots, I thought the 757 was one of the sexiest airplanes I'd ever seen, at least on the ground. It had long legs, a narrow body and big, uh, engines! It looked like it was going fast while just sitting there.

After the usual two weeks in ground school and two weeks in the simulator, it was time for my IOE. This time it was out of SNA, an airport known by three names: Orange County Airport, Santa Ana, and later, John Wayne Airport.

I had flown in and out of John Wayne many times in the MD-80. The runway is only five thousand seven hundred feet long, almost half the length of a typical big airport runway. If you were heading to Chicago, you were weight restricted. You could not carry full fuel and full passengers. The 757 was so powerful it could take off with full passengers and full fuel and climb straight to 42,000 feet.

When landing, the 80 had only four main wheels, meaning four sets of brakes.

Landing must be just right in order to get stopped on that short runway.

On the 757, you had eight sets of brakes. Even though the airplane weighed a lot more, it would stop on that runway with ease.

Takeoff from SNA in a 757 was thrilling. Orange County has a strict noise abatement program to try to keep the wealthy residents happy, especially the ones in Newport Beach.

Starting with a max power takeoff, holding the brakes until the engines are spooled up, then releasing the brakes, the airplane accelerates quickly. At rotation speed, you pull the nose up until you feel like you're going straight up. You're not, but I've seen 30 degrees on the attitude indicator at times. It seemed you barely had time to get the gear up when, at eight hundred feet, the flight management computer would automatically reduce power to a lowerthan-normal climb setting. The engines roll way back, the nose drops forward, and the engines get quieter.

You continue the climb with the takeoff flaps still out to three thousand feet before putting them up and increasing to normal climb power and accelerating.

I once heard it described by a passenger on a radio station in L.A. He said, "The pilots shut the engines off and glided for a while before starting them up again and continuing the climb."

It's a precise maneuver and has to be done just right to avoid triggering the numerous noise monitors in the area. If you set one or more of them off, you will hear about it.

I flew the 757 for two weeks before I saw my first 767, where we did transcons from LAX to Miami, one leg a day, laying over at the beach again. It was great, and the flying was easy. There were also long hauls to and from Boston, Newark, or Dulles, sometimes two legs a day, unlike the workhorse MD-80. Occasionally, we flew Flight 77 from Dulles to Los Angeles.

More on that later.

The sleek, powerful Boeing 757

Once again, flying out of Los Angeles, especially to New York, we often had celebrities and movie stars on board. We would frequently see them at the terminal as well.

Sometimes I would make a note in my logbook if the flight attendant mentioned someone. One day, preparing to depart KAX, the number one flight attendant came up and said, "I think I have a passenger that's drunk." The captain asked me to go back and take a look. When she pointed him out to me, I recognized him and told her, "That's Ken Norten, the boxer. Don't worry about him; he's a nice guy." I'd met him a few years back when I was with Imperial Airlines. He had been a perfect gentleman. I'm afraid the years in the ring had taken their toll.

One thing that started bothering me was that when you came back to Los Angeles, descending into the Southern California basin, there was always a thick brown haze that you flew into. Often it was impossible to see the ground, and I would think about what that was doing to our lungs. The idea of living there became more and more disturbing; I couldn't wait to get out.

When I told the guys I flew with that I was moving to Texas, some of them who had lived in California their whole lives couldn't imagine leaving. I asked them why they stayed.

They would invariably answer, "Well… uh, the weather."

That wasn't enough for me anymore.

My horse trailer registration came due; it was $510. I called my realtor in Texas and asked him if he could register it there for me. He said, "No problem."

A week later he called and said, "Your new plate is on its way to you."

I said, "Great, how much was it?"

He said, "Don't worry about it."

"No, c'mon, I'll send you a check. How much was it?"

He said, "Five dollars."

Amazed, I said, "Five dollars a year?"

"No, five dollars for as long as you own it."

No wonder I was getting out of California.

The move to Weatherford, Texas, happened in early 1995, horses and all. The place we bought had two acres in the backyard for them. I spent the month of April commuting back to LAX until my transfer came through to DFW. Now I was driving less than an hour to get to the airport with none of the stop-and-go L.A. traffic. I love it when a plan comes together.

DFW

Same job, some company, different base. Being closer to the middle of the country, there weren't as many long flights, and some of the captains I flew with talked funny. There was that tourism commercial at the time inviting people to visit: "Texas, it's like a whole 'nother country." Many times, I thought, *Ain't that the truth!*

On an evening flight to LaGuardia, we were surprised when the flight attendant told us that Herb Kelleher was on board. Herb was the CEO of Southwest Airlines. He was well known, and his employees loved him. He was frequently on the television news talking about his airline. Now here he was riding with us. The captain told her, "When he finishes his dinner, tell him he's welcome to join us in the cockpit."

About half an hour later, the number one flight attendant unlocked the door with her key, and Herb walked in. He was on his way to a meeting in New York City and said Southwest didn't have any nonstop flights from Dallas. He sat down on the jump seat and entertained us for an hour. Being good friends with American Airlines CEO Bob Crandall, he had endless stories about Bob, good-naturedly making fun of him most of the time. He seemed very comfortable with pilots, and we had a great time meeting him.

As we approached the busy airspace of New York, he returned to his seat and we got back to business. I wouldn't have minded working for him, but I wouldn't have given up this job for the world.

On another layover, the captain and I showed up at the airport to fly home and were told that DFW had been hit by a vicious thunderstorm the night before, and one hundred airplanes had been grounded due to hail damage. Our airplane for the day had spent the night, so it was fine.

Upon arrival, we found the rest of our trip had been cancelled, so we could go home. Arriving at the employee parking lot, it looked like a war zone. Cars and pickup trucks looked like they had been beaten with ball-peen hammers. Windows were smashed, with some completely gone. Finding my 95 Monte Carlo, it looked the same as the rest. The front and rear windows were full of cracks, but at least they held so I could drive home. The car was less than a year old. When I took it to the dealer to have the damage fixed, the bill was $4,000. Welcome to Texas.

Flying over the vast countryside of Texas, heading west at five hundred miles per hour, it takes an hour to cross over El Paso before you leave the state. For years I had been looking down at all that open land and imagining riding horses from one horizon to the next. Kinda like the freedom on a motorcycle, only slower. I thought most of it was public land, like the national forest and BLM land out west. I was wrong.

Before long I learned that almost all of it was private land. There are only two national forests way down near Houston, and only a few small state parks in North Texas. Finding the owners of some of the open land near where I lived, I asked if they minded if we rode our horses on it. Their answer was, "Nope, I don't want anyone on my land." Even when there were no cattle or horses on it.

So, except around the neighborhood, we were left with putting the horses in the trailer, going to small state parks where you paid a fee to ride the trails. It was nothing like the vast amount of public land in the West.

***

One day at work, we killed time sitting at the gate at DFW because of a maintenance delay. The door was open, and a passenger brought his little boy up to meet us. It reminded me of my first tour of a cockpit. My parents could never afford to fly, but when I was very young, my father worked in the parts department for Pan Am Airlines at Miami Airport. While visiting his place of work with my mother, a woman asked if we wanted to see inside a Lockheed Constellation.

I was awestruck; it looked like a million dials, levers, buttons and switches. I asked how it was possible to see them all and made them laugh as I imitated trying to look everywhere at once.

Lockheed Constellation in Pan Am colors

Now, sitting at the gate, I explained to our guests how much fun it was to be a pilot. The little boy's enthusiasm seemed to melt away. He said, "I wish I could fly, but I could never be a pilot."

I said, "Sure you can. I don't believe that. Anyone can fly."

The captain indignantly squirmed in his seat and said, "Well, that's not true. It takes years of training and a lot of education. Not everyone can do it." He seemed to want to believe it took superhuman strength and intelligence to be a pilot.

It appalled me that he would say that to a kid. I felt it was important to support this kid's dream. So, I looked at the boy very seriously and said, "Anyone who wants to learn to fly can be a pilot."

He beamed and said, "Really?"

Acting as if it were the one true thing in the world, I nodded.

He looked at his dad and said, "I'm going to be a pilot."

His father smiled and nodded, thanked us and ushered the boy back to his seat. I felt like I'd done my good deed for the day.

When they were gone, the captain looked at me and said, "I can't believe you'd get his hopes up like that."

I said, "I can't believe you would try to take them away."

Europe

One morning I was in my airport car, cruising down Highway 30 with the radio blasting, heading to the Flight Academy instead of flying in and staying in a hotel. It was December 20, 1995. I'd been flying the 757/767 for sixteen months. Finally, I had been awarded 767 International. I would now be flying to Europe and the UK. Going south was also on the menu.

After buying the Eastern Airlines route, we now flew all over the place down there. Central America, South America and the Caribbean. Mostly out of Miami but also out of DFW.

Today's class was a South America Briefing. Some of the destinations out of DFW were Sau Paulo, Brazil, and Rio de Janeiro. It was adventurous, it was exciting, and it was all too often dangerous.

On the drive to the airport, a news flash interrupted the music on the car radio: "American Airlines Flight 965, a 757 from Miami to Colombia, has crashed in steep mountainous jungle."

It was stunning news—the same airplane I was flying. I turned off the radio and drove the rest of the way in silence. Arriving at the class with other pilots, the mood was somber. Everyone had already gotten the news. Taking our seats, the instructor began to share what he knew when Bob Crandall, the CEO of American, interrupted over the P.A. system. The announcement was being piped into all the classrooms in the flight academy.

He expressed deep sadness and remorse over the tragic accident and vowed to support the families of the passengers and crew, while investigating the cause of the crash. I didn't envy his job at a time like this. When the broadcast ended, the instructor began with the job at hand. I think his words about the hazards of flying in South America carried more weight than normal.

The pilots that crashed had made several errors in navigation while trying to hurry into Cali, Colombia, in the dark. Then they let the automation take them where they didn't want to go. Not knowing their exact location and thinking they were descending toward Cali, the ground proximity warning blared, "Terrain! Terrain! Pull up! Pull up!"

The copilot put on full power to climb, but he forgot to retract the speed brakes. The captain didn't notice it either. If they'd retracted them, they would have made it over the mountaintop. Rescuers had an awful time getting to the wreckage. One hundred-fifty-one passengers and all eight crew members died. Four people miraculously survived. After that, we were trained to pay more attention to the speed brake handle when putting the throttles up.

I remember many things from that day. The multiple ETPs, depending on whether your emergency was east or west of the Andes Mountains. There were many airports to divert into, but some of them were so primitive, you didn't want to. Only if it were a matter of life or death.

The one thing that really stuck in my mind that day was the Andes Mountains. In North America, only one peak rises above 20,000 feet (6,096 meters): Mount McKinley in Alaska.

"In South America," he said, "there are forty-nine." I never counted them myself, so I took his word for it.

In Cusco, Peru, the altitude at the airport is 10,860 feet. When airborne, if their cabin altitude exceeds 10,000, pilots are required to be on oxygen. So, at Cuzco, the pilots have to be on oxygen as soon as they get in the cockpit. The FO has to bring a walk-around O-2 bottle while he is outside the airplane. Landing and taking off in that high thin air is tricky, but the 757 with its massively powerful engines did it with ease.

The instructor warned us about several layover cities where we were advised not to leave the hotel because of crime. Even a taxi driver had robbed a crew at gunpoint. Some flight plans had as many as five ETPs because of the mountains reaching up to space. At times, there were riots and political unrest. My main thought was, *I don't really want to go down there.*

The allure of London and Paris was more my style. I preferred cosmopolitan cities where, I'd heard, even most French people speak English. When I got on the line, I bid trips going east, not south.

I was given another check ride so I could get type rated in the airplane. It was easy since I flew it every day. I now had my fourth and fifth type ratings on my license, saying B757 and B-767 along with Learjet, Cessna Citation and DC-3. I was qualified to sit in the captain's seat while he was off on his break.

Pilots either love or hate international flying. The long legs and extreme time zone changes take their toll—sometimes as much as eight hours in parts of Europe, depending on the time zone you left from. Or sixteen hours into the next day when you cross the international date line heading to Japan. Some people adapt; others never do. It probably depends on physiology. Jet lag becomes a way of life.

It helps to have a relief pilot. Under FAR Part 121, flights scheduled over nine hours require a second first officer. Different airlines have different terms for this role. At American, the regularly scheduled first officer is called FO, or First Officer-A, while the relief pilot is called FB, or First Officer-B. Both are commonly shortened to FO and FB. Since he doesn't do much else, it has also been known to stand for Food Boy. They are there to spell the other pilots during the long cruise portion of the flight. Getting to take a break to eat, watch a movie, or sleep does wonders to break up a long flight.

The FB must be in the cockpit for takeoff and landing. After takeoff, it is his/her job to figure the breaks for the three pilots and usually take the first one. The captain will frequently take the second one, and the FO usually gets the last.

Over the Atlantic there would be at least two ETPs because of possible diverts into either Gander, Newfoundland, or Keflavik, Iceland.

Once past Keflavik, you would head for Scottland or England. They were now figured into the flight plan by the dispatcher. Almost all flights are eastbound at night, taking off in the afternoon and landing in Europe or the UK the next morning. Westbound flights fly with the sun, getting in the same day.

Back then, American had an "up or out" policy, meaning that when it was your turn to upgrade to captain, you were required to do so. If you couldn't pass the check ride, you were out—fired! There were some FOs who didn't want to become captains, or simply didn't want to fly domestic. So even though they had upgraded, after their one-year lock-in was up, they would bid back to international FO and stay there. At least until they could hold the international routes as captain. I flew with several guys like that.

There were a lot of good reasons to bid international—less work and higher pay, and the layovers were cool. My first trips were to Orly Airport in Paris. The layovers were about twenty-four hours or more. For example, if you landed at ten o'clock in the morning, you might leave again at ten o'clock the next day. It sure beat flying three or four legs a day, through hubs and laying over in Des Moines or Bakersfield.

Our hotel in Paris was right on the Seine River and a short walk to the Eiffel Tower. I quickly learned to love the restaurants and brasseries, with their French cuisine and wine that was cheaper than beer.

A typical layover in Paris

Like all international trips, sleep was a problem. By the time you got to your room, you'd been up for nearly twenty-four hours, and your body was begging for eight hours of rest. But if you gave in, you'd be wide awake all night—and just when you were ready to fall asleep again, it would be time to leave.

So there were two options. The first was to skip sleep entirely: change clothes, hit the ground running, meet some of the crew for sightseeing, and try to stay awake the rest of the day. Then go to bed early. The second was to take a short nap—no more than two hours. But waking up was brutal. It felt like being ripped out of a sound sleep, like you were trapped in a deep, dark well and had to claw your way out. Your eyelids felt welded shut. It was like you had died and were trying to fight your way back to the living. Your body wanted eight hours, but you only gave it two.

Still, it was worth it. You'd be somewhat rested, able to enjoy the afternoon and go out for dinner. You'd get back to your room around eight o'clock, get a full night's sleep, and feel refreshed by the time it was time to leave the next morning.

Gargoyles on Notre Dame Cathedral in Paris

Some of the attractions in Paris, especially for writers, are the memories and writings of Ernest Hemingway. He lived there in the 1920s before he was famous. There have been many books written about him and the city, and there are so many places that he talked about that are still there. Places where he lived, ate, drank—La Closerie des Lilas, Sylvia Beach's Shakespeare and Company, Jardin du Luxembourg, the quays of the Seine. The city is alive with his spirit and memories.

He and his friends, like Pablo Picasso, F. Scott Fitzgerald, and many others, bring back memories of a lost time, the so-called Lost Generation. Part of the romance of that time stems from his love affair with his first wife. It was the happiest time in his life; he would later write. The marriage and the happiness would not last.

But my focus was flying airplanes and being the best at it I possibly could. At that time, I knew nothing of the literary and emotional connection to the city. Today there are dozens of places to keep you busy: the Louvre Museum of Art, the Arc de Triomphe, Napoleon's Tomb, Montmartre and the beautiful gardens and parks. The city is full of monuments and statues, and it is easy to get around; the subway system works well, even if you can't read French.

Who needs the Eiffel Tower?

One day, I showed up for duty in operations at DFW, this time flying as the FB. Some pilots liked the position because they worked less, but it wasn't my preference—I didn't get to fly the airplane. My destination was listed as FRA. I had been flying to Paris, so for some reason I assumed it was an airport in France.

There were only two other pilots in the international operations room, so I asked, "Are you guys going to France?"

Together they replied, "No," and continued to ignore me.

Pulling up my flight information on the computer, I realized—obviously—that flights are never to a country but to a specific airport. I was mortified to discover that FRA was Frankfurt, Germany. I had never been there before.

What was I thinking? Feeling like an idiot, I had to swallow my pride and say, "Oh, I guess I'm going to Frankfurt. Is that where you're going?"

The look they gave me matched exactly how I felt. Yes, I must be an idiot.

Their mood and lack of friendliness didn't improve for the entire trip. I guess my initial display of ignorance was unforgivable. So, my first excursion to Germany wasn't all that pleasant.

I started to wonder if flying international routes was worth it—if it meant working with people like that.

Fortunately, the next time I went to Frankfurt, the crew was friendlier. I discovered what made international flying worthwhile: wonderful layovers, visits to Hofbräuhauses with good German beer, and hearty dishes like Jägerschnitzel and Schweinshaxe. Germany wasn't so bad after all.

Our hotel was in Darmstadt. In the city, there were a couple of massive concrete towers. Marveling at their size, I was told they were flak towers—anti-aircraft gun emplacements from World War II.

German flak towers

One funny thing about flying internationally was the baggies full of foreign currency: German marks, French francs, and British pounds. Every country had its own money before the European Union started using the euro, which simplified travel for everyone, especially pilots and flight attendants. The United Kingdom did not participate.

Out of DFW in the 767 when we flew to London, it wasn't to Heathrow, which is just west of the city. We landed at Gatwick Airport. I had only been to London briefly in 1985 on the way back from Africa after a safari, so it felt special to spend more time there.

Gatwick was an unusual international airport with its single runway. Located halfway between the city of London and the English Channel, it feels like the middle of nowhere. Our hotel was a short walk from the terminal, and there was a train station where you could hop a ride to the big city.

The train went north into Victoria Station, where you could take the subway to other parts of the city. A short walk from Victoria will take you to nearby locations like Buckingham Palace, Hyde Park, the Thames River, or Big Ben and the Parliament building.

There are plenty of the ever-present pubs, or public bars. At the hotel in Gatwick there was a restaurant, but it wasn't the same as going to pubs, some of which had been there for hundreds of years. I loved the atmosphere and the food.

I heard many pilots say they did not like English food, but then some did not like crew meals or McDonald's either. I thought Bangers and Mash or Beef Wellington was great, and then there was the beer. My favorite food, which you could get anywhere, was fish and chips. There was one place in Kensington that served great beer, and the side with the fish and chips was mint mushy peas. I don't much like peas, and it may sound weird, but imagine cooking down peas like refried beans and adding mint. I thought it was great.

After a day of sightseeing with the crew, then dinner and a few pints, we had to get back to the hotel. If you missed the last train of the night, you'd be stuck in the city with no place to stay unless you paid for a room. More than once we rode the last train of the night, fighting to keep our eyes open.

We would be dead tired, so we would assign someone, usually the FB, to watch for our stop at Gatwick. If we missed it, we'd end up in Brighton Beach, where the train stopped for the night. Staying awake on the train was almost as hard as getting up after a quick nap after a long flight. More than once you'd wake up to find the designated lookout asleep and panic, thinking we missed our stop, but never got stuck in Brighton for the night.

On one layover, the other pilots and I, along with some of the flight attendants, took the train south to Brighton Beach on a rare sunny Saturday afternoon. We spent hours sitting on the porch of a restaurant on the beach talking and drinking beer, watching people enjoying the sand and surf. It was windy, and we thought it was freezing cold, but I guess the Brits thought it was normal.

There is never a shortage of places to see in London, and with its efficient subway system, it's my favorite city besides Paris.

***

One hazard in aviation is our feathered friends. Almost all pilots have had bird strikes. They can range from a sparrow to a goose or a vulture. The cockpit windshields on jets are designed to withstand the impact of a one-pound bird at 250 knots. Or, as we like to joke; a 250-pound bird at one knot. There are many accounts of large birds coming through the windscreen and injuring or killing pilots.

One dark night, while flying the Bandeirante for Imperial Airlines, we were heading to LAX at six thousand feet with the lights of Laguna Beach below when there was a loud bang. Our eyes went to the engine instruments, but everything looked normal. It sounded as if someone had whacked the fuselage with a baseball bat. Using my flashlight, I checked the windows for damage, and the large pane right in front of me was covered with blood and feathers. A seagull, perhaps? What was he doing way up there at night? On the ground, we could tell that it had hit the aluminum body just below the plexiglass. We wondered what would have happened if that bird had been just a fraction higher. Would the windshield have held?

Chesley Sullenberger found out the hard way what birds can do when his A-320 Airbus hit a flock of geese over New York City. With both engines knocked out, and through some expert flying, they ended up in the Hudson River; nobody was hurt except the geese.

Sometime in the 90s, an American Airlines 767 departing Orly Airport in Paris center-punched a flock of cormorants. A friend who knew the captain sent me pictures of the aftermath. The airplane looked like it had been shot with twenty-millimeter cannon fire.

There were several large holes in the nose of the airplane and the wing roots on both sides. One of them came into the cockpit, landing in the captain's kit bag. He had blood all over his shirt and pants.

Bird strike damage in Paris. It could have been much worse.

Both engines were spared, and they landed safely back in Paris.

I shudder to think if some of them had come through the windshield, would the plexiglass have held? Glad I was not on that flight.

When possible, I always tried to fly FO rather than FB. Depending on the schedule, even as FO you may only get four landings a month. A low workload that some pilots enjoyed, but it can be hard to stay current when you are working so little. You get plenty of flight time per month, but most of it is at cruise altitude on autopilot. The problem comes when you go back to the schoolhouse for recurrent training, and you are out of practice.

Better pilots than I probably had no problem with it, but I felt I needed to keep current by getting more flying in. As much as I liked flying less legs and laying over in Europe, I decided I needed to go back to domestic. And besides, there was the goal of upgrading to captain.

I'd flown with hundreds of captains over the years, but two of them out of DFW on the 757 stick in my mind. Next to the last guy I flew with was Vic Vasquez. He was of Mexican-American descent, born in a poor small town in the Big Bend country of the Rio

Grande in South Texas. He worked his way out of that little town, went to college and joined the U.S. Air Force. At that time, he still flew C-141 cargo planes in the Texas Air National Guard. Like most captains, he was very competent, but what struck me was that he was one of the calmest, easy-going captains I had ever flown with. I made up my mind that when I upgraded to the left seat, I would try to emulate his laid-back demeanor.

The other one was the last captain I flew with; his name was Bob Gregson. Not just a nice guy to fly with, he was a laid back good ol' boy who, on short final, always said out loud in his strong southern drawl before every landing, "The wheels are down, the flaps are down, and the girls are down." (You must make sure the flight attendants are seated.)

For the rest of my career, before every landing, Bob's words would run through my head.

Chapter 14
Captain

*"Successful people are not gifted;
they just work hard, then succeed on purpose."*
–G.K. Neilson

Captain wings have a star on top

It is often said in the airline industry that the pilots who work the hardest make the least money, and vice versa. As easy as the international flights were, I felt I was getting out of practice not getting to fly the airplane and land it as much as I had been. I had been with the company for almost ten years and was eager to upgrade to the left seat. Flying domestic routes again would be harder work, but at least it would pay a little bit more. Perhaps I needed to prove to myself that I could do it.

In 1991, American started taking delivery of the new Fokker F-100. Made in Holland, it was actually a stretched version of their shorter model F-28 jet, designated the F-28-100, or F-100 for short. Unlike the MD-80, it was very modern and simple, easy to learn and easy to fly. It had an FMS just like the 767 and could also Auto-Land.

There were only two crew bases, DFW and ORD (Chicago). It was used on shorter routes between one and three hours. It flew to the east coast and west only as far as Colorado Springs, then south to Leon, Mexico, north to Toronto and everywhere in between.

Watching the seniority list on the computer, I saw that I could hold captain on the F100 on reserve. I hoped it would only be for a short time. American's smallest and most junior equipment was also called the Barbie Jet or the Little Fokker. Having a capacity of 97 passengers, it only required two flight attendants. They said it was designed 'by pilots, for pilots.'

The cockpit was smaller than I was now used to, but somehow it seemed bigger from the left side. It was clean and uncluttered.

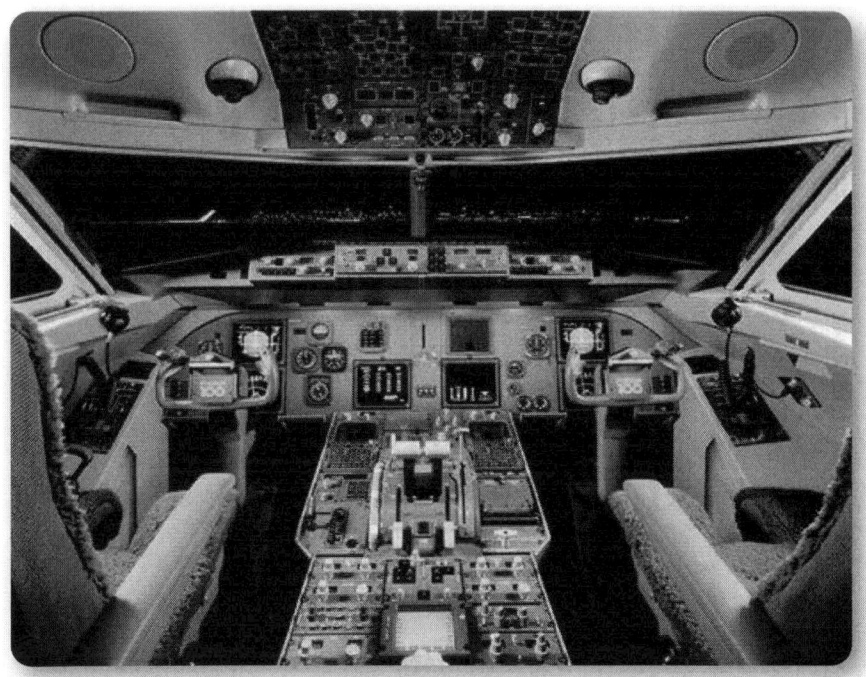

The F-100 cockpit

Unlike most transition classes, I wasn't paired with a first officer. Instead, I was placed in a class of ten captain upgrades. It was a different dynamic than I was used to, but we made it work. As usual, there was a two-week ground school. The guys seemed to compete to see who knew the systems best.

Then it was time to get to work in the simulator. We took turns in one seat or the other.

Part of that advanced cockpit was a set of six CRTs—cathode ray tubes—displaying flight instruments, engine data, and system information. The top screen was the PFD, or primary flight display.

Fokker display screens.
The gauges to the right are analogue backup flight instruments.

Just below it was an ND, or navigation display, with a moving map mode for situational awareness. It showed all kinds of information about your direction and route.

Today, cars have that feature, but back then, starting with the 767, it was new.

When pilots learn instrument flying, they must develop a scan to gather information from multiple instruments at the same time and put it all together to keep the airplane right side up and pointed in the right direction.

Instead of scanning six or more instruments to get all that information, the Fokker pilot only had to look at two screens. Hence the term "Fokker Stare." Your scan got a lot smaller, just one of the many things that made it easier to fly.

In normal operations, pilots always share the legs, so half the time the captain is not flying. He is usually the one who operates the landing gear handle. Normally, it's on the copilot's side of the instrument panel, but on the F-100, they put it in the middle so either pilot could easily reach it. It's the only airplane I've ever seen done that way.

Power was provided by two Rolls-Royce Tay 650 engines mounted at the rear of the fuselage, like the MD-80. Each engine was powerful enough to fly the airplane, even on takeoff with the gear down, if the other one failed. That's a requirement for transportcategory airplanes. They were also touted as very tough in the event of bird strikes.

The airplane could be hard to slow down, so it had a large clamshell speed brake in the tail to help. It could be used with any flap setting or configuration. It wasn't unusual to see an F-100 on final approach with its speed brake fully deployed all the way to touchdown.

The little Fokker

Most wings on jets are *high speed, low drag*. Flaps and leading-edge slats turn it into a low-speed wing for takeoff and landing. The Fokker had a high-lift, low-speed wing. It didn't have any leading-edge slats and didn't need them. It was one less thing that could go wrong. We used to joke that the wing on the Barbie Jet was 'high drag, low speed.'

The plane's maximum Mach was 0.77, which meant we cruised it at 0.72, which seemed very slow. That's about 475 knots compared to roughly 500 knots when cruising at 0.76, like on an MD-80. For comparison, a DC-10 could cruise at 0.88, which is 582 knots or 610 miles per hour.

You had to be patient when climbing to altitude. With some of the short hops, you may not get there before having to start down.

We normally used flaps for takeoff most of the time, but I was surprised to learn that at high gross weights and high altitudes, like Colorado Springs, we would do no-flap takeoffs. All I could think of were two bad accidents where pilots forgot to put the flaps down. One was Northwest Flight 255, an MD-80 in Detroit in 1987, which killed 151 people. The other was Delta Flight 1440 at DFW, a 727 in 1988, which killed 14 people. I didn't like the idea of no-flap takeoffs, but because of the wing design, I got used to it.

American had a program called 'Captain's Duties and Responsibilities,' or D&R. It was designed to teach you how to be a captain, not just fly the airplane from the left seat. I was anxious to attend that program. When I had upgraded at Imperial and Devarian there was no specific captain training. Just a check-ride to see if you could fly the airplane from the left seat and handle all kinds of emergencies. No intense simulator training like at AA.

Both times I was just cut loose to figure out the whole *being in charge thing* for myself. No wonder some of the captains I flew with were so bad. They had not been trained either.

But now with a big airline, I was going to be taught the ins and outs of being the boss; being in command, running a cockpit, how to act like a captain. I watched my schedule looking for the class, but it hadn't shown up yet.

The check ride in the simulator was a non-event, and I received my sixth aircraft type rating. I was now qualified to fly the airplane as captain, but I still needed a real-world check ride. Other than at a distance at the terminals, I had not yet seen or been in a real F-100.

By October 1998, I was off on an IOE with a check airman named Mike. He was not very friendly at first but warmed up as we got to know each other. Over dinner and beers, the first night in McAllen, Texas, since I hadn't had a captain's D&R, I peppered him with questions like, "How do I know what the right thing to do is? How do I know what decisions to make? How do you keep from getting in trouble?"

Mike thought about it and said, "If you make your decisions with the company's best interests in mind, they will back you up."

That was of course, if you follow all the company regulations and the federal aviation regulations. If you can remember them all.

It reminded me of when I was a kid and asked my father, "How do you know when you're doing a good job?"

His reply was, "If your boss is not yelling at you, you're doing okay."

My father was a carpenter, a job he enjoyed, creating things with his hands. I had just turned eighteen when he died. I was an aspiring biker and had already been to juvenile hall several times and was still recovering from a motorcycle accident. As I grew a beard and long hair, I think he was dismayed that I would never amount to anything. I sincerely wished he could see me now.

Then I asked Mike, "I haven't had a captain's D&R yet. How do I find out about that?"

He said, "Ask your chief pilot about it. He'll get it scheduled."

On one leg, an FAA inspector rode in the jump seat. It was like having a traffic cop in the back seat while driving your car. He was a good guy though, and it was all routine.

A new captain's IOE required twenty-five hours with a check airman, so that took more than one trip. The next guy was with me for less than two days, when the required hours were met and he left in the middle of the trip. The next leg on my own as a new captain was to Monterrey, Mexico. I'd never been there before. I'd never even flown to Mexico. Studying the airport information, I saw it had high terrain around it and only one main runway with a circling VOR approach. Checking the weather revealed a low ceiling; it was windy and raining and very dark.

Walking to the gate, I met my first F-100 copilot. His name was Stu.

I said, "I'm brand new on the airplane, have you been to Monterrey before?"

He said, "Sure, lots of times."

I said, "Good, it's your leg."

Because it could be a tricky airport to get into, not long after that they started requiring new captains to have a Mexico Checkout, with a check airman going with them on their first time.

The F-100 was built as a regional jet, so the routes were more limited. The furthest west we went was Colorado Springs, but all up and down the east coast and as far north as Toronto and as far south as Leon, Mexico. Naturally, we spent a lot of time in hubs like DFW, Chicago (ORD), Nashville and Raleigh Durham. Once again, I was back to carrying foreign money, Canadian dollars and Mexican pesos.

Although we got around quite a bit, it wasn't unusual to fly all day and not leave the state of Texas. From DFW to El Paso, back to DFW, then McAllen, back to DFW and then to Amarillo for the night.

I was still waiting for my captain's D&R. I suppose I expected to be awarded my captain wings in that class. One day, I was in operations at DFW talking to two FOs when one of them pointed at my chest and laughed, saying, "Who ever saw a captain with copilot wings?"

Embarrassed, I said, "Nobody has given them to me yet."

One of the guys said, "Go ask the chief pilot."

So, having some time, I marched over to the chief's office and asked the secretary if I could get some captain wings. She said, "Just a moment."

Getting the chief from his office, he came out with a pair of wings and said, "We have to ring the bell."

As he clanged it, he said, "Like angels, you know when they get their wings."

I said, "I'm not ready to be one of those yet." He laughed, congratulated me and shook my hand while the secretary snapped a Polaroid, then handed me the picture.

1996, DFW. The small bell is behind him.

I asked him about the D&R. He said he would notify the flight academy, and they would contact me.

***

Many of my first officers were former military pilots, some even fighter pilots. At every first meeting, the question would come up: "So, what's your background?"

That old hierarchy thing was raising its head again. Mostly, they were looking for common ground to see if they'd flown the same kinds of airplanes and if they knew the same people. But they also wanted to see where you stood in the pecking order. With me, the conversation was usually short. When I told them my background was all civilian, they'd usually get quiet because we had nothing in common. One guy even said, "No formal training, huh?"

What they were really asking was: What service were you in? What did you fly? Who did you know? Often, they had mutual acquaintances; military flying is a small world. I witnessed this camaraderie many times in three-man cockpits or when someone was in the jump seat. Sometimes they were on the same level — mutual respect. But other times, one guy was an F-4 fighter pilot and the other was a helicopter pilot. So now the guy who flew helos was on the bottom rung of the totem pole.

I always thought that was very unfair. I have a lot of respect for the helicopter guys in any operation, but especially in combat. They have the more dangerous job — many times slugging it out with the enemy toe to toe, looking the enemy in the eye, getting shot at, while the fighter guys zoom by at twenty-five thousand feet dropping bombs. In Vietnam, the loss of non-college-educated Army helicopter pilots far outweighed that of the fast movers.

Of course, I'm taking a friendly poke at them; I love them all and have huge respect for military fliers. Not having been part of that hierarchy, they are all my heroes. I wish I could have been one of them. Not only was I not dealt the cards in their game, but I had also been in an entirely different game altogether.

When this good-ole-boy military chatter was going on, I was always left out. I was not part of their club, and I wasn't about to tell them which club I had been part of.

Chapter 15
Not Everything Goes as Planned

*"Death is more universal than life;
everyone dies but not everyone lives."*
-Andrew Sachs

A fine Air DC-8 in Miami

Walking through the terminal at Dallas-Fort Worth between flights, I passed an openair tavern and was surprised to see an airline pilot in uniform sitting at the bar. I had visions of the old comedy skit with Dean Martin and Foster Brooks about a drunk pilot.

As I got closer, I saw I knew him. His name was Pat Thompson, and he had been a copilot of mine on the Learjet at Devarian. One thing I remembered was that his middle name was Dale.

Walking into the bar, rolling my suitcase and kit bag, I looked around nervously, noticing a mixed drink on the counter. Sticking out my hand, I said, "Hey Pat, how have you been?"

He said, "Dale, it's good to see you. I've been okay; you're looking good, captain now, huh?"

"Yeah, I'm on the F-100, living here in Texas. I haven't seen you in ten years! Who are you working for?"

"I'm at Fine Air out of Miami flying DC-8s."

"How are they to work for?"

"Okay, I guess, typical freight outfit flying mostly to South America and the Caribbean, not the big time like you."

"Yeah, but you're flying four engines, as captain, that's pretty cool."

"It's a living, but I'd trade places with you," he said distantly.

"So, what are you doing sitting in a bar in uniform? I'd get fired for that; in fact, I shouldn't even be standing here."

He waved his hand and said, "Oh, they don't care. I'm not working today, just deadheading through and will catch another flight in an hour."

Still feeling nervous in the bar, I said, "I'd better get out of here. Be careful on those old DC-8s. It's good to see you, Pat."

"Hey, you too. I'll see you around."

Two months later, Fine Air Flight 101 crashed taking off from Miami. Pat was the captain.

The crew of three were killed, along with an onboard security guard. Miraculously, after sliding in flames across a busy highway, only one person on the ground died.

After investigating the background of the pilots, they found out Pat had two DUIs on his record. That may have been why he wasn't working at a major airline. Like me, he had a past to hide, although I never had a DUI. But listening to the cockpit voice recorder, they scoured every action the crew had made and found they weren't at fault. The NTSB discovered that the cargo had been purposely moved rearward by the loading crew, who had no understanding of weight and balance. This shifted the airplane's center of gravity so far back that it became dangerously tail-heavy and couldn't fly.

When they realized the cause of the crash, the lead examiner said of the pilots, "They didn't stand a chance."

Mary Schiavo, who was FAA director at the time, said. "South Florida had a reputation for being an 'anything goes type of place'."

It wasn't the first—and wouldn't be the last—time that misloaded or unsecured cargo caused a takeoff accident.

***

One of our destinations out of Chicago was Rochester, Minnesota, home of the Mayo Clinic. As one of the best places for medical care in the world, many of our passengers into that airport were going there. Some of them were wheelchair-bound, and they were always boarded first because of the extra time it required.

Crews, pilots and flight attendants, know that in case of a ground evacuation, the crew is responsible for getting everyone off the airplane, and the ultimate responsibility is the captain. It is your duty to be the last person off the airplane and cannot leave anyone behind.

On one flight into Rochester, we had thirteen wheelchair passengers. I couldn't help but think, what if there is an accident on takeoff or landing, and the airplane catches fire? What if the airplane has been evacuated, and I leave the cockpit to find thirteen passengers unable to walk, still in the cabin? I cannot leave until they are safe… Now how is that fire coming along?

At the time, I could find nothing in the operations manual, so I sent a message to flight operations inquiring whether we should limit the number of wheelchairs per flight. I never heard anything back.

Flying reserve can be great, or it can suck, depending on your situation. When first on the F-100, I was on reserve. Just filling in for trips that had sick calls or misconnects. It was easy. Most of the time you hang out as if you're unemployed, then get a phone call, put on your uniform and rush to work. You frequently had more time off than a line-holder, but it's not really your time since you can be called away at any moment. It wasn't a bad deal if you are reasonably close to the airport. But making plans is difficult. Just about every airline pilot has been on reserve at some point and can relate. For the whole eighteen months on the F100, I was on reserve. And it wasn't like when I was at LAX, where I had to go to Hawaii. At least then people felt sorry for me for having to go to work. Not really, of course; it was a kind of joke; many people would have loved to have my job.

One evening after landing at Austin, Texas, and were about to go to DFW. As we taxied back out, we could see lightning to the north. Then a note came over the ACARS printer from the dispatcher saying there was a huge line of thunderstorms between us and our destination. Airplanes were not getting through it. Good old Texas. The dispatcher had rerouted us way out west to San Angelo to drive around the back side of the storm, then head to DFW. It turned a one-hour flight into two. Now we had to go back to the gate for more gas and pick up the new flight plan.

First, we had to wait for a gate, then after we got our extra gas and the new flight plan, there was another surprise. We were getting a line check from an FAA check airman. Could this night get any worse?

The check airman showed up, and I was surprised to find it was Ross Saddlemire, the American Airlines Chief Pilot who had pinned my wings on ten years before at the flight office in LaGuardia. We welcomed him into our little office. He had retired from AA at age 60, which was required back then, and gone to work for the FAA.

I hoped that our shared background and his deference to our company would work in my favor. Still, there's that traffic cop looking over your shoulder feeling you can never shake. Ross was a good guy, but he had a job to do.

With a full airplane and almost full tanks, and with Ross on the jump seat, we were finally cleared for takeoff. It was late as we lifted off and contacted departure control, expecting to be cleared westbound toward San Angelo. Instead, the controller said, "Cleared direct Dallas-Ft. Worth."

Mike, the first officer, said, "What about the thunderstorms?"

The controller said, "They've dissipated and moved east; you've got a clear shot."

Mike and I looked at each other and shook our heads. We knew we were going to have a problem. We were loaded with several tons of fuel to avoid the storms, and now they weren't there.

Jet aircraft have landing weights. They can take off heavier than they can land, and it is a violation to exceed that weight. The landing gear has not been certified for it. We needed to burn off a bunch of gas; the F-100 could not dump it like a 727, and we weren't in an emergency.

Mike got us to a lower altitude and went fast trying to burn off that extra fuel. It did little good. By the time we arrived at our initial approach fix, we were still way over our landing weight. Limitations must not be exceeded unless in an emergency and especially in front of an FAA inspector. Besides, today the computers will snitch on you; you just can't get away with it.

I said to Mike, "Tell approach control we need delay vectors for our landing weight."

We were sent into a box pattern northwest of the airport. At three thousand feet at night, we put the gear down and the flaps to full as we proceeded to grind around for over an hour to burn off all that excess gas.

Ross was patient, acting as if this happened all the time. I made several P.A.'s to the passengers, explaining why we were in this silly predicament of boring holes in the sky to waste gas we normally tried to save.

Driving around at maximum flap speed with gear and full flaps, the airplane shook, and the noise was much louder than normal. Watching the gauges, we finally got down to a number where we would be legal to land by the time we got to the airport. Ross said nothing; he knew we had no choice but to burn off that gas.

We finally landed at DFW several hours late. The passengers were just happy to get there. Getting to the gate, Ross thanked us for the ride and got off the airplane. Mike looked at me and said, "I'm exhausted."

Not only was the F-100 easy to fly, it was also reliable. I had very little trouble with it. My one emergency happened one afternoon. Landing at Chicago when we put the flaps out for the approach, we got an asymmetry warning light and the flaps stayed at zero. One flap had come out further than the other, or one had not come out at all. The built-in safety feature caused them to stop working at all.

We pulled out the quick reference handbook and were surprised to find the procedure to be, "Override the flap inhibit switch, land with no flaps."

Izzy the FO said, "That's all?"

I said, "That, and add twenty knots to the Vref approach speed."

On an MD-80 or 737 would have been an emergency, but not on this airplane. That high-lift wing was ready for it.

I told Izzy, "Tell them we need a long landing and rollout."

The tower controller said, "I'm not sure if we can do that. Stand by." He probably wondered why this little jet needed so much runway.

I said, "If he doesn't give it to us, declare an emergency and demand the longest runway they have."

There was a pause, then the controllers said, "Long landing and rollout approved." I flew the approach faster than normal. In the flare, the nose came up higher than usual—it felt like a 727. I popped out the clamshell speed brake in the tail to help slow us down. The landing was normal, and we didn't roll as far as I expected. We turned off the runway, and no emergency was ever declared.

That aircraft was taken out of service for repairs; they assigned us another one.

I did have one engine failure, but it was while taxiing to the terminal, once again at ORD. On those airplanes with tail-mounted engines, we would frequently taxi on one engine. Having just cleared the runway, both engines were still running—I had not shut one down yet. We were surprised when one of them decided to take the day off.

We notified maintenance over the radio that an engine had quit. At the gate, we were swarmed by excited mechanics and supervisors asking all kinds of questions, like, "Why didn't you declare an emergency?" and "At what altitude did you lose the engine?"

We laughed and said, "Zero, it was on taxi-in. I don't think that's considered an emergency."

It took a while, but we convinced them it was no big deal.

There was an incident coming out of Rochester, Minnesota, one day. The FO was flying the plane, and we were in the clouds, climbing through about twenty-thousand feet, heading to Chicago again.

He had the autopilot on when the aircraft started an uncommented slow roll to the left.

In unison we said, "What the hell is it doing?"

When the bank reached thirty degrees, I said, "Get that autopilot off." He grabbed the yoke and, instead of disconnecting the autopilot, pulled it to the right. With that much overriding force, the autopilot disconnected, and the airplane snapped back to the right. He leveled the wings and began hand-flying.

I said, "Don't use the autopilot again." He hand-flew it the rest of the way to landing.

The roll had been very abrupt, and the flight attendants who were standing in the aisle serving drinks were thrown against the overhead baggage doors, hitting their heads and wrenching their necks. All passengers were in their seats with seat belts fastened, and no one else was hurt. Fortunately, both flight attendants were men, having stronger necks and thicker skulls than females, so it could have been worse, but still on arrival at ORD they took the rest of the trip off and reported to medical. I felt bad; it was the only time anyone had been hurt on my airplane.

The maintenance crews wanted to know what we had done wrong. We told them we'd done nothing wrong; the autopilot just started an un-commanded bank. It would be in the report, but for now that airplane was out of service.

You can't fly in the atmosphere of this planet without dealing with the weather. You can't go swimming without getting wet. Somehow, as captain, you find that weather is more important than ever, because you are ultimately responsible for the safety of the flight.

As copilot, you should be paying attention to every aspect of the flight, and I tried to. But it is easy to let the captain watch the weather enroute and at the destination, and at the alternate. When you're in the left seat, there is no one else to pass the buck to. It's all on you.

Flying in California is easy, smog in the L.A. basin and the occasional rain shower to keep it interesting, sometimes fog in San Francisco or Santa Ana winds in Ontario. But the rest of the country really keeps you on your toes. Snow and icy runways in the winter and the summer gets very challenging with thunderstorms, windshear, microbursts and wet runways that can cause hydroplaning.

I had now flown throughout the country for the last twelve years, but now that I was in charge, it seemed different. I wasn't flying checks anymore; our cargo was people. They wanted to be comfortable; they wanted to arrive on time… they wanted to arrive alive.

Okay, that's not asking too much, and it does make you more alert.

Of course, you want to arrive alive too. How else can you complete your career? It's nice that we all have the same goal. To me, the most important part of the job was staying out of trouble and not making mistakes. If you can do that, you will not only be okay, but your passengers will also be okay, and you will finish your career with your license intact, with your body intact, then you can retire. That was my goal, so I looked at the long-term result. That's what kept me going. I made decisions not only to keep my passengers safe, but to keep myself out of trouble. If I could do that, everyone would be happy.

Flying in the Midwest means dealing with snow and ice in the winter—and sometimes going head-to-head with thunderstorms in the summer. They can be the bane of aviation. In West Texas, storms can build into a solid wall across your intended path, sometimes reaching seventy thousand feet. No commercial jet could get over them, and the F100 was limited to just thirty-five thousand.

But I was about to face another kind of deadly threat. It wasn't hiding in the corners of the sky or lurking in the complex inner workings of an airplane. It was following me through life while I moved along, completely distracted and thinking I was invulnerable.

Chapter 16
I Have What...?

"The future is promised to no one."
-Wayne Dyer

For a couple of months when shaving, looking in the mirror, I noticed a mole on my left upper arm. I thought it was new, so when I saw the flight physician for my six-month checkup, I asked him about it.

He glanced at it and said, "It's probably nothing."

Later, talking to a nurse, I showed the mole with an inquiry. The answer was, "It's probably nothing."

My neighbor across the street was an emergency room physician. Hanging out with him one day over a beer, I brought the mole up again.

He asked, "Does it bleed or itch?"

"I don't think so."

"I wouldn't worry about it."

But something was nagging me in the back of my mind — this wasn't right. I made an appointment with a dermatologist in Granbury, just south of Weatherford.

Arriving at the appointed time, the waiting room was typically Texas, looking like it was built in the sixties. It was quaint, clean, and empty. Soon the receptionist sent me in. I walked into a large room with big windows and plenty of light. He said pleasantly, "Hi, what have you got?"

Without sitting down or taking my shirt off, I pulled up my left sleeve so he could see the mole. He didn't get out a magnifying glass or even take a close look. With one short glance he casually said, "We've got to get that off of there… right now!"

I was surprised. I thought it was nothing, but still…

He said, "I'll call a surgeon I know and get it set up as soon as possible."

"Do you think it's that important?"

He patiently looked at me as if I were not all there and said, "That's a melanoma."

I instantly recognized the word after hearing about famous people dying from it.

"Do you have a cell phone?"

"Yes,"

"Make sure the receptionist has your number?"

"Okay."

"As soon as I hear from the surgeon, I'll give you a call."

I thanked him and left. I was in and out in less than five minutes.

An hour later, I was visiting a saddle maker in Azle who was making a custom saddle for my favorite horse, Doc. My flip phone rang; it was the dermatologist.

He said, "Can you be in Fort Worth in two days at ten o'clock to have that biopsied?"

Knowing I was off that day, I said, "Sure."

"My receptionist will give you the address. Don't be late. This is important." I thought, *Should I be worried?*

Two days later, I showed up for the appointment. He was a plastic surgeon. The doctor was very personable, and after some numbing shots in the arm, he carved off the offending mole before I knew it. He put a bandage on it and said, "We'll check this out and be calling you with the results."

I thought, *Well, I'm glad that's over with.*

After flying a two-day trip over the weekend, I was surprised when on Monday, I got a call from the surgeon's office. He said, "Can you be back at our office on Thursday for a wide excision?"

I said, "What's that?"

"That mole was a malignant melanoma, and it was deep enough to metastasis. We have to take out a large area of the surrounding skin. You may need a skin graft from your thigh. You'll be off work for a while."

Going from "It's probably nothing" to "This is critical" was unexpected. My wife was worried. I told her, "It's not a big deal."

The next day I drove into the airport and went to the chief pilot's office and gave him the rundown. As a fairly junior captain, I needed to play this by the book. He told me, "No problem, we'll take care of you. You just do what you need to do." I didn't realize it would get the FAA involved.

Later, other pilots told me, "Don't ever let the FAA know about critical health problems." But I didn't know how I was going to hide something like this.

I had limited sick time, but that didn't seem to be a problem then.

Thanks to the chief pilot, I got some time off for the surgery; it was the first I'd ever had. How lucky is that for being a motorcycle rider?

The drugs were great! They put you out, and you don't know a thing until they wake you up, which feels like just a couple of seconds later. I was very groggy. My wife drove me home and put me in bed. Fortunately, I didn't need a skin graft from my thigh, so the recovery was easier than expected. I attributed that to having lifted weights for many years, though not recently, and having loose skin that could be pulled together. They removed a seven-inchlong elliptical piece of skin and were able to pull the rest together. While they were at it, they decided to do a lymph node biopsy to check if the cancer was spreading. That left an incision in my left armpit. They also sliced out another cancerous mole on my forehead.

I can always appreciate getting multiple things done at once. When I finally got out of bed and looked in the mirror, I was shocked. I felt like the Frankenstein monster. There was a long row of stitches on my upper arm and another on my forehead, not to mention the swelling and disfigurement. At least the scar on my forehead looked like something from a motorcycle accident or a knife fight in a bar.

The results from the biopsy said the melanoma mole was 1.1 millimeters deep, enough to metastasis, or spread to important places like the liver, lungs, or the brain. I was sent to an oncologist who looked like Morticia Adams, only not as pretty. She had black hair and dark circles under her eyes as she practically demanded that I go on interferon treatments. The same thing used for hepatitis C.

I said, "Why interferon? Why not chemotherapy?"

"Because if a melanoma metastasizes, it does not respond to chemo."

"So, it won't affect my job?"

"The treatment takes a year, and the side effects are like having the flu, including blurred vision."

"Is there any guarantee it will work?"

"No, it's experimental."

"I can't do that — be off work for a year; I don't have that much sick time."

"You must or you're going to die."

"No, I'm not doing it."

"You must!"

"No!"

She insisted again, "If you don't, you're going to die."

"You don't know that - you said it was experimental."

"You have no choice."

"We'll see about that."

It was a gloomy drive home, feeling like I'd just gotten a death sentence.

I sought out my neighbor Alan, the ER doctor, and asked his advice. He said, "If I were you and had the ability to travel, I would go to the best medical facilities in the world: Duke University, the Mayo Clinic, or M.D. Anderson in Houston, and get another opinion."

After a couple of weeks, I got the stitches out and was back to work.

I called M.D. Anderson, just down the road in Houston. As they say, "There is no such thing as a short drive in Texas," but American had direct flights there, so I made appointments to see oncologists.

It seemed I needed more time off to see doctors. I was still on reserve on the F-100 and couldn't hold a schedule, so I went back to flying 767 international where I could hold a line and have more designated days off.

After getting back on the line, I had a follow-up with the surgeon who had taken off the melanoma and done the wide excision of the lymph nodes. He was a very nice guy and was excited when I came into his office. He said, "Hey, I was a passenger on one of your flights!"

Surprised, I asked. "Why didn't you come up and say hi?"

"Oh, I didn't want to bother you; it looked like you were busy, but I gotta tell you,

I've never felt so safe on an airplane than when I knew you were flying."

What a nice guy. I thanked him, but I thought, *How does he know I'm a good pilot or not, just because he operated on me? I appreciated it, though.*

If I went back to flying international, three-day trips and working nine days a month would give me the time off I needed to make appointments with doctors and travel to places like M.D. Anderson in Houston and appointments in Fort Worth. I put in for the transfer while pursuing oncology visits and doing things like lymph node biopsies to try to see if the cancer had spread. Also, there were CT scans, blood tests, and more tests than I can remember. Then the FAA required me to have an MRI of my brain every year. Apparently, brain cancer can cause seizures.

Meanwhile, I had to go back to training as a copilot on the 767. But instead of the normal month of training, they gave me the short course. Five days!

I was paired with a captain who had been off flying status for two years on medical leave due to sciatica. Either he was completely rusty or he wasn't a very good captain in the first place. He was absolutely no help during the training and checkride. I had been off work a lot and had not flown the 767 in almost two years and still had the Barbie Jet in my head. No doubt the stress of the illness was a bit of a distraction too.

During the checkride, I botched a single-engine ILS approach because I had no help from this guy and was basically flying single pilot. The check airman busted me, but the captain passed. Probably because of the help I gave him.

Now my job was on the line, as well as my health. Once again, I was devastated. How could I let this happen? All the old doubts started flooding back. I didn't know which was more crushing: the cancer or failing the checkride. I felt like a failure, like my life was falling apart. Everything I'd worked for all these years was going down the drain. My wife's support made all the difference; she knew we were going to beat this.

More visits to M.D. Anderson did not dispel the specter of interferon treatments, even they were advising me to do it. But it was able to push it back since their tests showed the cancer had not metastasized… yet.

After a ton of stress and a few days refresher course in the simulator, I took another checkride in the simulator, this time with an FAA inspector watching. I passed it with flying colors, and there was a different, more competent person in the left seat.

The same check airman remarked, "That was just about perfect! If you'd done that well the other day, we wouldn't have had a problem."

I just said, "Thank you."

My neck was released from the guillotine.

Now I was back to laying over in Europe and flying one three-day trip a week. Plenty of time to see doctors and have a myriad of procedures done.

Back to the 767 and international trips

In the confusion and distraction, one month I flunked bidding - again.

When I showed my next month's schedule to my wife, she said, "Oh, you're going to be flying to Paris on our anniversary."

I considered hitting my head against the wall for my stupidity, but I recovered and said,

"Well... I thought you could go with me, and we could have dinner in Paris for our anniversary."

She said, "That is so thoughtful! What a wonderful idea!"

I thought, *I sure hope there's room on the plane.*

Fortunately, there was—she got first class. In Paris, we hit the ground running, with no sleep that morning. Making our way down the Quai Jacques Chirac, we stopped at street vendors, buying ham and cheese baguettes and melba toast. Then, we visited a small *marché* (market) and bought a bottle of wine, goat cheese, and caviar.

When we got to the Eiffel Tower, we took one of those almost sideways elevators in the four legs to the second level, where we huddled out of the wind to have a French-style picnic. It was memorable.

I entertained her with local history, telling her the story of how the tower got its name.

"When it was finished, they stood back in awe. Nothing had ever been built so big and so strong. One of the men exclaimed, 'Boy, that sure is an eyeful.'"

"So, they called it the *Eyefull* Tower."

Gustave Eiffel would roll over in his grave.

After touring the Musée du Louvre—where there's never enough time, especially on one short, sleepless afternoon—we picked out a cozy brasserie on the Champs-Élysées and had an exquisite dinner of something I will never be able to pronounce. And, of course, another bottle of wine.

With the sun setting in the watery sky, the walk back to the hotel seemed to take forever, through the narrow streets and dim lights with old buildings, never more than five stories high. The old worn doors, and the old worn streets with smooth cobblestones. Finally arriving at our hotel and retiring to our company-paid, four-star room, we promptly passed out after one of the happiest wedding anniversaries ever.

We started to tire of Texas. For the last two summers, they had over one hundred days in a row with temperatures above one hundred degrees. But that didn't include humidity. With the heat index—heat plus humidity—it was even worse. One day, returning from a European trip and driving home, I was listening to the radio; they said the heat index was 129 degrees. Some people without air conditioning were dying. I hadn't heard about horses dying from it, but mine had to stand out in the heat every day. They would stand still and sweat.

Trying to fly home during the holidays to see family was impossible because the flights were always full, and it was too far to drive. Gremlin, my old friend from the Hangmen motorcycle club, lived in Arizona, but not in the desert; he was up in Prescott. Not wanting to stay in Texas and not wanting to go back to California, I decided I would do what I said I'd never do—commute!

American did not have a Phoenix crew base at the time, so I could work out of any other crew base, as long as I could get to it. LAX, Chicago or DFW were closest.

A lot of pilots and flight attendants commute. It means getting on an airplane to go to work. You can fly free and sometimes, if the plane is full, for pilots, you can ride in the cockpit; flight attendants can sit in cabin jump seats. Not much of a treat when you spend all your working hours there, anyway.

I can never seem to be able to do anything halfway, so I didn't just commute on an airplane; I added in a two-hour drive to get to the airport. A double commute!

I was still doing medical tests and lymph node biopsies, locally in Fort Worth and at M.D. Anderson. Phoenix had a branch of the Mayo Clinic where I could continue those examinations.

Chapter 17
The 737

"Progress is impossible without change."
-George Bernard Shaw

The new 737-800 cockpit

American Airlines had announced that it was buying the new Boeing 737-800 and that one of its bases was going to be out of Los Angeles.

Checking the seniority numbers, I saw I could hold captain, so I put in a bid for it. LAX was closer, and even though AA didn't fly the route, it had more flights available because I could ride on Southwest and America West. There were a lot—about two per hour. It seemed to be a piece of cake.

After visiting Gremlin and checking out the area of Prescott, Arizona, and finally buying some property, we found a builder; everything was coming together. On trips to Arizona, when leaving DFW, it was 90 degrees and 90 percent humidity; it was hot and sticky. Arriving in Phoenix in a 105-degree dry heat, it felt cool by comparison. Yes, the dry heat makes a big difference.

I went to training on the 737 in the fall of 1998. After a month of ground school and simulators on the new airplane, I took my checkride and got my seventh type rating. I thought for sure I would get my captain's D&R this time and inquired about it. They said, "We'll let you know." I probably didn't need it by then, but I always wanted to learn more to be the best captain I could be.

When I first flew the MD-80 in 1987, it only had VOR and NDB for navigation. It was basically 1940s technology. The new 737 still had VORs and NDBs but also the same laser-ring-gyro system as the 767, but on top of that, GPS. Global Positioning Satellite receivers.

Man, this thing was magical; it felt like the space shuttle. It would do RNAV (Area Navigation) approaches that other aircraft couldn't do. The captain's side had a really cool, space-age HUD, which stands for heads-up display.

Example of a heads-up display during landing

It was like flying a video game; it used the same technology that modern jet fighters have. None of the other aircraft in the fleet had that. It was all integrated and worked together to give you the finest, most accurate and safest navigation system ever. Being very easy and precise to fly, you could do hand-fly CAT-3 approaches while other aircraft could only do it on the autopilot.

I was all ready to go. There was only one small hitch—we didn't have any airplanes yet, so the deliveries were running late. I was sent back to 767 FO and the international flights for about five months.

The move to Arizona happened in December of '98. After getting settled, I started commuting from Phoenix back to DFW, still flying to Europe. Even though AA only had six flights a day in each direction, it was easy commuting, usually three times a month for threeday trips. The flights to Europe left late in the day to fly through the night, so I could usually make the commute in each direction in one day.

In April of 99 the first 737s started showing up. After going back to the schoolhouse for a refresher course, I did my first commute to LAX for my LOE. Meeting my check airman in operations, we walked out onto the ramp to see my first ever live in the flesh American Airlines 737-800. I liked the airplane, partly because it reminded me of one of my favorite jets, the legendary Boeing 707. It had the same narrowbody fuselage, but only two big fuel efficient, turbofan engines producing as much thrust as four of the sleek old pure jets of the past, and at a much lower takeoff weight.

The 737's grandfather, the elegant Boeing 707 in the classic Astrojet paint scheme

Though nowhere near the biggest, the 737-800 was the most advanced airplane in the fleet. I especially enjoyed the cockpit because it featured a HUD, or heads-up display.

Unfortunately, when they were delivered, the HUDs had not been certified yet by the FAA, so they were taken out. For all its automation, when I flew it, it was only a CAT 1 airplane.

(Approach category one. Please see the glossary under ILS.)

It had more than enough range to fly coast to coast, and at first, American used them that way. Many times, I flew Flight 77, five and a half hours from Washington Dulles to LAX. Some of you will recognize that flight number. Although passengers did not seem to like being cooped up in a narrowbody for that long. Widebodies had spoiled them.

The airplane was highly automated, and the flying was easy, usually only one or two legs per day. Having the same old 707 nose designed in the 50s, some pilots complained it was too noisy, although being half deaf from too many loud motorcycles, guns and jet engines I didn't notice. The MD-80 was quieter because the engines were so far to the rear of the fuselage.

The 90s were rather stagnant, with not much upward movement on the seniority list and often furloughs. It wasn't unusual to see backward movement instead of forward. I hoped that by the time I got on the 737, my seniority would move up and I would be able to hold a line, but no, I was on reserve again.

Reserve availability was only one hour by ground transportation. Now living in Prescott, Arizona, I could not get a call and tell them, "I'll be there in three and a half to four hours."

Back then, there was no long-call option like there is now.

I was happy with my position, captain on the 737, but not happy with my living situation and getting to work. I loved where I lived, and I loved my job, but the two did not jibe. The result was a lot of driving, commuting flights and hotel rooms, on my own dime.

On days when I had to be available, I had to be somewhere in Southern California within an hour of the airport. Luckily, a friend of mine was a sergeant with the Los Angeles County Sheriff's Department. He offered to let me stay at his house when I had to be available, so I took him up on it. Leaving my car at LAX, I'd fly in and drive to his house and wait to be called. He had an office with a couch where I could sleep. I'd kill time by reading or going to the beach, working out in a local gym and running in a nearby park.

Sometimes, I would do a ride-along with him when he was on patrol. It was a different world for me, being on the other side of the law. I thought it was fun and exciting; sometimes, it felt dangerous.

I was usually on call for five days, then had two days off, frequently away for twenty days a month. It was normal to fly at Thanksgiving and Christmas. Not a good recipe for a happy marriage.

Some pilots don't like to fly all night, so many of the trips I got assigned to were allnighters. Leaving LAX at eleven o'clock at night for the red eye to Chicago. It was normal to get up early in the morning, then turned into a long day. Nothing new in the airline industry.

One night on our way to Chicago, Joe, the FO, and I were drinking coffee and chatting about anything to keep each other awake. We arrived over the airport at five in the morning; we seemed to be the only airplane in the air. There was a flat layer of clouds below us at three thousand feet that went almost to the ground. An orange glow on the eastern horizon faded up to deep blue where you could still see stars. It felt quiet and peaceful. Even with millions of people below us in the city, we still felt isolated. The base of the clouds over the airport was two hundred feet, with half a mile visibility — Category One minimums!

Without the HUD, that was the lowest we could legally go.

Zooming along, skimming the cloud tops in the morning sky, I was following vectors, maneuvering for the approach when the autopilot kicked off. I was still new on the airplane and, having been up all night and all the previous day, I was tired and in no mood for games, so I switched it back on. It stubbornly clicked off again.

Not wanting to force the issue with a possible electrical problem, I left it off and started hand flying the jet. Usually we make coupled approaches, meaning letting the autopilot do it, especially in the clouds. It's smoother and easier on the passengers. The autopilot does such a good job; you get used to letting it do the work.

I don't know when the last time was that I had hand-flown an approach in real conditions, but I said, "Here goes."

Joe was also new on the airplane. His background was flying F-15s for the Air Force.

I was impressed, so I didn't want to screw this up.

Just as the controller cleared us for the approach, the auto-throttles clicked off too. We entered the clouds, and it got very dark. I thought, *Just like in the simulator!*

The flight director and the speed cursor made it easy, but in my fatigued state, I still had to work at it. There was a slight crosswind. I drifted off the localizer and fought to get back. I was above the glide slope, then below it. I was working way too hard. When was the last time I'd done this?

At two hundred feet, Joe called "minimums," and the runway appeared straight ahead. I had nailed the crosshairs of the flight director perfectly. The glide slope and localizer came together and were perfectly centered; we were right where we were supposed to be, in perfect position for landing. Joe exclaimed, "That was awesome. I couldn't have done better myself." I didn't think it was that smooth, but I smiled and said to myself, I'll take it. He was impressed, and I didn't look like an idiot in front of him. I decided he was a very good copilot. We taxied in and parked the jet. As the passengers got off, I wrote up the autopilot and auto-throttles for the mechanics to fix while we headed off to the hotel to get some sleep.

Narrowbody flying not only had you going through all the hubs, you also flew into some of the more challenging airports. Short runways and frequently swerving visual approaches, following highways, rivers or sometimes just landmarks.

Compared to a standard straight-in ILS approach, they were fun. LaGuardia Airport in New York was old, crowded and challenging. You had to be on your toes. My favorite approach there, along with many other pilots, is the Expressway Visual to runway 31.

Descending from one landmark to the next, having to meet your crossing altitudes with the dense city of Brooklyn below you. Fly to the big cemetery, turn right to follow the Long Island Expressway, turn left over Flushing Meadows Park, then a hard left again to line up with runway 31.

At night it was even cooler with a million lights below you as you picked the ones you needed to follow your desired track. Yanking and banking at low altitude, following ground references, makes you feel like a real pilot.

After the last tight, low-altitude turn, you level the wings to line up on runway 31, try to land short and get a good touchdown, but don't try too hard; you don't have that much time. Hit the brakes and thrust reversers, then try for an early turnoff to keep the controllers happy. (New York controllers are never happy). Besides, you don't want the airplane behind you to have to go around.

The River Visual 19 at Washington National, or DCA, is another fun one. You start way out over the Potomac River and follow it as you get lower and lower. As you get in close, you are pointed straight at the Watergate Hotel. You point straight at it until the river takes a sharp right, and you do too; you can see kayakers in the river just below your right wing. When the wings roll lever, you can see people in the windows of the hotel. Just off your left wing is the most restricted airspace in the country besides Area 51. It contains the White House, the Capitol Building and dozens of monuments. They wouldn't tell us specifically, but there were rumors of surface-to-air missiles that would be fired at you if you got too close to the White House. Nobody wanted to try to find out if it was true.

Descending a little lower with the Lincoln Memorial just under your left wing, you resist looking at the National Mall and the Washington Monument. After another low-altitude turn over the 14th Street Bridge, you line up with Runway 19. Almost immediately after rolling out of the turn, you're in the flare. Once again, the runway is not that long, so you don't take your time. Like LaGuardia, it's a busy place.

The 737-800 at Chicago

Everybody who flew the narrowbodies—the 737, 727, MD-80, the F-100 and the big 757—had a chance to do those approaches from time to time. The company didn't even charge us extra for them.

I was flying all over the country again; it even felt rather international, going to Toronto and Montreal and Monterrey and Puebla, Mexico.

When venturing into the atmosphere, you have to deal with the weather. Many times, it was sunny and clear, or a smooth, peaceful night. But in the Midwest in the spring, summer and fall there were all too often thunderstorms, lightning and heavy rain. In the winter, it was snow and icy runways. Thunderstorms are relatively easy to avoid, and the new Doppler radar gives an extra safety margin when taking off or landing.

Snow caused a lot of delays. We waited for the runways to be plowed or inspected for braking action. There were delays getting deiced, sometimes more than once. You're not a real airline pilot until you've flown in the snow in the Midwest or Northeast.

Buffalo, sitting at the east end of Lake Erie, is known for its lake effect snow. One evening, landing there, the tower was closed and airport operations told us the latest conditions over the radio.

Operations, "The runway was plowed about an hour ago, but the snowplow broke down and it now has another foot of snow on it."

We were the last flight of the night, so we didn't have to get back out.

"Then she said, "The taxiways haves not been plowed at all and have at least two feet of fresh snow on them."

That was a game-changer. I had no idea how this airplane would react trying to push through that much snow.

Operations, "Do you still want to try to land?"

As the captain, it's all on you. Are you going to take the chance if something goes wrong?

Mulling over my options, including diverting to Rochester or Syracuse, I asked the first officer, "What do you think?"

He said, "I think we can do it."

He was not responsible; I was.

Never wanting to back down from a challenge, I told operations, "Sure, I'll give it a try."

She said, "Good luck."

I wasn't sure I liked the sound of that.

We saw the runway right at minimums. The touchdown was as soft as a feather in the snow. The deployment of the ground spoiler lever was our only hint that we were on the ground. I could hear clapping from the back.

The airplane jerked as the anti-skid grabbed and released; the tires fought for traction.

The thrust reversers enveloped us in a cloud of snow.

We came to a stop in the middle of the runway—now for the hard part. You could barely see the taxiway lights, so I pointed between them and hoped for the best.

Getting into the two-foot snow took a lot of power to keep that bird moving. The hard part was when I turned the tiller in my left hand to steer, the plane would keep going straight. I had to stop, turn the front wheels in the direction I wanted to go, and use asymmetric thrust to coax the airplane into the turns.

The turns on the taxiways were ninety degrees. When I needed to go right, after turning the steering tiller, I would run up the power on the left engine to swing the airplane around.

While trying to go straight on a taxiway, the snow would pile up on the nose wheels and the airplane would start diving left or right. I had to stop, straighten the nose wheels and use the same asymmetric thrust to try to get straight on the taxiway.

The taxi light made the white landscape glow in the surrounding darkness. Snow crunched and groaned loudly under our wheels, the engines whined, and the airframe rumbled and shook as we slid and struggled on our way to the gate.

Buffalo is a small airport, but it still took me twenty minutes to get to the terminal. It normally would take two or three.

Fortunately, the ramp area was partly plowed, and getting parted at the jet bridge was not so bad. When we finally set the parking brake and shut down the engines, the agent came onboard and into the cockpit and said, "I can't believe you made it!"

I signed, "That makes two of us."

After reading the parking and shutdown checklists, we felt we had earned our pay that night.

That hotel bed was going to feel really good.

Buffalo, New York

Chapter 18
The Fun Never Ends

"Life is either a daring adventure or nothing at all."

-Hellen Keller

I still had no instruction on 'how' to be a captain. I continued to hope for my D&R class, thinking the world's largest, and I thought best airline would surely want to teach me how to be the best possible cockpit manager. I assumed military pilots had been taught leadership, but a lowly civilian guy like me should get a leg up. In the meantime, I read books on leadership from people like General George Patton and others. Whenever I enquired about the class, the answer was the same; "We'll let you know." Maybe I should be happy that they trusted me enough to think I didn't need one, or did I just fall through the cracks?

I thought the HUD was great and used it a lot in the simulator while training on the airplane. When one instructor cautioned me, "Don't use the HUD too much. You'll get dependent on it and won't be able to go back to regular instrument flying if it stops working."

As everything electric or mechanical does at one time or another.

My answer was, "I've been flying for twenty years without a HUD; I don't think I will forget anytime soon."

When Boeing delivered the 737's to American, they had the HUDs installed, but they have not yet been certified by the FAA. So, in true AA fashion, rather than just pulling the circuit breakers or deactivating them in some way, the company flew them up to Mojave airport north of Los Angeles to have the HUDs removed.

While on reserve one evening, I got a call from a copilot, not from Crew Schedule.

This was quite unusual. This guy was the junior member of a two-man crew called the Tulsa Tech Pilots for the 737. He normally worked with a captain, and together they did things like picking up new airplanes from the factory or when an airplane had a maintenance issue. They were like company test pilots; each fleet of airplanes had its own crew.

His normal tech teammate was off on vacation, so he needed a captain for the simple job of picking up an airplane and delivering it to LAX, and since I was L.A. based, I got selected.

He said, "Don't wear your uniform, just show up in street clothes with your kit bag.

We'll be driving to Mojave and fly an airplane back.

That sounded easy enough. The next morning found me in operations, where I met Phil, and we were off. Picking up a rental car, we hit the freeways and passed the time talking about what his job entailed and the usual airline gossip and rumors. Two hours later we arrived at the small old airport at Mojave, now called The Mojave Air and Space Port.

I had been there many times for the Mojave Air Races, where I first saw Bob Hoover.

Once I had applied for a job with an outfit based there, towing targets in old Korean war era F-86 Saber. I'm kind of glad I didn't get the job since your target was getting shot at with live ammunition.

As previously stated, the 737s were delivered to American with the HUDs installed.

They were delivered to Mojave, where a company was contracted to remove the HUDs. When that was completed, the airplanes were ferried back to L.A. to be put into service. That was our job today—a short one-hour ferry flight in a brand-new airplane.

Arriving at Mojave, Phil left the rental car with the company, where someone else would return it locally. Having been picking up and dropping off airplanes for months, he was well acquainted with the crew of mechanics who worked there. Today they had a special request.

The foreman said to Phil, "Bob here is retiring; this is his last day. Do you think we could get a fly-by in his honor?"

Phil looked at me and said, "What do you think, Captain?"

Always up for a little fun, I said, "Sounds good to me!"

After doing our checklists, with both engines running, we taxied out to receive our clearance, Phil called the tower and said, "Boeing Three Alfa X-ray requesting a low pass after takeoff."

"Roger Three Alfa X-Ray, taxi to runway One-Two. After takeoff, plan a left turn to line up for runway Two-Six for your low pass."

The controllers at Mojave see a lot of unusual things, and I'm sure a low pass from an occasional airliner was not out of the ordinary to them.

Completing our checklists just like it was a normal revenue flight. As we lined up on runway One-Two the tower cleared us for takeoff. Pushing the throttle levers forward, the engine RPM gauges swung up to takeoff power as I called for autothrottles on; they set the precise takeoff power, which was preset in the Flight Management Computer.

We lifted off quickly with no passengers or cargo and a minimum of fuel. When the gear came up and flaps were retracted, we accelerated quickly to two hundred knots, which was the speed limit in what was then called an 'Airport Traffic Area.'

As I nosed over to level off at thirty-five hundred feet above sea level, we were only seven-hundred feet above the ground. We don't normally get to do this kind of flying in airline operations, so I was having a blast.

Phil completed the after-takeoff checklist as I rolled left into a thirty-degree bank for the two-hundred-twenty-degree teardrop turn to line up with runway Twenty-Six.

Angling in to line up on Two-Six, I pushed the nose down and, with my right hand, spun the speed select knob to two hundred and fifty knots. The plane quickly accelerated. I didn't think the tower controllers at Mojave would mind, so I didn't ask.

Lining up with the centerline of the runway, I kept diving down. Out of the corner of my eye, I could see Phil looking nervously at me as we raced toward the ground. The asphalt runway was rising in front of us; it seemed to fill the windscreen.

We had not discussed how fast or how low we would go, and to tell the truth, I hadn't thought about it. There was no plan. But like doing a wheelie on a chopped Harley, I had never had a plan for that either. Sometimes, it didn't work out well.

So today, I was flying by the seat of my pants and, most of all, I was having fun! It's also possible that the blue jeans and cowboy boots made me feel a bit too unconstrained.

Closely watching the radar altimeter, Phil called out three hundred feet, then two hundred. He sounded a bit nervous at one hundred and got even louder at fifty feet.

At forty feet his voice got higher, and at thirty feet, it sounded more like panic mode. I was going to go lower, but I decided to leave well enough alone. We raced down the runway at two-hundred-fifty knots with Phil calling over and over; "Thirty feet, thirty feet, thirty feet." His voice got a bit louder and higher-pitched each time.

I thought, *This is the most fun I've had with my clothes on in a long time.*

Down in ground effect and heat waves, the jet bumped a little. It felt like driving a huge high-speed bus down a wide asphalt road; the runway was so close beneath us. I didn't think of it until later, but the radar altimeter reads from the belly of the aircraft, but the engine nacelles hung down quite a bit lower than that. So, we were even closer to that hard, uncompromising asphalt than I thought. A banked turn would have dug in an engine or a wingtip. But I didn't plan on turning.

I was very focused on staying over the centerline of the runway, and Phil's callouts were very helpful in keeping me from descending any further.

There was no time to look left to see if our fan club was lined up on the parking ramp to watch and take pictures. We rocketed down the length of runway Two-Six in a flash, and when the end of the runway disappeared under the nose, I pulled back on the yoke to get some altitude.

The airplane responded like a space shuttle launch, and it seemed like we were going straight up, approaching a thirty-degree pitch up. I glanced to my left to see State Highway 14 just below us. Damn, we were low! There were people in cars glued to their windshields, looking up wide-eyed, with mouths open, pointing. We were an unexpected sight.

It finally occurred to me that I could get in trouble for this. I suddenly had an image in my mind of an American Airlines 737 on the front page of a newspaper, at low level over a highway and going almost straight up. Possibly causing traffic accidents. How would I ever explain my way out of this? I may be retiring earlier than I had planned.

Climbing to our assigned altitude, I banked off to the south. Phil's voice returned to normal as he said, "Thanks and goodbye" to the tower, then contacted L.A. Center to pick up our IFR clearance to LAX.

I didn't know how many FAA and company regulations I had broken. Phil looked at me as if he thought he'd made a huge mistake choosing me for this flight. His only salvation would have been to sell me out in the hearing and say it was all my fault. I had tied him up and gagged him with duct tape. He had no choice.

But he calmly said, "Well… that was fun! I think the guys on the ground enjoyed that."

That saying came to mind again: I try not to make plans for the day because the word premeditated starts getting thrown around the courtroom.

The rest of the short flight to LAX was busy with radio communications and arrival routes. After landing and parking at the maintenance hangar, Phil said, "If I get any pictures from those guys of the fly-by, I'll put them in your mailbox in ops."

I caught a ride to the employee parking lot; he got a ride to the terminal to fly back to Tulsa. He thanked me for joining him to get the job done, and we said goodbye.

I never saw any evidence… I mean pictures of the fly-by, and although I worried for months, never heard a word about it. Phil never called me again to 'help out.' I think he felt that his career was more important.

***

In the 737, like the 727, the stabilizer trim in the cockpit is a large, noisy wheel on both sides of the throttle quadrant. It's very visible right next to your leg. One day I started a trip at LAX with a first officer I hadn't met before. Even though she was pretty new on the airplane. I decided to let her have the first leg.

On takeoff, rolling down the runway, trying to look everywhere at once, engine gauges, airspeed, while looking out the windshield to make sure we're going straight. Then back to the gauges, glancing at the airspeed indicator, I called out V1, then Rotate. Suddenly, the stabilizer trim wheel next to my right knee started spinning rapidly. Surprised, I looked down and said, "I think we have a runaway trim."

I reached for the emergency trim cutout switches when she casually said, "Oh, that's me doing that."

Not wanting to have a discussion at a critical phase of flight, I just said, "Don't do that."

I had never seen anyone use the trim to pull the nose up on takeoff before or since. When we got up to cruise altitude, I said, "Please don't change the trim setting on takeoff; it's preset for a reason. If we lose an engine, you'll have enough to do without trying to retrim the airplane."

She said, "Okay."

It amazed me that someone would be too lazy to pull back on the control column and use the trim button under her thumb instead. Or maybe someone taught her that, or maybe she thought it was clever and cool. I didn't. I've always disliked it when pilots get 'creative'. When you are a copilot, it can be difficult to say something. As a captain, I not only had a right to correct a bad technique, but a duty.

Night Moves

It was a dark and stormy night, as Snoopy would say. At the end of a three-day trip, we were tired. The airplane shook and bumped along from the turbulence, and the cockpit lights were turned up high as rain rattled loudly on the fuselage. We could see nothing outside except bright flashes in the opaque clouds as lightning lit up the outside world.

I'd already told the flight attendants to prepare for landing and take their seats so they would be safe from the sometimes-violent shakes the atmosphere was throwing at us. Maneuvering over Los Angeles, following vectors from Air Traffic Control, we were down to three thousand feet and slowed to two hundred knots. The coastal city was getting a rare dose of thunderstorms coming in off the ocean.

I was at the controls with the autopilot on. My hands on the yoke and feet on the rudder pedals just in case. Because of the wind shift from the storm, ATC was turning the airport around, sending airplanes out over the water to land to the east instead of west, which is more common.

The approach controller told us to turn right to 300 degrees to avoid a large red cell on the radar. Brian, the first officer, said, "Man! That's a big cell for this part of the country." I said, "Yeah, I wouldn't want to fly through that thing. I hope we're far enough away from it."

"We should be fine."

"I'm worried about hail. It can come out the top and be flung as far as thirty miles away."

He said, "Oh, hadn't thought of that."

The plane bucked and shuddered as the heavy rain continued to abuse the cockpit windows and the aluminum fuselage. We tried not to look outside because the flashes could temporarily blind you if you looked directly at them when they hit.

The cell was almost over the airport. We were close, but would clear it with plenty of room.

Then Los Angeles Approach Control announced, "Attention all aircraft: LAX is getting heavy rain and lightning. The airport is closed, expect holding."

When we cleared the big cell, the controller gave us a heading of 260 to parallel the runway heading and take us out over the ocean, telling us, "Stand by for holding instructions."

We had been looking forward to getting on the ground, getting in our cars and heading home for the night and a couple of days off.

I looked at the gas gauges, did some math in my head and told Brian, "It looks like we can hold for forty-five minutes before we have to divert, what do you think?"

He checked the gauges and said, "I agree."

Suddenly, the cockpit lit up as if someone were using an arc welder, and there was a tremendous bang. It felt like Babe Ruth had tried to hit a home run off the bottom of the rudder pedals.

We were stunned and temporarily blinded for a few seconds.

It felt like we'd hit a small part of the sun. Like you'd just died, only you didn't, you're still here, and the airplane is still flying. Did that really happen?

For a second you could smell the ozone, my ears were ringing and my feet stung as I held my breath, waiting for something to go wrong with the airplane, for an engine to quit, maybe both… for the electronic flight instrument to fail… and the cockpit would go black. I could hear screams from the cabin. I hoped mine wasn't one of them.

After a couple of seconds of silence, Brian said, "Damn, that was close. I wonder if it hit us?"

Relieved to see them still working, we scanned the engine and flight instruments looking for something that had failed, but everything looked okay.

I said, "Tell ATC we took a lightning strike at this location."

He did, and the controller responded with, "Do you need any assistance?"

He looked at me, and I shook my head.

"Negative, everything appears normal."

"Okay, keep me advised."

I cleared my throat, took a deep breath and made a short P.A. to the passengers in the calmest voice I could muster, telling them what they already knew, that we'd had a close lightning strike, (if not an actual hit), but the airplane was fine, and we would be landing in a few minutes. I thought I heard a sigh of relief from the back, or maybe I imagined it.

Soon, the big red blob on the radar screen moved east, away from the airport. Other flights ahead of us were being cleared for approach. The controller told us to forget about holding.

After a few more vectors and descents, we were cleared to intercept the localizer, then the ILS approach to Runway 7 Right. Descending through one thousand feet, Brian said,

"Landing checklist complete."

We broke out of the clouds at six hundred feet and were treated to a light show. The usual airport lights glowed in the foreground, while beyond them, the skies over South Central Los Angeles flashed almost continuously—bright electric bolts reaching from cloud to ground. Rain poured down in a torrent.

At five hundred feet, I asked for the noisy windshield wipers to be turned on.

The landing was normal, and as we taxied in, I took the ground control radio while Brian called maintenance to report the possible lightning strike.

Before climbing out of the cockpit, I logged the lightning strike in the maintenance book but didn't stick around for the inspection results—I wasn't about to go hunting for damage in a downpour. The usual evidence of a direct hit includes tiny pinholes and scorch marks at the point of impact.

Modern airliners are designed to withstand direct lightning strikes in several ways. The fuselage acts as a Faraday cage, static wicks bleed off electrical charges, and specially designed fuel tanks help mitigate the effects of a strike.

Because of these fixes, lightning has not brought down an airliner in over sixty years, even though direct hits are common nowadays because there are so many planes in the air.

This exact same thing happened to me ten years earlier over Detroit one night when I was a first officer on the MD-80. The result was the same: loud, bright and scary, but other than our heart rates, there were no malfunctions or damage to the aircraft.

***

I found that I could hold a line in Chicago, so I bid there for a couple of months. The commute there was only six flights a day each way on AA, instead of 25 to LAX, and those flights seemed to always be full. It was a lot harder. Again, I frequently had to stay in hotel rooms at my own cost. I even rented a small apartment for one month to keep from commuting back and forth. It was doable, but it didn't solve my problem of not being home for long periods of time.

After fourteen months of staying in Los Angeles on reserve five days a week—or Chicago for a whole month—my wife had had enough of me being gone so much. She said she might as well not be married. I took the hint.

Checking the options on the computer, I had to make a decision. As captain, I could have gone back to the F-100, the 727, or the MD-80 in Dallas-Fort Worth or Chicago. All were more junior bases than Los Angeles but with a longer commute. I could have been stuck flying all-nighters or getting kicked back to reserve again.

Whether I went east or west, I was doing a double commute to get to work, driving two hours to Phoenix's Sky Harbor airport, then getting on a flight of one hour (west) or two and a half hours (east). It added a lot to your workday, and you weren't even getting paid yet. Getting to Phoenix meant parking in a remote lot that I had to pay for, then catching a van to the airport. You had to have a backup of at least two more flights to make your sign-in. So, to be in Los Angeles at noon, I had to catch a flight out of Phoenix by at least nine o'clock and leave my house by six.

It took six hours to get to work. If the sign-in time was too early, I would have to fly out the night before and pay for a hotel room again at my own expense just to get to work on time.

On the flip side, after finishing a trip, if you were lucky, it only took four hours to get home. But if it was late and there were no more flights that night, you had to pay for another hotel room and fly home in the morning, which cut your day in half. It was normal to get into Phoenix at midnight. By the time you reached your car and grabbed some fast food for dinner, it was three a.m. when you got home. After flying all day, fighting fatigue became a way of life. This is why I said I'd never commute. But here I was, doing it.

If you're going to be married in this job, you need to pick a woman who is independent enough to take care of things at home when you're not there—because you can be gone a lot. I was extremely lucky to have a wife who not only handled problems and took care of the house, but also the horses—and, when I was home, me. I couldn't have done the job without her.

I looked at other possibilities and how I fit in on the seniority list. One of the nice things about being an airline pilot is having options. One of the bad things about being an airline pilot is having options. What airplane to fly, which seat to take, what base to work out of, where in the country to live, to commute or not to commute. I felt lucky to have so many choices.

I've flown with people who lived in places like Anchorage, Alaska, or Bozeman, Montana, and commuted to work on other airlines. Commuting can seem like a job in itself.

***

Walking down the terminal at Washington's Dulles Airport with my first officer Jack. We were looking for some coffee and maybe some lunch. Looking through the big glass windows, we saw an enormous airplane parked at a gate. It stopped us in our tracks. I thought it was a 767, but it was too big. It was a Boeing 777, the first one we had ever seen in person.

It belonged to United Airlines.

Jack said, "I wonder if we can go aboard?"

I looked around the waiting room. There were no passengers and no agents at the ticket counter, so I said, "I don't know. Let's find out."

The door to the gate was open. We were in our airline uniforms with IDs on our chests, so we walked right through. Looking out the jet bridge window, we could see the huge engine on this side of the airplane and one of the main landing gears with six wheels on each side—fourteen wheels total. When we got to the airplane, the entry door was open and nobody was around, so we walked onboard. There wasn't a soul on the airplane, and the cockpit door was open. We walked in to check it out. With security today, we would never get away with that.

The cockpit was powered down. Instead of round gauges, there were five big cathode ray tube (CRT) screens, all blank. There were myriad dials and switches everywhere, like any modern jet. But we were totally impressed by the spaciousness of the huge cockpit.

Looking out the windshield, we could see down into the terminal windows instead of up.

Like all modern airliners, it was built for only two pilots and had plenty of room for two jump seats. It seemed you could hold a party inside that cockpit, and maybe room for some dancing. But the air traffic control radio was rather hard to dance to. A United first officer showed up to pre-flight it. We told him we were admiring his airplane, and he proudly gave us a tour and answered our questions. He hit a few switches, and the cockpit came alive.

The screens powered up so we could see the displays. Just outside the cockpit door was a bunk room for pilots to sleep on long flights.

I asked, "How do you like flying this thing?"

He said, "I love it. It's roomy, fast, and feels as nimble as a 737. You can't make a bad landing in it."

After we departed to let him get to work, Jack and I decided we would both like to fly that monster if American ever bought them.

Chapter 19
The Triple Seven

"Progress is the ultimate motivation"
~Tony Robbins

The Boeing 777 lifting off in London

In 1999, we got our wish. American started taking deliveries of the Boeing 777, or Triple Seven. Out of LAX, they flew it non-stop to London, and I could hold a line on it as first officer.

After four years of flying captain on the F-100, then the 737, and being on reserve the whole time, I bid the 777 as first officer and got it immediately. I was way too junior to hold the left seat.

Soon I was off for another month of training at the Schoolhouse, where I was paired with a captain named John for the month of July 2000.

Technology-wise, the Triple Seven was similar to the 737-800 I had been flying, except there were no laser-ring gyros; they were not needed anymore because of the GPS.

The cockpit was huge, like the rest of the airplane.

The training was straightforward and easygoing. John and I would go out to dinner and have a couple of beers, so the training passed quickly. The systems and multi-function displays in the cockpit were typical Boeing—it was an easy airplane to learn. John had been flying the 767, and he took to it easily as well.

The check ride went off without a hitch, even though both of us were getting a type rating—my eighth one.

The first time I flew the actual airplane was with Justin, another FO. We met at DFW with a check airman named Mike. He took us for a walk around. It was impressive looking up at that huge airframe, those engines, and the immense trucks with six wheels each. It was a clear day as we did a training flight over to Amarillo Airport for some touch-and-goes. At one point, Mike said, "Ya' know, this thing handles so well you can forget how much airplane there is behind you."

He was right; it was responsive and light on the controls. Each of us did three takeoffs and landings with the last one being a full stop. As we taxied back to the end of the runway, Justin and I swapped seats. We got three bounces each to make us current, just like in the Learjet so many years before.

Except now, in the landing configuration, the main gear was almost one hundred feet behind you and about twenty-five feet below you. It helps immensely to have the radar altimeter giving the countdown to the runway: "50, 40, 30, 20, 10." Every landing was a good one—not bad when you're new on an airplane.

At the time, the pilot schedules out of LAX on the 777 were mostly six-day trips.

After getting back from one, I would have a week off. With two of those per month, suddenly I was home a lot more. My horse and my wife started to remember who I was. The cats didn't care.

We would go from Los Angeles to London's Heathrow Airport, a ten and a half to eleven-hour flight. Getting in about ten in the morning, we'd go through the routine described earlier, either hit the ground running, or nap for two hours, then struggle to get up and go out on the town. Staying in the room and watching television or reading a book was not an option. You'd just fall asleep again.

After about twenty-one hours, we would take off again for either New York, Chicago, or Miami and layover again. The fatigue factor was not so bad for the US layovers, being closer to our own time zone. We'd layover downtown, except in Miami, where we would be at one of the hotels on the beach. In the wintertime, it was the place to be.

The next day it was back to London again for another long layover, then the long flight home to Los Angeles, against the wind, which could take eleven to twelve hours at certain times of year. Four long flights and three short nights. You had to make the sleep count. The break you got on the airplane helped a great deal. After six days, it was no wonder we were tired when we got back. Those time zones can be brutal.

Sometimes it was just over and back, three-day trips with two flights and one layover. I tried to avoid those because there were three per month, more commutes to LAX and back, and there was less flight time and therefore less pay.

Whether three-day trips or six, they all left in the afternoon, so I could commute to work the same day and got back early enough that I didn't need to get a hotel room and spend the night. Life was looking up. Too bad I was never smart enough to live ten minutes from the airport.

Back on the long international flights, as stated earlier, an extra pilot is required so that each pilot can take a break. Depending on your circadian rhythms or level of exhaustion, you might get some sleep. One of the nice things about the airplane was the bunkroom just behind the cockpit, where you could lie flat to sleep. But the union had also negotiated for us to have a first-class seat blocked off for us, along with the seat next to it. We could watch movies or eat a meal. At least at first, we had a choice.

Before long, the company decided that if we had bunks for our break, we didn't need seats. Or if we had two seats blocked off, we didn't need bunks. I would have much preferred the bunks, but nobody asked me. The company removed the bunks—it was now just an empty closet. I was used to sleeping in a seat—that's the way it was in the 767. But still, sleeping in my uniform in first class with the passengers was not my preference. In the private bunk room, I could take off my shirt and pants, so it wouldn't look like I had slept in them. Back in first class, I had to stay dressed—and what if I snored!?! Before they took the bunks out, I got to use the bunk room once.

Now that our bunk room was an empty closet, flight attendants started bringing air mattresses and slept on the floor during their breaks. Years later, I heard the FAA ordered AA to put the bunks back in. The company spent money to take them out so we couldn't use them, then they spent money to put them back in. They could have just left them alone.

Ever since the old days of long-distance flying over oceans, position reports have been a requirement. The advent of radar made it easy to provide separation of airplanes over land. But out over the oceans, pilots have always had to call in their positions and altitudes so that their presence is known and nobody runs into each other. It still makes a lot of noise, even if nobody on the ground… or water hears it.

I had been doing it since flying the DC-10 to Hawaii, and later across the Atlantic to Europe and the UK. It involved monitoring the long-range

HF radio. HF stands for high frequency. It was very annoying as there was a lot of static, and you could hear other airplanes calling in their position reports as well. Sometimes when you needed to send your report, you had to wait until other aircraft were finished.

That was now old school. The 777 did position reports for you. When you made a selection in the flight management computer to do automatic waypoint reports, it would send in a flash. When passing a waypoint, you just verify the computer made the report, and the computer is always right. You were still supposed to keep track of your location and passing waypoints and ETPs, but you didn't have to listen to that damn HF radio static all the time and try to talk to that faraway disembodied voice. International flying just got easier.

Out there over the Atlantic, the worst thing that could happen was to get off course or off your "track." It didn't happen very often, but when someone did, they were in big trouble. In that dark, empty sky, it could feel like you were all alone. That is an illusion. There are a lot of airplanes out there with you at any given time, day or night. Being off course risks a midair collision. There is nothing worse. The FAA does not take it lightly. All the procedures are meant to prevent that. If you follow them to the letter, it should never happen.

Like the Los Angeles to New York route, going to London we frequently had celebrities onboard. I've lost track of all the big names that were on my airplane, but one flight in particular was memorable because we had Britney Spears onboard. The gate agent would almost always tell us if we had a VIP on board, although it made no difference to us.

Their life was no more important than anyone else's. Right then, at the top of that food chain was us. As pilots, we felt if we survived, all of our trusting passengers would survive too. So, we didn't worry about them too much. We just wanted them to be comfortable.

I was flying with an old friend from the 757-767 days named Ron Mulhern. He liked to call himself Captain Ron, like in the movie with Kurt Russel. He was a jovial guy and loved to laugh.

Normally the extra pilot is the most junior, but on this trip, we had a very unusual FB. His name was Sandy Sanders, and he was not only a General in the Air Force Reserve, but a check airman on the 777. I forget why he requested this trip as FB when he could have flown it as captain, but he insisted he was not there to watch anyone and was just working the trip.

He was quite a character, African American, good-natured and had a million jokes and funny stories. He made the job seem more like a party. He even did the walk-around, cockpit preflight, and other FB-related chores. I was amazed, and that's why I remember the trip.

None of the cockpit crew went back to look at Britney. We were all used to celebrities; they were just regular people as far as we were concerned, and there was no reason to bother them.

The funny part was that when we were airborne, Sandy had gone back to use the lavatory. When he returned, he was beaming from ear to ear and laughing. We asked,

"What's up?"

Sandy said, "I just can't wait to tell my granddaughter that my butt sat on the same toilet seat as Britney Spears!"

Apparently, he had run into her coming out of the lav as he was about to go it. He was enjoying the joke so much we all laughed as it added to the party atmosphere of the three-day trip.

***

I loved laying over in London, despite the challenges of the large time zone difference from the West Coast of America. Once you got past the struggle of napping and then fighting your way back to the land of the living, there were always so many places to go. The city is full of history, and there is so much to see. It's like Disneyland times one thousand—only it's all real. You'd have to spend a long time, or have a lot of layovers there, to see everything.

The Globe Theater in London

A fascinating and historic place is Shakespeare's Globe Theater on the south side of the Thames River. Originally built for plays in 1599, it was used continuously until 1613, when a prop cannon fired during a performance of Henry VIII caused a fire that burned it to the ground. They rebuilt it the next year, and the actors continued to perform until 1644, when it was finally taken apart to make way for tenements. In 1997, it was rebuilt again as close to the original specifications as possible. After three hundred and fifty-two years, another Globe

Theater now stands where Shakespearean plays are performed once more—a piece of history London is so rich in.

Inside the Globe Theater

On a layover, another pilot and I took the tour of the theater but didn't stay for any plays. They were scheduled for later in the evening, and we had plans—dinner and a pint at a local pub, then off to bed early to be ready for our flight out the next day.

Buckingham Palace is only one of the many castles in and around London. The Tower of London is possibly the most famous. It is also right on the river. Built in 1078 by William the Conqueror from Normandy, it is a must-see. The colorful Beefeater Guards are still in charge of the place, along with the big black ravens, which are considered good luck. Be sure to check out the Crown Jewels of the United Kingdom while you are there.

The Tower of London

Whether I was touring a castle, or sitting in a pub, I would often contemplate how I got here. With my background as a high school dropout and former biker with an arrest record, I could have been sitting in prison, or maybe doing construction again, or driving a truck. Not that there is anything wrong with those professions, I did them for years, and any honest work beats sitting in jail. But as much as I dreamed about having a flying career, I still never dared to imagine I would get this far. Once again, I had to chalk most of it up to luck. I was still careful not to mention my shady background to my fellow pilots. Besides, they may not have believed me anyway.

During the two years of flying 777 trips to London, we stayed at several different hotels. To stay awake and get the blood pumping, I would go for a jog in Hyde Park when we stayed at the Marble Arch Hotel, right near the monument of the same name at the northeast corner of the park. The park was established in 1536 by King Henry VIII. At first, I wondered if it was named after the story of *Dr. Jekyll and Mr. Hyde*. It wasn't, of course.

One captain I flew with was named Ric Tanney, who was the grandson of Vic Tanney, a fitness guru on television in Los Angeles in the 1960s who owned a bunch of gyms named after him. He was a competitor of Jack LaLanne, also a TV fitness guru.

Ric was young for a captain, good-looking and very fit. I guess it ran in the family. He was the only captain that ever ran with me.

One time, I went to the Museum of Natural History. It seemed like every single animal—except the domestic horse—was listed as "threatened" or "endangered." Even the American coyote. I imagine a lot of people who've lost beloved pets to coyotes wouldn't mind seeing them endangered.

Occasionally on a layover perhaps, on the rare occasion I might wear a short-sleeved shirt, a flight attendant or another pilot would see the tattoo on my forearm and say, "What's that?"

I would let them see the tattoo better. When they say the initials MC after Hangmen, they would say, "Oh, Marine Corps, huh?" I would usually just smile and not say anything, then change the subject. I would never claim to have been a Marine, but I didn't want to admit the truth either.

Most pilots had their favorite pubs, with different beers and different food. Some wouldn't go to pubs at all because back then, in the late '90s and early 2000s, smoking in public places was still allowed in England. Most of the people I flew with lived in California, which had already outlawed smoking in any public place.

Many of the California boys and girls were no longer used to a smoke-filled room. I never smoked, but I grew up with a father who smoked, so to me, for better or worse, secondhand smoke was normal. I thought women who smoked were sexy. Perhaps watching all those 40s and 50s movie stars like Ava Gardner and Elizabeth Taylor puffing on a cigarette skewed my judgement.

When in a bar or pub, cigarette smoke was just part of the atmosphere. I didn't think anything of it. The only bad part was getting home and finding your layover clothes still smelled like cigarette smoke.

I rarely went to a regular restaurant. Sometimes the crew wanted to go to an Indian place, so I would go along, but most of the time it was pub food: Beef Wellington (named after the Duke of Wellington, the hero of Waterloo), bangers and mash, or shepherd's pie. In my opinion, the best fish and chips were in England, and it didn't seem to matter where you got them. Whether from a street vendor outside Buckingham Palace or your favorite pub, they were always good.

One pub in Kensington served, along with their fish and chips, "mint mushy peas." I never liked peas when I was a kid. My mother tried to get me to eat them, and I would refuse.

I was suspicious when I first saw them. Then I took a taste and thought they were great. Think of refried beans smashed into a paste, or something pudding-like, similar to good Mexican refried beans, then add fresh mint. I think I liked the peas even more than the fish and chips themselves. Or maybe it was just the good English beer, like Boddington's, or the Irish Guinness, or one of a hundred other great tasting beers.

Sometimes I would go to some of the local markets, like Harrods, which was always a fun place. I would buy jars of caviar to take home with me. My wife and I loved caviar. It was like a little slice of Paris, and it brought back memories of the picnic on the Eiffel Tower all those years before.

It cost a fraction of what it did in the States and was twice the size and twice as good. On one trip, returning to America, I went through customs as we always did. I dutifully filled out the customs form and said that I had three jars of caviar. Four ounces each.

The customs officer looked at the form and said, "Sir, I must inspect your bags."

I said, "Okay, help yourself."

When he found my caviar, he said in a haughty manner, "Sir, do you know how much caviar is legal to bring into the United States?"

I only knew that you were allowed one liter of an alcoholic beverage, but I had no clue about caviar.

I said, "No."

"Sir, you are only allowed to bring two ounces of caviar into this country at any one time. I must confiscate this caviar."

It was only about twelve dollars' worth. I shook my head and said, "Go ahead." Thinking surely, he and his buddies will be eating it in the back room on their break. Keeping the world safe from cheap caviar was part of their mission, and I'm sure they enjoyed it. I supposed this was all negotiated by lobbyists in Washington, D.C.

On our way back to the States, the crew meal choices were usually filet mignon, salmon, or lamb chops. The captain had first choice, but most of the time, being good leaders, they would defer and take whatever was left. I didn't care what I ended up with since it was all good.

The three of us were not allowed to eat the same entrée. This was possibly a holdover from the movie *Airplane* or the original it was copied from, the Canadian movie *Zero Hour*, where the pilots both ate the fish, got sick, and passed out, leaving someone else to fly and land the plane.

There's something about food in Europe and the UK. They just seem to know what they are doing. I never had a bad meal, in a restaurant, a pub, or even on the airplane.

Back then, we flew the 777-200. Now American Airlines has the 777-300. It is longer than a 747-400 and has ten exit doors instead of eight on the -200. The thrust from the huge engines on the -200 produced 77,200 pounds more than a single 747 engine. The -300 produces 115,300 pounds each and has a range of 8,555 nautical miles. Again, way more than a 747.

That's a lot of range. A very long flight. No wonder they require four pilots. You can start to believe you live in the air, like in Richard Bach's book *Stranger to the Ground*.

Chapter 20
To Fly or Not to Fly

"The only person you are destined to become is the person you decide to be."

~ **Ralph Waldo Emerson**

A Boeing 777 taxing for takeoff

Did you know you can be a working airline pilot and hardly ever fly an airplane?

On flights over nine hours, an extra pilot is required to spell the other two, so they can get some rest and be fresh for landing. For flights over twelve hours, a fourth pilot is required by FAA regulations.

Naturally, FO means First Officer, or FO-A. They can't call them FA because that already means Flight Attendant.

FB means First Officer-B, and FC means First Officer–C. Some companies call them international officers.

However, with airline parlance, and pilot and flight attendants' sense of humor, FB, because he was the first to come back and eat, became known to mean Food Boy.

And the FC on the really long flights, had to take his break first and was not sleepy yet, he almost always watched movies in first class, so he became known as the Film Critic.

Although I enjoyed the international trips, one leg a day and laying over in exotic cities, I discovered a problem with them, even when I was on the 767.

For the most part, FBs and FCs don't fly the airplane, meaning they don't handle the controls and take off and land the airplane. Their job consists of sitting in the seat during cruise flight while the airplane is on autopilot. They're fully qualified but in normal operation rarely get to. Which is why they are required every ninety days to go to the flight academy to do three takeoffs and landings in the simulator to stay current.

A lot of time off is a compelling reason to bid international. One guy I flew with was a professional jet ski racer. I didn't even know that was a sport. He said he became a pilot so he could have as much time off as possible and still make good money. He always bid FB, so when he did fly, he didn't have to work much. So much for having a love of flying.

The good part was that you worked less. The bad part was that you worked less. It was nice to only fly one leg a day, but other than making radio calls for frequency changes and, in the old days, position reports. On the 777, we didn't even do that. In any kind of flying, the real work is in takeoffs, approaches and landings.

In some months, you might fly three trips a month. Just over and back, that's six legs.

If the landings are shared normally, that's only three approaches and landings per month. With the six-day trips we were doing, that's only four legs per trip, two trips per month, that's eight legs with four landings per pilot.

Flying domestic you might fly as many as four legs per day and anywhere from eight to twelve legs in a three-day trip. That's four to six landings per pilot, then multiply that by four trips per month. All that up and down keeps you busy and makes you a better pilot.

Flying international is easy, but you don't get to do as much pilot stuff. You get rusty.

I learned this years ago on the 767, so later on the 777 I always bid first officer, the right seat. Not FB, the extra guy, or girl, who just filled in during cruise flight. If you go ninety days without at least three landings, you have to go back to the flight academy to do them in a simulator. Back then, because of union rules, if you had to go to the schoolhouse for any reason, you got to exceed the monthly maximum and make more money, so some people were gaming the system and going non-current on purpose.

Personally, I worried about not being a good pilot. Maybe those other guys were so good it didn't matter, but for me, I knew I needed more stick time to be proficient.

That all hit home one night when I was in the simulator doing recurrent training.

Instead of pairing me with a captain, they put another FO like me in the left seat. I'll call him Tony. Like me, he had previously been a captain, so he wasn't an inexperienced pilot. He was senior to me, having gotten hired in 1984. Tony had gone non-current and was there to do his three takeoffs and landings. In other words, he had not flown or landed the airplane in at least three months.

It was a training session, not an actual check ride, so there would normally have just been an instructor that we call a Sim-Pilot, telling us what maneuvers we needed to do or simulated emergencies we should handle. His name was Dave. However, this time, standing in the back of the dark cockpit was John, a check airman. He claimed he was there to give Dave an evaluation, so we thought nothing of it.

Not being the line captain, Tony was no help during my portion of the flying. It was like I was flying single pilot. But I was current by flying first officer all the time, and I got through it okay.

When it was Tony's turn, we switched seats. I took the left, and he got into the right seat, his normal job. We adjusted them and got comfortable. The sim instructor told Tony to program the flight management computer, or FMC. It's rather complicated if you're not used to it.

Initially, it takes a lot of training, but like me, Tony had been flying Boeing jets for years. Plus, he was type-rated on the 777, which the FAA required for copilots or international officers on long-distance over-water flights.

Dave asked Tony to build a fix from the runway we were sitting on at Chicago and then construct a holding pattern off that fix.

At American, all pilots except the 727 guys knew how to use the flight management computer or FMC, the control head for the flight management system. But Tony was flustered and couldn't figure out how to do it. Maybe he was just nervous. He apparently had not planned on this. He was only here to do three landings. If he'd been flying as FB, he must not have touched an FMC in months, perhaps longer.

Studying before any recurrent training is an unwritten rule. If you don't know the answer to a question, an instructor or check airman will wonder what else you don't know.

We're supposed to know everything relating to our job.

The request was relatively simple, akin to entering a longhand DOS command on an old computer. I leaned over and started to open my mouth when I felt a bump on my shoulder. Looking up, I saw John, the check airman, not Dave. He looked at me with a frown and shook his head. The meaning was clear: don't help him.

Somehow, dark cockpits are always more stressful than daylight settings, so simulators are almost always a nighttime scenario. I think you sweat more that way.

After an uncomfortably long time of Tony fumbling with the FMC and not being able to build the fix and holding pattern, John was now in charge and getting a bit impatient he said, "Okay, let's forget that: I want you to take off from this runway and fly straight ahead and level off at three thousand feet."

After all the hoops we jumped through in the simulator, it was a simple task.

Outside the windows, the clouds suddenly vanished, and we now had clear VFR conditions. In the simulated night, you could see stars and the lights of buildings on the ground all the way to downtown Chicago.

The engines were running, so when cleared, I did captain stuff like turning on the landing lights and releasing the parking brake and said, "Your airplane, Tony."

He put the power up, and I turned on the autothrottles. As the big airplane started moving, I made the standard callouts. "Power is set, eighty knots, V1, Rotate."

All was going well. Tony flew the airplane just fine. I pulled up the landing gear and flaps, made some more callouts and ran the after-takeoff checklist.

At three thousand feet, he leveled off and said, "What do you want me to do now?"

John said, "I want you to go back and land on the runway you just took off from."

I thought, *In VFR conditions, that'll be easy.*

Pilots always help each other, so I leaned down to the FMC to pull up the ILS to Runway 09 Right at Chicago so he would have a reference to fly to. But I felt another sharp tap on my shoulder. Once again, John shot me with that look and shook his head.

The little runway symbol from where we'd taken off was right there on the map mode of the CRT screen, but Tony didn't seem to see it. He appeared confused. He said, "I don't understand what you want me to do."

It was something student pilots learned—flying a traffic pattern to a runway. Turn right or left for a few seconds, then turn right or left and you will be paralleling the runway; you'll be able to see it. Just fly past it, turn base leg, then turn final and land. Piece of cake!

But I guess Tony didn't know how to bake cakes… and he couldn't understand what John wanted. I wanted so badly to give him advice, but John wouldn't let me. He was determined to see what Tony was capable of, or not.

Tony seemed lost over O'Hare Airport in VFR conditions. It was inconceivable to me, but here we were. He made it worse by arguing with John about irrelevant things.

Finally, frustrated, he angrily said, "I just want to do my landings."

John said, "Yes, fine, go land back on that runway."

Tony said, "I need an ILS approach." Glancing accusingly at me.

John said, "No, it's VFR conditions; you don't need an approach, just go back and land.

Tony flushed again and said, "I don't know what you want me to do."

This went back and forth a bit longer until John had Dave turn off the simulator, the outside went dark and the lights in the cockpit came on bright.

As he waited for the big virtual reality box to settle on its hydraulic legs so he could open the door, John said, "Sorry, I'm busting you. Check with the training department to see what you have to do next."

When the red 'In Motion' light went out, John opened the door and left. Dave said,

"I'll see you in the debriefing room, and he left too."

Tony looked at me with a mixture of disbelief and anger. "He just busted me? I don't believe it! All I was here for was my landings."

I didn't know what to say. He couldn't run The Box, as we called the FMC. He couldn't do a VFR pattern, a rudimentary procedure in any airplane. I said nothing as he fumed.

He said, "Why didn't you help me?"

Once more, I just stared at him and said nothing. He shouldn't have needed help.

Tony said, "I'm going to the union. That asshole didn't have the right to do this.

As I got my flight bag out of the cubicle next to my seat, I thought, *Yes, he did, and I would have busted you too.*

Now Tony would have to take a full check ride, something we normally practice for weeks. And as a type-rated FO, it had to be to the standards of a captain. If he couldn't do the easiest part of our job, how was he going to do the most difficult?

If he were to flunk a check ride, a report would go to the FAA, and then he would have to take another exam with them on board. Talk about pressure. If he flunked that, the FAA would pull his license, and he would lose his job. It was a grim scenario.

I knew many FBs I had flown with were gaming the system and going non-current. How many others were forgetting how to fly? Was John, the check airman, laying a trap for people like Tony? Had they been doing such a bad job that they had gotten the attention of the flight training department?

About six months later, I saw Tony in operations in Dallas Ft. Worth. I was surprised he still had his job. He said he'd complained to the union that he'd been ambushed unfairly. They arranged for him to get five hours of training and then take an easy checkride with a union official present, and he passed.

"I showed them," he said.

I was amazed. How had he let himself get that incompetent? When was the last time he'd flown an actual airplane? Lives are at stake. I didn't understand the arrogance. Even flying as first officer and getting four landings a month, I felt I was getting rusty. Flying is a perishable skill—use it or lose it. Tony was an experienced pilot. If it could happen to him, it could happen to me. I started thinking about working for a living again, going back to domestic.

Chapter 21
How Not to Be

"There are no friends and no enemies, only teachers."
-Charlotte Malony

Over the North Atlantic in a Triple Seven, still wearing long sleeves to hide the tattoo

I still wasn't out of the woods with the melanoma. After moving to Arizona instead of going to M.D. Anderson in Houston, I started going to the Mayo Clinic in Scottsdale. They ran all kinds of tests, checking to see if the cancer had metastasized. When the FAA got wind of the situation, they required me to have an MRI of the brain once a year for the next five years, since brain cancer could cause seizures. After each scan, I was sent the results—a certificate stating that I had a normal brain. I took great pleasure in having proof that I was indeed normal, even if nobody believed it.

Back on the line, it was always difficult when we arrived in London. Coming from the west coast of the USA, you were eight hours out of your time zone. Having been up for almost twenty-four hours, we had flown all afternoon and all night, into the morning. The level of alertness is deceptive, and now that you can relax, it's like coming down off speed.

Not that I would know.

Often, we got off the bus after an almost hour-long ride from the airport and were near the end of our endurance. I've always marveled at bus drivers in the UK and Europe who can maneuver those big buses through narrow streets. They always spoke good English, except for one Scottish driver.

Often, we would get to the lobby of our hotel mid-morning to find they had no rooms ready for us. People had not checked out yet, or the maids had not cleaned them yet.

So, it became all too routine to sit in the big comfortable chairs in the lobbies of expensive hotels and fall asleep in your uniform. Initially, we tried to act dignified and stay awake until our name was called, but before long we gave in to the fatigue and snored loudly in the lobby, hoping we would annoy the hotel staff enough to give us a room ASAP.

One memorable trip into London was on the fourth of July. We left Los Angeles on the third and on the morning of the fourth, checking in on the radio to London Approach

Control, we were surprised to be greeted with "Happy Fourth of July," or "Happy Independence Day." Instead of 'Happy Traitors Day' or 'Happy Insurrection Day.'

That continued with the tower, then ground control, and even the American Airlines ramp. We thought it was very generous of them.

I've already explained the sleep, or not, strategy for European layovers. You can't sleep all day and be up all night when nothing's open. By morning you're ready to go to sleep again, but now you have to go to work. It's better to try to force yourself into the local time zone. Fatigue be damned.

Some pilots and flight attendants thrive on the time zone changes, and that is all they ever want to do—fly international. Some can't stand it or don't want to.

One day on a westbound flight, London to Chicago, we were over the North Atlantic, approaching the Canadian coast. After seven hours in the air, I was on my break in a firstclass seat, since the bunks had been taken out. While eating dinner, a flight attendant came up to me and said, "We need your help."

I said, "What's up?"

"I have two very drunk men in back. They're bothering other passengers, talking loudly and swearing. There are kids around them, and the parents are very upset. We have tried to get them to settle down, but they're being abusive and will not comply."

"Okay, I'll talk to the captain."

I went up to the cockpit and explained the situation to him, thinking he might want to handle it himself. He looked at me and said, "Go take care of it."

Happy to be acting on his authority, I said, "Roger that, Boss."

The company required us to look official if we had to deal with passengers, so I put on my jacket and hat and went back.

Following the flight attendant on the long walk to the fifth row from the back of coach, she pointed to two young British men, probably in their early twenties. They were sitting on the left side of the airplane. I stood in the aisle and looked at them, then leaned forward with my elbow on the seat in front of them and, putting my face into theirs, I said in a deep voice, "What do you two think you're doing?"

The guy against the window was very drunk and obviously the problem. He immediately started loudly talking trash. Slurred gibberish was more like it. Meanwhile, his friend, not quite as drunk, kept telling him, "Shut up, shut up, you've started enough trouble already, shut up."

Spotting a bottle of Jack Daniel's whiskey in a paper bag on the folding tray, I snatched it away. That is highly illegal on any flight, especially an international flight. I held the bottle by the neck, thinking I might want to hit this guy over the head with it.

One solution that came to mind was to duct tape them both to their seats and duct tape their mouths for the rest of the flight, but I decided to try the easy route first.

Recognizing that the not-so-drunk guy in the aisle seat was trying to keep the peace, and the guy in the window seat was too far gone to try to reason with, I focused laser attention on the guy closest to me.

Getting louder, I said, "You're both in violation of international aviation law. I'm taking your whiskey. If you don't keep control of your friend here, I'll have you both arrested when we get to Chicago.

That seemed to register with the guy; he nodded and said, "I'll take care of him, I promise."

"Good, it's that, or go to jail. Your choice."

I left and gave what was left of the bottle of whiskey to a flight attendant and told her to dump it out and let me know if they had any more trouble. Then I went back to the cockpit and briefed the captain, then sat back down to finish my meal and the rest of my break. It struck me as ironic. Here I was, someone who had been behind bars, threatening to put someone in jail.

In Chicago, after all the passengers had left, I walked off the airplane to find our still drunk friends looking very upset in the jet bridge. The problem guy glared at me as if it were all my fault. I just smiled back. A tough-looking customer service agent was doing a great job of handling these guys. She told me they were connecting to Mexico City, but they were not being allowed on a flight until they sobered up. They might be put on the next flight six hours later. If they didn't behave, they would be sent back to England.

I thanked the customer service agent and headed off to my layover. It's always nice when the company backs you up.

***

We were over Lake Superior, an hour out of Chicago, when the intercom bell went off. Ding ding. I picked up the telephone-sized handset and answered, "This is Dale."

A nervous voice said, "Hi, this is Melissa at Door 3R."

"Hi, what's up?"

"We have a passenger who is experiencing chest pain and shortness of breath. It could be a heart attack."

"Is there a doctor on board?"

"I've already made a P.A. No one has responded."

"Okay, I'll inform the captain. Stand by."

"Hey Boss, we seem to have a medical emergency in the back. They don't appear to have a doctor available. What do you want to do?"

"Nothing. Tell her to keep us apprised of the condition. We'll be landing soon."

"Would you like me to declare a medical emergency?"

"No."

"Are you sure?"

I thought, *Should we hurry if the person dies?*

"Just tell the flight attendants to keep us informed. Notify the company to have EMS on site when we get to the gate."

I called back and relayed the information. Melissa was surprised, but said, "Okay, we'll let you know."

I said, "Keep the defibrillator ready."

"We will," and she hung up.

Calling the Chicago operations, I requested medical personnel to meet the flight.

It seemed to take forever as we slowly trudged along at a slow 250 knots in the line of other airliners. After landing as we taxied in, I asked the FB to call the flight attendant and ask about the condition of the passenger. After a short conversation, he reported there was no change. The purser made a PA asking the passengers to keep their seats so medical personnel could get to the patient. When we finally got to the gate, EMTs rushed onboard and took the afflicted passenger off on a gurney. Then, the rest of the folks deplaned.

If we had declared an emergency, air traffic control would have cleared us directly to the airport as fast as we wanted to go, getting everyone out of our way. We would have had priority, landing in less than half the time and expedited taxing. I was mystified as to why the captain wouldn't do that.

Normally, a medical emergency is not something you want to take chances with. A possible heart attack, for example, could turn out to be nothing, a panic attack perhaps. But it could also be the real thing. Minutes can mean life or death. Is a doctor or a medical professional onboard? A pilot is not a doctor; if possible, you want to get a professional opinion if one is available. If a doctor or nurse advises you to get the airplane on the ground, you should do it. In the best-case scenario, you may save someone's life. Worst case, you did it for nothing, but you still got to the head of the line and did something unusual.

Conversely, if you do nothing and the patient dies, both you and the company could be found liable in a wrongful death lawsuit.

These medical emergencies happened twice while flying the London to Chicago route. Both were within an hour of the airport. Both were chest pain and shortness of breath. My immediate reaction was to declare a medical emergency and ask for expedited handling to the airport.

But I wasn't in charge. When advising that to the captains, different guys both times, they denied the suggestion.

It was exasperating. It would have been a huge breach of protocol for me to declare it myself. In both cases, to my knowledge, both passengers survived. But to me, just taking the chance that things would be okay and not expediting to the runway was taking a big risk.

On the other hand, maybe they knew something I didn't. Maybe passengers pulled this all the time to get attention or whatever. Or maybe getting to the runway quicker would shorten the flight time, causing the captain to make less money? Or was it just the extra time needed to fill out the paperwork?

Maybe I was naïve. But my reaction then, and later as captain, was to take any report seriously and do my best to take care of the passengers. Racing to the airport at the head of the line would be exciting, something you normally didn't get to do. I didn't understand treating a medical problem so casually.

***

In the old days as commuter pilots, we looked up to the guys in the big leagues, flying the big jets. At Imperial Airlines, pilots frequently rode with us to go to work or back home. I remember talking to copilots who told me they were having to retire at age sixty, never having upgraded to captain. That sounded awful; the movement was so stagnant. Flight engineers, it seemed, could fly forever. We called it "Fly till you die."

At the airlines, pilots in narrow-bodies on domestic routes worked harder and made less money doing it. Sometimes flying four, five and six legs a day, dealing with thunderstorms part of the year and snowstorms the other. Laying over in places like Little Rock or Twin Falls, Idaho, or Baltimore.

Then there were the guys in the big iron, the DC-10s, 767s, and 747s. The 777s came onboard in 1999. On international routes, flying one leg a day and working two or three trips a month, with long layovers in exotic locations and eating exotic food, they were living it up, working less and making more money. It was like two different worlds within the same airline.

There were stories of pilots having wives and children in other countries, while they had families at home. I couldn't imagine the stress of that kind of balancing act—living two different lives and living the lies.

If you could handle the time zones, or the lack of stick time—not actually flying the airplane—international flying was great.

***

Cruising along at 38,000 feet, the brilliant white of the snowcapped mountains of Greenland contrasted with the deep blue of the Atlantic Ocean. On our way home from London, we were chasing the sun. The twelve-hour flight was daylight all the way, unlike the eastbound leg where you flew through the night to arrive in the morning. We lounged at the controls in the roomy Boeing Triple-Seven cockpit, which seemed so big compared to the narrowbody jets it reminded me more of the bridge of the Starship Enterprise. The captain was in the back taking his break while Ray, the FB and former fighter pilot, was talking my ear off and insisted that we, the pilots, needed to vote down the new union contract being negotiated with the company.

I said, "But the company is offering us United rates. They are the highest paid in the industry." United Airlines employee groups had managed to get union members on the board of directors and were now giving away the store.

He said, "So what? We can do better than that."

"Better than that?" I wasn't convinced. We had not had a pay raise in nine years. The industry had been stagnant, and upward movement had slowed.

"I'm tired of being taken advantage of; they need to pay us what we're worth!"

"And what are we worth?"

"Three hundred thousand dollars a year!"

My mouth probably dropped open a bit. I said, "How are they supposed to afford that?"

"That's their problem!"

I thought to myself, *If they can't, it'll be our problem.*

I voted for it, but the membership voted the contract down, thinking we could do better. It was back to the drawing board for the union negotiating committee. Not long after the subject was moot.

Chapter 22
Everything Changes

"Sometimes, you need to turn your world upside down to see it clearly."
-Jasper Thompson

At six in the morning, the sun slanted into the windows, lighting up my newspaper as I drank coffee at the dining room table. The day before I had come down from the mountains with my horses, riding Doc and leading the other two as pack horses. I'd been gone a week; it was deer season, but I think someone tipped off the deer. I came home empty-handed as usual.

The jingle of the telephone seemed unusually loud at that hour. Before I could say hello, my buddy Gremlin's voice said, "Are you watching TV?"

"No, why?"

"Turn it on."

"What channel?"

"It doesn't matter," he said, then hung up.

Taking my coffee to the living room, I grabbed the remote and pushed the red button, and the whole world changed.

It was September 11, 2001.

The television screen showed a tall building on fire; it was the World Trade Center in New York. A place I had just toured a couple of months ago on a layover. It had been astounding to walk onto the observation deck of Tower Two and see an identical building at that high altitude seemingly feet away. The view of the city and surrounding area had been stunning.

There was speculation that an airplane that hit it, but no one knew what size airplane it had been, but it was a big fire.

That speculation ended when out of the side of the screen a large dark airliner swooped into the picture and smashed into the other tower in an enormous ball of flame and debris spewing out the opposite side.

I don't know how long I sat there before I realized my coffee was cold.

Facts came dribbling in. The Pentagon had also been hit. Two of the planes used in the attack were American Airlines. That hit me hard. Who were the crew members? Were they people I knew? What bases were they from?

Just over an hour after being hit, each tower collapsed. It was unthinkable; this couldn't be happening. It was like watching a science fiction movie you know it is not real.

But it was.

My head said, "This is not happening."

The guardian angel on my shoulder kicked me in the neck and said, "Yes, it is, Bucko... Man up."

I had flown past the World Trade Center towers dozens of times; you couldn't look at the city without seeing them. Now that they were gone, it didn't seem possible.

It became even more obvious that the country was under attack. After the Pentagon, there was another crash of an airliner in Pennsylvania. The air traffic controllers heard fighting in the cockpit over the radio.

I turned on the VCR and slid a new tape in, and set it for an eight-hour recording cycle. No matter which station I tuned in to, the news was all the same. The phone started ringing off the hook and didn't stop all day. I must have gotten a call from everyone I knew, wanting to know if I was working and if I was safe. Ironically, I was on vacation all that week. The next day I saved the front section of the Arizona Republic and its headline and photos of the attack.

I was supposed to go back to work on the Los Angeles to London run in a few days, but now the skies were shut down, no one knew what was going on and rumors were rampant. Later I heard all kinds of dramatic stories of pilots and flight attendants who were working that day and, after having their flight cancelled or diverted, how they had to be creative in getting home.

Some crews reported having some very agitated Middle Eastern men get off their canceled flight, some glaring at them, some threatening; pointing a finger in a flight attendant's face saying, "You have been very lucky today."

As the details came out, after checking my logbooks, I didn't know the crews, but found that I had flown the very same airplanes that were hijacked that day. Also, Flight 77 that hit the Pentagon was a Dulles to LAX non-stop. I had flown that same flight number many times. Not only as first officer on the 757 but also as captain on the 737.

I felt very lucky, and a bit guilty that day, and I still do. I had not been flying. I had not been targeted; my coworkers had. Any pilot and flight attendant in the company could have been on those flights that day. Why were we spared, and they were not? It's called survivor's guilt.

With the United States airspace now shut down, there were no flights anywhere by anyone except the military. I wouldn't be going back to work anytime soon.

I had been lucky while someone else was not. I was home and safe while my coworkers died.

Others, I heard later, had stories of having to divert into small airports or big hubs— whatever was the closest available. They were ordered by ATC to land immediately. It was chaos. They were stranded along with their passengers. Some had to rent cars and drive home, sometimes across the country.

Everyone—pilots, flight attendants, and passengers—has a story from that day: what happened, what they went through, and how they got home. It was a life-changing event. For the people on four airplanes and on the ground, it was a life-ending event.

Some were out of the country, in Europe, South America, Japan, all over. The small town of Gander, Newfoundland, was temporary home to thirty-six wide-body airliners and almost seven thousand people.

For every flight crew's story about being stranded, there are a hundred passenger stories. All over the country, all over the world. Sometimes in expensive vacation spots, being forced to spend more money than they could not afford.

During this time of hatred and murder, it was also a time when people came together and helped one another. It was the worst of times. It was the best of times, to paraphrase Charles Dickens.

Immediately, there was talk of arming pilots so they would never be helpless victims again. Late-night comedians foolishly made jokes about it. The president was against it, but Congress supported it. They don't have Air Force One—they fly with us. The program eventually came to pass and is still active today.

Within a few months, someone decided that pilots and flight attendants should be fingerprinted and background checked by the FBI. That struck fear in my heart. My world felt like it was crashing in. It wasn't the first time I'd been fingerprinted, but with my background, I held my breath, not knowing how much they might dig up about my past.

Would I lose everything I had worked so hard for?

Coming up on the twenty-fourth anniversary of that terrible day, it still feels like yesterday. The day the world changed. When innocence was lost. When we woke up to the fact that there were people out there who hated us. Since then, because of the resulting War on Terror, many more people have died than on that day.

I still try to remember the victims of September 11, 2001, who were just trying to live their lives, and didn't hate anybody.

Epilogue

Eventually, we went back to work and adjusted to life after 9/11 as the new normal.

Hardened, reinforced cockpit doors were quickly installed. Congress passed the Federal Flight Deck Officer program.

On a flight from London to Los Angeles, a flight attendant came to the cockpit and said, "Captain, we have a white powder spill in one of the lavs."

At that time, there had been many incidents of anthrax spores being sent through the mail to media outlets and government offices. The FBI was investigating. Five people died and seventeen more were infected.

I went back to take a look. When the flight attendant opened the lavatory door, I saw white powder on the floor, but no footprints. It looked like someone had opened the door, thrown it in, and then closed it. I told her to lock it off to make sure no one used it.

Brad, the captain, was based in DFW. When I told him what I saw, he didn't seem concerned and said, "Let the company know." I did over the radio. Then he went to the firstclass cabin to take his four-hour break. Greg, the flight engineer, and I took control of the airplane.

Approaching the coast of Newfoundland, I gazed down at the pale bluish-white icebergs in the ocean as we speculated about what would happen when we arrived at LAX. This was going to be a mess. Would they send us to a remote location at the airport with firetrucks and hazmat teams? Would the passengers start panicking? Would the news media be watching? Would we be delayed for hours and miss our commute flights home? We would probably have to answer a lot of questions and file reports.

Then I said, "Ya' know, it will either be that or a janitor with a mop."

Hours later, as the tension mounted, we finally landed at LAX. Contacting ground control, we were given a clearance to taxi to our gate. Greg and I looked at each other in surprise. The captain said nothing.

Arriving at the gate, I found everything was normal. There were no police, no emergency crews, no fire trucks. The agent opened the door, and the passengers flooded off. When the shutdown and parking checklist was complete, I left my seat, put on my jacket and hat and went back to see what was up with the suspected anthrax. Arriving at the lav, I found a cabin service guy cleaning up the white powder off the floor.

I walked away, shaking my head.

***

Two months later, on November 12, American Flight 587 took off from JFK airport in New York bound for Santo Domingo in the Dominican Republic. It was a fully loaded Airbus A-300. Inexplicably, it crashed in the Belle Harbor community of Queens, killing everyone on board, plus five on the ground. Naturally, the terrorist threat was suspected, and as always, an investigation was launched.

Four years prior, American had a program that all pilots were required to attend. It was called the Advanced Airplane Maneuvering Program, or AAMP. Designed in part to instruct how to recover from unusual attitudes, since many pilots had never done aerobatics or been upside down. The class was held in a large auditorium at the flight academy. One key thing I took away was that in a high angle of attack situation, the ailerons become less effective. To get the nose down, you need to use the rudder to roll the aircraft and let the nose fall through the horizon to regain normal control. It was a form of unusual attitude recovery—something you should never experience in an airliner.

The accident investigation found that terrorism had nothing to do with it. Flight 587 had gotten into wake turbulence from a previously departing Japan Airlines 'heavy' 747. The Airbus was heavy also, but not as big as the jumbo jet. The National Transportation Safety Bureau found that the first officer who was flying over-controlled the airplane to the degree that the flight control surfaces failed, the whole vertical stabilizer and rudder broke off and left the airplane impossible to control.

The NTSB decided that the accident was caused by faulty training by American that led to the FO using too much rudder during the wake turbulence encounter. But I disagree. Looking into the FO's past, they found he had done the same thing seven years before, three years before the AAMP class. He had a history of overreacting in wake turbulence.

The copilot simply used too much input, too quickly, kicking the rudder full deflection in one direction and then the other three times. This caused the tail to tear off. All they had to do was ride it out and, like any other flying, use only the amount of control input needed. I've always thought it was unfair to blame the training at American Airlines for this accident.

After 9-11, contract negotiations were forgotten. A year later, after losing a billion dollars, both United and US Airways declared Chapter 11 bankruptcy. In 2005, Delta and Northwest followed suit. Retired pilot pensions were put on the chopping block. Instead of pay raises, all the airlines were implementing layoffs, pay cuts, and early retirements. I guess we weren't going to get paid what we were worth after all.

Because of the downsizing, the company told us there was going to be a system-wide bid run. Whatever you got, you could expect to be there for a long time. They called it MOAB, the Mother of All Bid Runs, named after Saddam Hussein's Mother of All Battles. I enjoyed flying the 777 and laying over in London, New York, or Miami, but I didn't want to be stuck as a copilot forever.

Change was coming whether we liked it or not. No one knew what to expect. Who would survive in the airline industry?

The photo that went viral around the world

Six months after 9-11 my brother-in-law in Denmark sent me an email with this picture asking, "Is this really you?"

I said, "Yes, where did you get it?"

"From a buddy of mine in Italy."

"I was trying to keep it quiet; I don't want to get fired."

But it was too late. I had it taken as a joke. There was a lot of talk about arming pilots.

There was nothing more unsuitable for use in a cockpit than a fifty-caliber rifle. I'd emailed it to two people. One, my friend Marc, a former navy pilot who was now an American Airlines first officer. He thought it was funny but said, "Don't let anyone else see that. You could get in big trouble."

The other was a captain I had flown with years before, and I knew he was into guns. Social media had not been invented yet. He forwarded it to everyone on his email list. In a couple of weeks, it seemed to go around the world.

People took it as an anti-terrorism statement. Crewmembers and passengers recognized me at work. Copies were posted on bulletin boards in flight operations around the country. Two flight attendants I met had printed it out and carried it with them. They asked for an autograph.

A mechanic in Minneapolis walked up and looked at me in awe and said, "I just want to shake the hand of someone who has some balls."

I didn't have the heart to tell him it was just a joke.

Others were sure I would get fired. At some point, it was going to get back to the company.

So much for keeping a low profile.

A Sneak Peek at From Outlaw Biker to Airline Pilot and Beyond Book 4

And the next chapter of my flying career

Simon sat forward, peering through the windscreen and said, "What's all that smoke?"

The sun was almost straight overhead, and the tall black plumes cast long shadows across the brown city of low buildings and barren landscape.

I said, "Well, we *are* flying into a war zone."

"Yeah, but it's all over the place, are they fighting all over the city?"

"Maybe they're throwing a party or celebrating something."

Picking up the microphone, Simon said, "Kabul Tower, November Five-Four-One Papa Tango is with you thirty miles west at one five thousand feet."

An American sounding voice said, "Roger Papa Tango, you're radar contact, descend and maintain five thousand."

"What's all that smoke from?"

"Oh, the natives seem to a little restless because of that thing in Benghazi last night."

"How are things at the airport?"

"We're on heightened alert, but the airport is secure so far. Continue inbound."

The date was September 12, 2012.

We were delivering a used MD-80 to Kam Air of Afghanistan. It was still in its Scandinavian Airlines paintjob.

Simon looked at me and said, "I wonder what happened in Benghazi?"

Staring out at the smoke I shook my head. We had been in the air since yesterday except for a gas stop in the middle of the night and had heard nothing.

The closer we got, the more ominous it looked. We strained to see the airport through the smoke. Further in the distance rose the towering Hindu Kush mountains, gleaming white with snow all year round.

We leveled off at five thousand feet above sea level, less than that above the ground, now over the city we could see roadblocks in the intersections made from burning tires with people milling around in the streets.

Simon spotted the airport and called it in sight. The tower said, "Cleared for the visual approach to runway one-one."

After reading it back Simon said to me, "I hope nobody down there has any RPG's they don't need."

I said, "I'm more worried about Stingers."

Handheld surface to air missiles was a new and disturbing thought. In all the deliveries of airliners over the last few years, we never had to worry about that before. At least the airplane was empty.

We'd been flying ten and a half hours since spending the night in Keflavik, Iceland and a stop for fuel in Varna, Bulgaria. It had been a long two days since we left Roswell, New Mexico.

There was tension in the cockpit but neither of us would admit to being scared, we tried to act like the cool, calm, experienced pilots we were.

The wind noise got quieter as I pulled back the throttles, to descend further and slow to one-eighty. The temperature in the cockpit was cool, but I was embarrassed to notice my armpits were getting damp.

The closer we got to the ground the more uncomfortable we felt. The thickness of the smoke in the air reminded me of the smog in Los Angeles when I was a kid. We tried to focus on the job at hand; landing this airplane at an airport we'd never seen before… in a country at war.

To be continued in Better Lucky Book 4

A Personal Request

If my story lifted your heart, sparked a thought, or simply kept you soaring through the pages, I would be so grateful if you left a short review. Your words don't just remind me that sharing my journey matters—they also help other readers interested in this topic discover a book they might enjoy.

You can leave your review on the site where you purchased the book, and on Goodreads if you enjoy connecting with other readers there. It takes only a minute, and it means the world to me.

Thank you for flying beside me through these pages.

Stay Connected!

If you'd like to keep flying with me beyond these pages, I'd love to stay in touch. Join my readers' community to get:

- Early news about upcoming books
- Behind-the-scenes stories and sneak peeks
- Special updates and exclusive content

Sign up for my email list here: https://www.dalearenson.com.

You can also connect with me on Facebook:

Follow my author page: Dale Arenson

Join our readers' group: Dale's Adventures

As a thank-you, subscribers and group members often get bonus content, sneak peeks, and insider updates. Thank you for flying beside me through these pages!

Acknowledgments

Once again, unlike my first three books, I did not do this one all on my own.

First, I would like to thank Kathy Dishington for her tireless help in proofreading these stories, for her love and support, and for sharing in my life today.

To my second wife Jeri, who shared my whole life with American Airlines, with all the trials and tribulations and the doubt and the triumphs. I could not have done it without her.

A big thank you to my friend, editor and publicist, A. G. Billig, founder of SelfPublishing Mastery, for all her help with marketing and advice.

To Dawn Black in Turkey for her excellent work in formatting this fourth book for me. I highly recommend her. She can be contacted through Fiverr.

Finally, thanks to all of you readers who have read this and my other books and who give me the confidence to keep writing.

About the Author

Dale Arenson is an award-winning, bestselling author of gripping memoirs inspired by his risky and unconventional life.

A high-school dropout in sunny Southern California, he found the supportive family he always craved as a member of the famous Hangmen Motorcycle Club.

After many run-ins with the law and brushes with death and animated by the desire to better himself, Arenson decided to give up his dangerous lifestyle. With extraordinary grit and determination, he reinvented himself as a commercial pilot and had a successful career in aviation for 35 years.

Always up for a good challenge, later on he became a World Champion and Record Breaker Rifle Shooter.

A big admirer of classics such as Plato, Hemingway, and Marcus Aurelius, Arenson is now taking his turn at writing books that entertain, inspire, and stand the test of time. He currently lives in Clarkdale, Arizona. Exploring the high desert on his Harley, reading, and writing are his favorite pastimes.

By the Same Author

From Outlaw Biker to Airline Pilot and Beyond Book Series

Better Lucky Than Good

In this gripping follow-up to his bestselling memoir, Hangmen, Dale Arenson lets you in his early days at the helm of an airplane. He also shares incredible stories of learning and survival. From the first day in his Cessna 140 to being at an airshow with the legendary Bob Hoover, each moment of this new chapter in his life is an adventure.

The outlaw biker becomes a construction worker, then a salesman, until he fulfills his dream of working as a professional pilot. His unorthodox path to success nearly gets him killed many times, but he perseveres.

Better Lucky Than Good is an inspirational story full of drama, humor, and fun flying stories. It will keep you at the edge of your seat, make you laugh and cry, and inspire you to follow your own dream.

The Lucky One

The Lucky One is the second memoir in the From *Outlaw Biker to Airline Pilot and Beyond* series and picks up right where the first book left off. The storyline will captivate your imagination with its unexpected twists and turns, keeping you at the edge of your seat. Arenson's unique writing style, vivid and entertaining, will you take you right next to him in the cockpit and make you turn the pages, wishing this airborne adventure would never end.

In his quest to becoming the finest pilot possible, Dale must confront not only adverse weather or unforeseen aircraft malfunctions but also his own old beliefs and self-imposed limitations. As he pushes through driven by his newfound passion, he finds expansion, fulfillment, and joy. Becoming a flight instructor in his classroom in the sky reveals to him his gift and love for teaching. His job as a pilot flying on forest fires for the California Department of Forestry teaches him how to be strategic in his thinking and endeavors. By setting small goals, he works his way up from flying small airplanes, then twin-engine Cessna O-2 to being at the helm of the sleek Learjet and interviewing for a job as a commercial airline pilot with American Airlines.

Motorcycle Adventure Stories

HANGMEN: Riding with an Outlaw Motorcycle Club in the Old Days

When 15-year-old Dale drops out of school, he's not sure if he wants to be a Marine or a biker. Neither of them pays well, but both fulfill his need for adventure and excitement. As soon as he gets his first Harley, the decision comes easily, and the young man falls into the dangerous life of a 1% outlaw biker in Southern California.

For nearly a decade, Hangmen Motorcycle Club has been his family, and Dale, passionate yet kind-hearted, finds true brotherhood with this extraordinary group of men. Caught up in gang brawls, run-ins with the law, partying and some romance, there is never a dull moment in his day. Perennial values such as honor, loyalty, and freedom also become part of his life. For Hangmen Motorcycle Club—a modern version of the gunfighters of the Old West—is all about living life to the fullest as free spirits, preserving one's liberties, and protecting one's kin.

With hundreds of raving reviews, *Hangmen* is a page-turner to be enjoyed from beginning to end whether or not you are a biker. It is packed with unexpected twists and turns, and the author's sense of humor brightens up even the bleakest situations. Ultimately, Hangmen is a book about humanity and probably the most authentic and raw immersion in the motorcycle club subculture of the 60s and 70s.

Against The Wind:
A Motorcycle Ride

Take a ride down the forgotten backroads of America — where the journey matters more than the destination. This is a story of solo travel, rediscovery, and living fully in the moment. With nothing but a chopper, a small gas tank, and a big imagination, the road opens up into an unpredictable adventure. Along the way, you'll find the joy of simplicity, the thrill of uncertainty, and the quiet beauty of life when you stop chasing the future and start embracing the now.

Aviation Glossary

Notes on Aviation Jargon:

When it comes to numbers, we don't say "runway fourteen." We say "One Four," or "Three Two Right," "Three Six Left." They're numbered that way because of their magnetic headings: one hundred forty, three hundred twenty, or three hundred sixty degrees.

Aircraft call signs aren't "Air Attack Four-Forty." It's "Four Four Zero" or "Tanker Seven Six."

However, there are other times when the number is just a number. A Bell 206 is just "Two-Oh-Six," not "Two-Zero-Six."

A Boeing 727 can be a "Seven Two Seven" or a "Seven Twenty-Seven." Sometimes there are set rules, and sometimes there aren't.

An acronym like VOR isn't pronounced "Vor." It's "V-O-R," although I've heard amateurs say the former. It's like GPWS, which stands for "Ground Proximity Warning System," being called "Gypwis." Uh… no. We say the initials: "G-P-W-S."

ACARS: (From Wikipedia) An acronym for *Aircraft Communications Addressing and Reporting System*. It is a digital datalink system for transmitting short messages between aircraft and ground stations via airband radio or satellite. The protocol was designed by ARINC and deployed in 1978 using the Telex format. More ACARS radio stations were subsequently added by SITA.

ADF: Automatic Direction Finding. In the cockpit, it consists of a dial that points a needle homing to a ground-based station known as an NDB (Non-Directional

Beacon). It is the oldest air navigation system still in use today. (See NDB below.)

Airspeed: There are four kinds of airspeed:

- Airspeed in miles per hour.
- Airspeed in knots, or nautical miles per hour.
- Indicated airspeed, which is what is read on the instrument panel. It reflects what the airplane *thinks* it is doing.
- True airspeed, the real speed corrected for thinner air at altitude and temperature, measured "relative to the air mass through which it is flying."

Then there is **ground speed**, the actual speed (miles per hour or knots) over the ground depending on air density, headwinds, or tailwinds.

- If you're flying a small airplane at 100 miles per hour with a 50-mile-per-hour tailwind, your ground speed is 150 mph.
- If you make a U-turn into that 50-mile-per-hour headwind, your ground speed drops to 50 mph. The cars on the interstate will be passing you.

Altitude: There are two kinds of altitude:

- **MSL (Mean Sea Level):** Needs to be corrected for pressure altitude with an altimeter setting in inches of mercury, adjusted for temperature.
- **AGL (Above Ground Level):** Helps prevent collisions with terrain or obstacles.

APU: Auxiliary Power Unit. A small turboshaft jet engine built into airplanes to provide electrical and pneumatic power. It allows the aircraft to operate autonomously without ground support for cooling and engine start. Otherwise, a GPU (Ground Power Unit) might be needed.

ATC: Air Traffic Control. A service provided by the FAA to direct aircraft through controlled airspace and offer advisory services in uncontrolled airspace. Its primary purpose is to prevent collisions, organize and expedite air traffic, and provide pilots with important information and support.

ATIS: Automatic Terminal Information Service. A recorded message giving pilots all pertinent information about airport conditions. It is usually updated once per hour, or more often as needed. When a pilot informs the ATC that they have received the recording, the controller knows the pilot does not need to repeat it. Each ATIS recording is coded alphabetically from Alpha through Zulu.

Auto-Feather: A device that automatically turns the propeller edge-on into the wind to reduce drag on a failed engine.

Barrel Roll: Rolling an aircraft in a circle as if going around the inside of a barrel. If done correctly, it maintains positive G-forces on the aircraft. Bob Hoover could perform it with one hand while pouring a glass of tea with the other.

Bidding: See also Seniority Number. When hired, pilots are assigned a seniority number in a line of those hired before or after them. Lower numbers are better; higher numbers often mean regret at not being hired sooner. When pilots "bid" for a seat, base, or monthly schedule, they are awarded it depending on who ahead of them wants it. The same applies to vacation each year. Careers often revolve around this slow, steady march of numbers, which advance only when people retire, quit, die, or are fired.

Carburetor Heat: A system that introduces warm air into the carburetor to eliminate or prevent ice from forming in the fuel/air mixture as it passes through the venturi. Ice can cause the engine to stop running. Pilots hate that!

Cerberus: The mythical giant hound that guards the gates of hell.

CFI: Certificated Flight Instructor — a commercially rated pilot licensed by the FAA to teach others to fly. Some say "certified" instead of "certificated." A seasoned instructor once stressed: "You have a certificate; you are certificated! Meat is certified!" **CFII:** A pilot qualified to teach advanced instrument flying.

Coffin Corner: For jets, a high-altitude envelope where stall speed and Mach overspeed converge.

Collective: A helicopter control that adjusts engine power and rotor blade pitch, controlling vertical movement. Operated with the pilot's left hand.

Cyclic: A helicopter control that determines the direction of flight, analogous to a fixed-wing aircraft but using a different mechanism.

Deadheading: Being sent as aircrew to cover a trip or return home after a trip cancellation.

You ride as a passenger but are still paid.

Density Altitude: Defined by AOPA: "Density altitude is pressure altitude corrected for nonstandard temperature. As temperature and altitude increase, air density decreases. It's the altitude at which the airplane 'feels' it is flying."

On a hot day, an airport 3,000 feet above sea level might have a density altitude of 9,000– 10,000 feet. This decreases lift and engine power (if not turbocharged), causing accidents if the plane cannot climb effectively.

DME: Distance Measuring Equipment, often paired with VORs or an ILS localizer.

Dumping Fuel: See Landing Weight.

ETP: Equal Time Point, formerly the Point of No Return — a decision point for emergencies.

FAA: Federal Aviation Administration. The U.S. government agency overseeing all aviation activities. Coordinates with military and foreign governments.

FARs: Federal Aviation Regulations (pronounced "F-A-R"). The national law governing aviation. Part 91 covers private pilots; Part 135 covers intermediate commercial aviation (airlines and large cargo carriers).

FBO: Fixed Base Operator. A business serving pilots and aircraft, selling fuel, performing maintenance, and more.

FB: First Officer – B. On international flights over nine hours, an extra pilot is required by the FAA. The crew jokingly calls this person the "Food Boy."

FC: First Officer – C. On flights longer than twelve hours, a fourth pilot is added for adequate rest. Known as the "Film Critic" because they usually watch movies first.

Feathering Propeller: Turning the propeller edge-on into the wind to reduce drag and stop windmilling, essential on multi-engine aircraft with a non-operating engine and critical on single-engine planes.

Ferry Flights: Repositioning or delivering an airplane empty, or moving it to a base for maintenance.

Flare: Raising the nose of an aircraft during landing to slow it and achieve proper wheel attitude.

First Officer (FO): The copilot, second in command, likely a term borrowed from the Navy.

Final Descent: Not an official term. Flight attendants announce it, confusing it with **Final Approach**, which is the alignment with the runway for landing.

Airport Traffic Pattern:

- **Upwind:** Runway heading after takeoff.

- **Crosswind:** Turning right or left to stay in the traffic pattern.
- **Downwind:** Opposite the landing direction.
- **Base Leg:** Turning to intercept runway heading.
- **Final Approach:** Aligned with the runway for landing.

Flight Engineer (FE): Also known as Second Officer or SIC (Second in Command). Operates complex aircraft systems (pressurization, hydraulics, fuel, etc.) and inspects the plane pre- and post-flight. Flight engineers once were mechanics; now almost extinct in civil aviation as computers replace them.

Flight Director: A computerized flight instrument that is overlaid on the attitude indicator and shows the pilot the attitude required to execute the desired flight path. They can be used with or without an autopilot system.

Flight Following: Kind of like being on an IFR flight plan where ATC is watching over you and warning of traffic, but it's strictly a VFR procedure.

FMS: From Wikipedia: A flight management system (FMS) is a fundamental component of a modern airliner's avionics. An FMS is a specialized computer system that automates a wide variety of in-flight tasks, reducing the workload on the flight crew to the point that modern civilian aircraft no longer carry flight engineers or navigators. A primary function is in-flight management of the flight plan. Using various sensors (such as GPS and INS, often backed up by radio navigation) to determine the aircraft's position, the FMS can guide the aircraft along the flight plan. From the cockpit, the FMS is normally controlled through a Control Display Unit (CDU), which incorporates a small screen and keyboard or touchscreen. The FMS sends the flight plan for display to the Electronic Flight Instrument System (EFIS), Navigation Display (ND), or Multifunction Display (MFD). The FMS can be summarized as a dual system consisting of the Flight Management Computer (FMC), CDU, and a cross talk bus.

The modern FMS was introduced on the Boeing 767.

FSS: Flight service station. Operated by the FAA, they provide information and services to pilots before, during, and after flights. Unlike air traffic control, they aren't responsible for giving instructions or clearances or providing traffic separation. They do, however, relay clearances from ATC for departure and approaches. They are an important source of weather briefings for pilots.

Helo: Slang for "helicopter." Pronounced 'Heelo,' or Hilo, like the city in Hawaii.

Hood: For IFR training, a plastic device not unlike the bill of a cap, only longer. It prevents the training pilot from seeing outside to aviate (stay upright) and navigate (get where you're going), so they have to rely entirely on instruments.

HUD: Heads-Up Display: From Wikipedia: A head-up display, or heads-up display, also known as a HUD (/hʌd/) or head-up guidance system (HGS), is any transparent display that presents data without requiring users to look away from their usual viewpoints. The origin of the name stems from a pilot being able to view information with the head positioned "up" and looking forward, instead of angled down looking at lower instruments. A HUD also has the advantage that the pilot's eyes do not need to refocus to view the outside after looking at the optically nearer instruments.

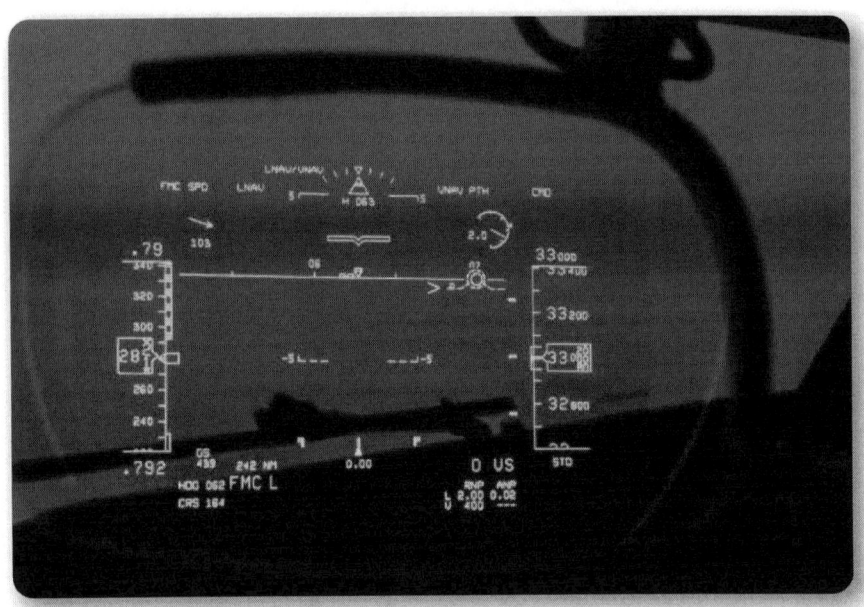

Glideslope: See ILS.

Ground Loop: Wikipedia describes it as a rapid rotation of a fixed-wing aircraft in a horizontal plane (yawing) while on the ground, which might cause the outside wing to touch the ground. In severe cases, the wing can dig in, causing the aircraft to swing violently or even cartwheel.

Icing: Atmospheric conditions that lead to moisture in the air freezing on aircraft surfaces, propellers, and jet engine inlets. On airfoil surfaces, it degrades lift and raises stall speeds. On jet engine inlets, ice can break off, go through the engine, and damage or destroy it. Many aircraft accidents have been attributed to icing.

Ident: See *Transponder*.

ILS: Instrument Landing System. A precision radio navigation system that allows pilots to find a runway through clouds or other reduced-visibility conditions. Because it is so precise, commercial pilots use this method constantly, even in good weather when the runway is plainly visible. The ILS provides both vertical and horizontal radio beams. The horizontal guidance comes from the localizer, while the vertical guidance comes from the glideslope. They are displayed as crossed needles in the cockpit that guide the aircraft to the touchdown zone of a runway. A pilot needs special training to perform this maneuver without being able to see outside. The hardest of all is doing it in a multi-engine airplane with one or more engines inoperative. Most modern jets can land themselves on autopilot.

ILS Categories

ICAO/FAA/JAA (EASA) precision instrument approach and landing[21]		
Category	Decision height	Runway visual range (RVR)
I[22]	> 200 ft (60 m)[b]	> 550 m (1,800 ft)[c] or visibility > 800 m (2,600 ft)[d]
II	100–200 ft (30–60 m)	ICAO/FAA: > 350 m (1,200 ft) JAA(EASA): > 300 m (1,000 ft)
III A	< 100 ft (30 m)	> 700 ft (200 m)
III B	< 50 ft (15 m)	ICAO/FAA: 150–700 ft (50–200 m) JAA(EASA): 250–700 ft (75–200 m)
III C[e]	No limit	None

Glideslope: See ILS

Ground Loop: Wikipedia describes it as a rapid rotation of a fixed-wing aircraft in a horizontal plane (yawing) while on the ground, which might cause the outside wing to touch the ground. In severe cases, the wing can dig in, causing the aircraft to swing violently or even cartwheel.

Icing: Atmospheric conditions that lead to moisture in the air freezing on aircraft surfaces, propellers, and jet engine inlets. On airfoil surfaces, it degrades lift and raises stall speeds. On jet engine inlets, ice can break off, go through the engine, and damage or destroy it. Many aircraft accidents have been attributed to icing.

Ident: See *Transponder*.

ILS: Instrument Landing System. A precision radio navigation system that allows pilots to find a runway through clouds or other reduced-visibility conditions. Because it is so precise, commercial pilots use this method constantly, even in good weather when the runway is plainly visible. The ILS provides both vertical and horizontal radio beams. The horizontal guidance comes from the localizer, while the vertical guidance comes from the glideslope. They are displayed as crossed needles in the cockpit that guide the aircraft to the touchdown zone of a runway. A pilot needs special training to perform this maneuver without being able to see outside. The hardest of all is doing it in a multi-engine airplane with one or more engines inoperative. Most modern jets can land themselves on autopilot.

IFR: Instrument Flight Rules. Flying by instruments is primary, while looking out the window is secondary. IFR flight is regulated by the FAA with a gazillion rules and regulations. Procedures and training are significantly more complex compared to VFR instruction. Pilots must demonstrate competency in conducting an entire cross-country flight and approach to landing solely by reference to instruments. Commercial airliners operate under IFR flight plans on every flight. A pilot must not only be licensed to fly IFR but also be current within the previous ninety days. The aircraft must be properly equipped for IFR flight operations and must have been recently inspected to qualify.

IMC: Instrument Meteorological Conditions

International Officer (IO): A second copilot on long international flights, fully qualified and type-rated in the aircraft. His or her job is to spell the other two pilots so they can get some rest on long flights. The IO also inspects and pre-flights the plane before departure. Different airlines have different designations for this position. That is what it was called at American.

IOE: Initial Operating Experience. See *LOE* for *Line Operating Experience*.

Knots: See *Airspeed*.

Landing Weight: The big jets are certificated to take off at speeds higher than they are allowed to land, due to the impact of a not-so-smooth landing. Normally, they burn off their weight during flight, but if they need to land right after takeoff, some jets can dump fuel overboard to get down to their maximum landing weight. If not, they have to circle to burn it off. Even at today's gas prices, it's still bad form to throw passengers overboard, so the fuel has to go.

Layover: A stopover long enough to sleep. A multiple-hour connection at an airport is not a layover unless you go to a hotel room. Airline crews call a delay in your schedule a "sit." **Leading Edge Devices:** Also called slats, they come out from the front of the wing to increase its camber and, like the flaps, increase lift, lowering the stall speed and therefore the approach and takeoff speeds. Along with the flaps, they turn a high-speed wing into a lowspeed wing.

Localizer: See *ILS*.

LOE: Line Operating Experience. From GROK A.I.: Line operating experience (LOE) in the airline industry refers to the practical, on-the-job training pilots undergo in actual aircraft operations, typically as part of their final stage of training before becoming fully qualified to operate flights independently. It's a critical step to ensure pilots can apply their simulator and classroom training in real-world scenarios under the supervision of a check pilot or instructor and it:

- Bridges the gap between simulator training and independent flying
- Ensures pilots can handle real-world operational challenges, such as air traffic control

(ATC) interactions, weather conditions, and airline-specific procedures

- Validates a pilot's ability to operate safely and efficiently in the airline's operational environment

Mach Number: Per Wikipedia: Mach number (M or Ma) (/mɑːk/; German: [max]) is a dimensionless quantity in fluid dynamics representing the ratio of flow velocity past a boundary to the local speed of sound. It is named after the Austrian physicist and philosopher

Ernst Mach. By definition, at Mach 1, the local flow velocity u is equal to the speed of sound. At Mach 0.65, u is 65% of the speed of sound (subsonic), and at Mach 1.35, u is 35% faster than the speed of sound (supersonic). Pilots of high-altitude aerospace vehicles use flight Mach number to express a vehicle's true airspeed, but the flow field around a vehicle varies in three dimensions, with corresponding variations in local Mach number

Mach Tuck: If you get into a Mach overspeed situation called "Mach tuck," the nose drops, and it wants to go even faster. When the supersonic shock wave gets far enough back over the wing to hit the ailerons, they can go into a flutter so fast that if you tried to grab the control yoke, it would break your wrists. You won't be able to pull the nose up to slow it down unless you grab the control column below the yoke and pull slowly, trying to slow it down. If the airplane gets too fast, it will disintegrate in the air. Learjets were known to do that, although it was mainly the older 20 series. We were flying the newer 30 series. Like I've said, they were exciting to fly.

Microburst: A vertical wind shear, usually from thunderstorm activity. Very dangerous to aviation, especially on landing or takeoff. Flying through it is like trying to go through an invisible waterfall. It can drive you into the ground and has, in several accidents, killed hundreds of people. It was figured out only in 1985 because of Doppler radar. Windshear/microburst recovery must be taught to pilots in simulators, and they must demonstrate the ability to recover. It's not fun.

Mixture Control: A knob next to the throttle that controls the fuel/air ratio (mixture) in the carburetor. It's used at higher altitudes to reduce the amount of fuel to compensate for lower air density: rich for more fuel, lean for less. The controls are normally set at full rich for takeoff.

N1 and N2: Two of the many gauges in modern fan jets. N1 is the fan, the high-by-pass portion that uses no fuel and produces more thrust than the jet portion. N2 is the jet portion, the turbine that spins at a higher rate. Both are shown on the gauges in percentage of RPMs, not actual. A modern jet engine will be spinning anywhere from 10,000 to 25,000 RPMs.

NDB: Non-Directional Beacon. A ground station that puts out a signal that can be used for navigation or approaches by the pilot using the ADF radio in an airplane. They're simple but effective. They aren't very precise, but even today most airports still have NDB approaches for pilots to land in IFR conditions. IFR pilots must prove competency on initial check rides and requalifying check rides.

Nomex: Fire-resistant cloth. From Wikipedia: Nomex has excellent thermal, chemical, and radiation resistance for a polymer material. It can withstand temperatures of up to 370 °C P.A.: Public Address system used to make announcements to passengers.

PFD: Primary Flight Display.

An example of the wealth of information on a PFD

PIC: Pilot in Command. Also called the captain.

Propeller: A large fan that keeps the pilot cool. Turn it off and watch him sweat.

Runway Heading: Runway 36 means three hundred and sixty degrees on the compass heading (corrected for magnetic variation). Runway 18 is one hundred and eighty degrees magnetic. Runway 09 is due east, runway 27 is due west, and so on.

Radial: As used in navigation, a VOR has three hundred and sixty radials in all directions that you can track inbound, outbound, or use when crossing an intersection.

Radial Engine: A reciprocating (piston) engine in which the cylinders "radiate" outward from the central crankcase like the spokes of a wheel. Often called a "round" engine. The S-2 tankers that used radial engines have now been converted to turbine engines, which has increased their load capacity, speed, and reliability.

RNAV: Area navigation (RNAV) is a method of instrument flight rules (IFR) navigation that allows aircraft to fly along a desired flight path, rather than being restricted to routes defined by ground-based navigation beacons. The acronym originally stood for "random navigation," reflecting the concept of flexible routing, though it now refers to a precisely defined method. RNAV integrates information from ground-based beacons, self-contained systems like inertial navigation, and satellite navigation (like GPS). This flexibility enables more direct routes, saving time and fuel, reducing congestion, and facilitating flights to airports lacking traditional navigation aids.

Sectional Chart: A local chart at 1:500,000 scale made for VFR pilots to navigate visually. It provides navigation aids and topographical information, including checkpoints such as populated areas, drainage patterns, roads, railroads, and other landmarks. Airports, controlled airspace, restricted areas, and obstructions are also included.

Seniority Number: See *Bidding*. When hired, pilots are assigned a seniority number, placing them in a long line of pilots hired before or after them. The lower the number, the better; the higher the number, the more you might regret not being hired sooner. When you 'bid' for a seat, base, or line for the month, it is awarded depending on who before you did or did not want it. The same system applies to vacation schedules. A pilot's career advances slowly as others retire, resign, or are fired.

SIC: Second in Command. A copilot. In airlines, they are called a First Officer.

Side Slip: Cross-controlling an aircraft using rudder and ailerons in opposite directions. Used to steepen a descent on approach or to land in crosswinds by slipping the aircraft into the relative wind.

Single Engine Service Ceiling: The maximum altitude a multi-engine airplane can maintain at a given weight with one or more engines inoperative. It varies depending on weight and density altitude.

Slats: See *Leading Edge Devices*.

Stall: In aerodynamics, a stall occurs when airflow over the wing is disrupted, not the engine. The wing provides lift; the engine propels the aircraft forward. If the wing stalls, the airplane will descend. Sufficient altitude allows recovery by lowering the nose; insufficient altitude results in a crash. Larger, faster airplanes require more altitude to recover than smaller, slower ones.

Souls on Board: Live people aboard an aircraft, as opposed to passengers in caskets (which are frequently transported by air).

S-Turns: Can be performed in the air or on the ground. On the ground, pilots use S-turns in a nose-high airplane to see ahead. In the air, tower controllers may request S-turns on final approach to create spacing for other aircraft.

TCA: Terminal Control Area. The airspace around large airports. This airspace is normally busy, with many commercial aircraft (usually jets) arriving and departing. Radio contact with air traffic control is mandatory.

Thrust Reversers: A temporary diversion of the engine's thrust. The engine does not reverse rotation, only the direction of the thrust output. Reversers slow the aircraft, reduce brake use, and can even back the aircraft out of a parking space. At American Airlines, this was called a "power back." Many turboprops, such as the Bandeirante and King Air, also have this capability.

Tower: Airports with an air traffic control tower manage operations on and around the airport, including ground movements, usually on a separate radio frequency. Contact is mandatory unless prior authorization is obtained for a Nordo (No Radio) aircraft. Towers can also provide coded light signals, which pilots must understand.

Touch and Goes: Practice landings in which the pilot lands and immediately takes off on the same runway without stopping. A complete stop is called a full-stop landing.

Traffic Pattern: The standard airport traffic flow:

- **Upwind:** Takeoff into the wind.
- **Crosswind:** First turn from the runway heading.
- **Downwind:** Parallel to the runway in the opposite direction of landing.
- **Base Leg:** Turn to intercept the runway heading.
- **Final Approach:** Aligned with the runway for landing.

Pilots practicing touch-and-go landings frequently fly this pattern.

Transponder: From "transmitter/responder." An automated aircraft device that emits a coded signal in response to radar interrogation. ATC assigns a four-digit code; when dialed in, the aircraft appears on radar as that number. "Ident" flashes the number on the controller's screen.

Trim: Adjusts control tabs on the elevator, rudder, or ailerons to reduce pressure needed on the control yoke. Small aircraft often have only elevator trim; larger aircraft have trim tabs in all three axes. Rudder trim is especially important in multi-engine airplanes.

Type Ratings: Required for large aircraft (gross takeoff weight ≥12,500 lbs) and nearly all turbojet-powered aircraft. Pilots must complete training and a check ride in each type to become PIC (Pilot in Command). The author holds nine type ratings, from a Learjet to a Boeing 777; all are jets except the DC-3.

VFR: Visual Flight Rules. Flying primarily by visual reference, with instruments secondary. Simpler than IFR, instruments are mainly for orientation and navigation. In small aircraft like the Cessna 140, VFR flying is easier and more enjoyable.

VG Registration Numbers: Most airplanes at Devarian used "VG" after their numbers, honoring Vic's wife, Grace. Others were leased.

VHF: Very High Frequency radio.

VOR: VHF Omnidirectional Range. Provides a radial beam for every compass point (360 degrees). Pilots can determine exact bearings, track inbound or outbound, or identify intersections from crossing radials. More precise than ADF/NDB navigation.

V-Speeds: "V" stands for velocity. Various speeds indicate what a pilot should or should not do. Some are fixed, others vary with weight and density altitude. See V-Speeds.

VSI: Vertical Speed Indicator. Displays the aircraft's rate of climb or descent. Critical for safe flight.

Wet Compass: Early compasses floated in alcohol, earning the nickname "whisky compass." Modern versions use kerosene. They are less accurate but better than nothing in an emergency.

WAC Chart: World Aeronautical Chart, pronounced "whack." Designed for VFR navigation. Less detailed than sectional charts but covers more territory, at a scale of 1:1,000,000 (one inch ≈ 13.7 nautical miles or 16 statute miles). Twelve WAC charts cover the continental United States.

Printed in Dunstable, United Kingdom